Making
David into
Goliath

*How the World
Turned Against
Israel*

JOSHUA MURAVCHIK

Encounter Books
New York   London

First American edition published in 2014 by Encounter Books, an activity of Encounter for Culture and Education, Inc., a nonprofit, tax exempt corporation. Encounter Books website address: www.encounterbooks.com

Manufactured in the United States and printed on acid-free paper. The paper used in this publication meets the minimum requirements of ANSI/NISO Z39.48–1992 (R 1997) (*Permanence of Paper*).

FIRST AMERICAN EDITION

LIBRARY OF CONGRESS CATALOGING-IN-PUBLICATION DATA
Muravchik, Joshua.
Making David into Goliath : how the world turned against Israel / Joshua Muravchik.
pages cm
Includes bibliographical references and index.
ISBN 978-1-59403-735-1 (hardback)—ISBN 978-1-59403-740-5 (ebook)
1. Arab-Israeli conflict. 2. Arab-Israeli conflict—Public opinion.
3. Public opinion—United States. 4. Israel—Politics and government—Foreign public opinion. 5. Israel—Politics and government—Foreign public opinion, American. 6. Arab-Israeli conflict—Influence.
I. Title.
DS119.7.M844 2014
956.9405'4—dc23
2013045687

For Isaiah, Aviv, Gabriel, Shai, Aaron, Erez, Ariel, and Quinn.
May the Lord bless you and protect you.

Contents

Acknowledgments

A great many people and institutions helped me in important ways as I worked on this book (and its companion e-book, *Liberal Oasis: The Truth About Israel*).

Two dear friends, Peter Collier and Neal Kozodoy, marvelous editors for whom I've spent a good portion of my life writing, helped and counseled me every step of the way, and Peter also edited this book with his unfailing skill and insight.

The entire project was made possible by the kind and generous financial support I received from the Lynde and Harry Bradley Foundation, Paul E. Singer, the Gale Foundation, Roger Hertog, the Lisa and Michael Leffell Foundation, the World Affairs Institute, Elliot Hershberg, Malcolm Thomson, the Morris Weiser Family Foundation, David Schimel, Rebecca and Laurence Grafstein, Olivier Sarfati, Joseph Aiken, Samuel H. Solomon, David Angel, a couple of other generous individuals whom I wish I could name but prefer to keep their privacy. My friends Joshua Landes and Theodore N. Mirvis, in addition to each making generous gifts themselves, hosted a breakfast at which other funds were raised. My dear old buddy, James Denton, took the initiative of directing a grant to me even when I was reluctant to ask. The Emergency Committee for Israel underwrote a research trip I made to Israel. Last but far from least I want to say a special thank you to Dianne Sehler who has offered me encouragement and support for many years. I am deeply indebted to each of these individuals and organizations.

I am happy and honored to be a Fellow of the Foreign Policy Institute of the Paul H. Nitze School of Advanced International Studies (SAIS) of the Johns Hopkins University, and I am grateful to Dean Vali Nasr, Executive Director Carla Freeman, and Program Administrator Kristine Kuehl Kunkel, as well as to the fine reference librarians at the SAIS library.

I was most fortunate to be able to call on the resourcefulness and diligence of two outstanding research assistants, Jared Sorhaindo and Moran Stern, and also the work of three interns, Ari Grazi, Hannah Elka Meyers, and Zach Novetsky.

I benefitted greatly in my knowledge and understanding of issues touched on in this book from conversations with, among others, Michael Allen, Shlomo Avineri, Joel Fishman, Abraham Foxman, Jeffrey Gedmin, Manfred Gerstenfeld, Tom Gross, Yossi Klein Halevi, Martin Kramer, Adam Levick, Michael Lewis, Noah Pollak, Steve Rosen, Rob Satloff, and Alexander Yakobson. My wonderful daughter, Madeline Muravchik, translated some French for me. Jennifer Burns, Eric Lee and Justus Reid Weiner provided or led me to materials that were helpful. Tony Badran and Badih Chayban went to pains to find and translate a speech from Arabic. Jamie Fly took solicitous interest in my progress. Thank you all.

And finally I want to thank Sally, my beloved wife of many years whose patience is the sine qua non of my books.

I am most grateful to each of these people and to any others whom my weakening memory has caused me to omit, for which I apologize deeply.

Introduction

In October 2009, a United Nations' investigatory commission chaired by the Jewish jurist, Richard Goldstone, accused Israel of "crimes against humanity" during the three-week war in Gaza the previous winter. This extraordinary category of crime was invented for the Nuremberg trials following World War II, which condemned the surviving leaders of the Nazi regime for the systematic mass murder of Jews and others. Now things had come full circle: the Jews themselves stood accused.

This moment underlined a dramatic change in international opinion that would have seemed unthinkable a few decades earlier. Little more than forty years had elapsed since underdog Israel had fought a six-day war against its Arab neighbors in which the Western world had cheered for its victory. For example, in Great Britain, where attitudes toward Israel had been chillier than elsewhere in Western Europe, virtually every major newspaper editorialized in support of the Jewish state. The British government took it upon itself to introduce UN Security Council Resolution 242, which affirmed Israel's right to live in peace behind "secure and recognized boundaries"—a formula that implicitly endorsed alterations to the pre-war armistice lines to allow Israel more favorable borders. Efforts by the Arab states to rally support for their cause in the General Assembly, where London and Washington wielded no veto, were rebuffed, with a substantial number of states condoning Israel's action.

But, by 2009, this sympathy seemed a distant memory in the United Kingdom and the rest of Western Europe, and the United Nations was arrayed overwhelmingly against Israel. Its Human Rights Council, which had created the Goldstone Commission, in the few years since its formation, had already adopted multiple resolutions condemning Israel for one thing or another, while rarely rebuking any other government even once. The Jewish state, once widely admired for its resolution "never again" to allow Jews to be targeted, now was denounced each time it raised its hand against murderous enemies.

In singling out Israel, the Human Rights Council was far from alone. Its predecessor, the UN Commission on Human Rights, had practiced the same one-sidedness, as had the UN General Assembly, which had lacerated Israel in countless resolutions, even going so far as to endorse terrorist attacks on Israel as legitimate "resistance."

Although the United Nations constituted an especially fertile field for denunciations of Israel, many other national and international bodies, including many in the West, joined this chorus. British teacher unions proclaimed academic boycotts of Israel; mainline Protestant churches in the United States divested from companies doing business with Israel; Norwegian supermarkets boycotted Israeli goods; Sweden's largest newspaper concocted sensational stories that Israel was slaughtering Palestinians to harvest and sell their organs; reputable international human rights organizations focused more on Israel than on the world's most egregious tyrannies; and a former president of the United States issued a book accusing Israel of practicing "apartheid."

In short, the "global community" had stamped Israel as an outcast. What had happened in the intervening decades to occasion such a dramatic turnaround?

On the surface, there were two explanations. First, the Arab cause, reactionary, overtly homicidal in its objectives, and expressed in bluster, had been replaced by the far more sympathetic and "progressive" Palestinian cause. Instead of proclaiming openly their determination to deny the Jews a state, Israel's enemies now accused the Jews of denying that same right to another people, the Palestinians.

Second, Israel no longer seemed endangered. The Egyptian and Syrian rulers who had mobilized their armies on its frontiers in 1967 had trumpeted their intent to annihilate the Jewish state. Although Israel had defeated Arab opponents in 1948 and 1956, it remained surrounded and outnumbered, and in 1967, with memories of the Holocaust still fresh, nobody felt certain that the Jewish state would survive this more determined threat to its survival. But four decades and several wars later, Israel appeared invulnerable. In a complete reversal of fortune, David seemed to have become Goliath.

Although superficially plausible, neither of these explanations was sufficient to account for the vehemence with which world opinion turned against Israel. It was true that the Palestinians had suffered at Israel's hands (as Israel had at theirs). And yet, no reasonable person could argue that Israel's abuses equaled, much less exceeded, those of scores of regimes that practiced violence, repression, and racial and religious discrimination without being rebuked by UN bodies or castigated by others in the way Israel now routinely was. Nor, conversely, could it be said that the suffering of the Palestinians, or the justice of their aspirations, surpassed that of others for whom world opinion showed little sympathy. Another Middle Eastern people, the Kurds, yearned for a state of their own, and by every measure their claim was more compelling than that of the Palestinians: they were five times more numerous, they spoke a language of their own, and their distinct ethnicity traced back roughly a millennium. But, aside from the Kurds themselves, who spoke up for the Kurdish cause?

It was also true that Israel had developed formidable military strength. But, if Israel was a Goliath, it was a miniature one compared to some of the members of the Human Rights Council that had so often condemned Israel, and that had charged Goldstone with a mandate that presupposed Israel's guilt. At the very moment that the Goldstone Commission was being called into existence, for example, the People's Republic of China was busy suppressing protests in the captive nation of Tibet by means of mass arrests and executions. This evoked scarcely a whisper of international protest although Israeli abuses of Palestinians paled in comparison to the Chinese treatment of Tibet. Indeed, were China to grant the Tibetans what Israel had offered the Palestinians, the Dalai Lama would have danced for joy.

Nor was it only the United Nations that gave Beijing a free pass, despite a record of butchery and continued repression that had few rivals. Neither Swedish tabloids nor Norwegian supermarkets nor British labor unions nor mainline Protestant churches rose to condemn the Chinese abuses. On the contrary, the People's Republic was viewed as a prime object for understanding and engagement— a member in good standing of the "world community" that self-righteously cast Israel as a renegade.

The contrast between the world's treatment of China and of Israel suggested that the true reason for the anathemas heaped upon the Jewish state was not that Israel was so strong but that it was not strong enough. True, Israel had proven its military superiority over its neighbors. But, when the Arabs finally came to terms with this, they shifted the contest to other planes, learning to exploit the political and economic advantages inherent in the sheer weight of their numbers as well as their control of vital natural resources.

The League of Arab States has twenty-two members, and their combined population exceeds Israel's by fifty-to-one. Moreover, for every Jew in the world, there are one hundred Muslims. Whereas Israel is the only Jewish state, fifty-seven states belong to the Organization of Islamic Cooperation. Once, such major Islamic states as Iran and Turkey had allied with Israel. But, carried along by the tide of radical Islam, the Muslim world had fallen into lockstep behind the Palestinian cause, making it the Islamic cause. Insofar as the Israeli–Palestinian or Arab–Israeli conflict is seen as pitting these two faiths against each other—as it is by most of the protagonists and perforce inevitably by those on the sidelines—the contest is hopelessly unbalanced. The Arabs had been unable to translate these advantages into military strength, but they made them pay off in political clout. They threatened those who crossed them with terrorism, oil cutoffs, and economic boycotts; and they rewarded those who appeased them with protection, economic favors, and the power of their diplomatic bloc, which largely controlled the United Nations through the Non-Aligned Movement.

Whereas people and countries quite often respond cravenly to such incentives, they seldom like to admit it even to themselves. Another factor, which may have been the most important of all in isolating Israel, made it easier to justify yielding to the power of numbers, the threats, and the diplomatic pressures; this was an ideological transformation that saw the rise of a new paradigm of progressive thought that Arab and Muslim advocates helped to develop. It involved multiculturalism or race-consciousness in which the struggle of the third world against the West, or of "people of color" against the white man, replaced the older Marxist model of proletariat versus bourgeoisie as the central moral drama of world history. In this paradigm, the Arabs, notwithstanding their superiority in resources and numbers, nor their regressive social and political practices, nor their recent alignment with the fascist powers, now, in the guise of the Palestinians, assumed a place among the forces of virtue and progress while the Israelis were consigned to the ranks of the villains and reactionaries.

Tutored by the Algerians, who had waged one of the twentieth century's most storied anticolonial struggles, the Palestinians executed a strategy that succeeded in yoking the support of almost the entire global Left. That support ran the spectrum from the diverse communist states and parties, with their cynical though formidable political apparatuses, to the idealistic "soft Left," throbbing with guilt over memories of imperialism and the enduring reality of racism. Championed by the Left's networks of organizations and intellectuals, a Palestinian state became a kind of Holy Grail to enlightened opinion, even while almost no one gave a fig for the aspirations of the Kurds or Tibetans or numerous other bereft peoples. Whether this state would rise alongside Israel or in place of it was of secondary concern.

These two forms of suasion—on the one hand, the raw power in Muslim numbers and Arab oil wealth, and, on the other hand, and the moral claims of the Palestinians and the latter-day ideology of the Left—were to some degree contradictory, but in practice they reinforced each other and created an enduring threat to Israel that might yet trump its formidable military machine. How Israel's enemies developed and deployed each of these methods of influence, and to what effect, is the story told in this book.

one
___

When Israel Was Admired
(Almost) All Around

"God Almighty," she whispered. "What have I done?"
All the months of fighting him, all the carefully built-up
resistance, collapsed in that mad second that had sent her
rushing to his side.

Thus did Kitty Fremont—tall, blonde, blue-eyed, beautiful, and the quintessential WASP—fall in love with Ari Ben Canaan despite herself. Having lost her husband in war and her daughter to polio, she was not ready to love again. And Ari was not easy to love. Kitty was still grieving and Ari was inured to human suffering, seemingly to all softer feelings. He was single-minded—obsessed with rescuing the remnant of European Jewry that survived the Holocaust and creating a state for the Jewish people. She had come to Palestine as a nurse, tending to refugees. Despite her personal tragedy, the direct experience of Israel's birth pangs filled Kitty's heart, and she gave it to Ari and taught him to love in return.

The two lovers are, of course, the main protagonists of Leon Uris's 1958 blockbuster, *Exodus*, the best-selling novel in America since *Gone with the Wind*. It became a major motion picture, was translated into scores of languages, and reached best-seller lists in numerous other countries.

Kitty was the invention of a Jewish writer, nurturing a wish that the gentile world should see the founding of the Jewish state as a story of heroism, sacrifice, and redemption. In this purpose, Uris succeeded beyond all measure. A romantic epic of deadly serious intent, *Exodus* framed the story of Israel for millions of Americans and other Westerners, helping to create a climate of opinion in the 1960s that was warmer to Israel than ever before and more convinced that the country's birth had been both just and necessary.

During the decades before the events portrayed in *Exodus*, Western publics had neither known nor cared much about the Zionist project, although wellsprings of sympathy could be found among devout Christians. The Jewish bible constitutes a part of Christian scripture, and the Jews hold an important place in Christian eschatology. Thus, for some, as Conor Cruise O'Brien put it, Zionism resonated with "a power" that activated "moral, spiritual and aesthetic forces, rather than calculations of material interest."[1]

Nonetheless, most of the time, such ephemeral "forces" were outweighed by *raisons d'etat*. With near unanimity, Arab leaders had denounced vociferously the idea of a Jewish state in their midst. Arabs outnumbered Jews many times over and, as the twentieth century unfolded, the world grew ever more dependent on oil from Arab lands. These considerations bulked large with the diplomats, generals, and others conducting the foreign affairs of Europe and America. When governments acted, as they usually do, primarily from motives of "realism," that is, of simple self-interest, then the Arabs held trumps. The Zionists or Israelis managed to prevail only in those rare instances when "idealism" prevailed.

Without two such moments—born of the convictions of an English foreign minister and an American president—Israel would not have come into existence. The first of these was the issuance of the Balfour Declaration in 1917 pledging the British government to foster "the establishment in Palestine of a national home for the Jewish people." This took on the force of international law when it was incorporated in treaties that formally settled World War I, establishing new countries and borders and a fragile new international order.

Arthur James Balfour was foreign secretary in the government of David Lloyd George, whom historian Paul Johnson describes as "a philosemite and a Zionist . . . also a Bible-thumper."[2] Following an audience he had granted to Zionist spokesman Chaim Weizman, Lloyd George was quoted as commenting that "when Weizman was talking of Palestine he kept bringing up place-names which were more familiar to me than those on the Western Front."[3] The prime minister's mind-set was mirrored in Balfour whose successor, Robert Vansittart, once said, perhaps in pique, that Balfour had cared for nothing but Zionism.[4]

To say that the two ministers acted out of unalloyed altruism would be an exaggeration. Historian Walter Laqueur notes that they "were aware that the goodwill of world Jewry was an important if intangible factor. The year 1917 was not a happy one for the Allies and they needed all the assistance they could get."[5] Yet, "by the time the Balfour Declaration was published, America had joined the Allies and there was no longer any urgent need to appease American Jewry." Thus, Laqueur concludes, "self-interest by itself cannot provide a satisfactory explanation for British policy on Palestine in 1917."[6]

Lloyd George's pro-Zionism was opposed from many sides within his own administration. Less than two years after its promulgation, "General Money, head of the British military administration in Palestine, advised London to drop the Balfour Declaration," writes Laqueur. "The people of Palestine were opposed to the Zionist program, and if Britain wanted the mandate [from the League of Nations to rule the territory] it was necessary 'to make an authoritative announcement that the Zionist program will not be enforced in opposition to the wishes of the majority.'"[7]

When, in 1924, Labour was entrusted for the first time to lead a government, Zionists might have taken heart. In general, around the world, their vision enjoyed more sympathy from the Left than the Right. But the Labour government proved to be steely realists with respect to Palestine. The colonial portfolio was placed with Sidney Webb, the avatar of Fabian socialism. He was stone cold to the Zionist idea and indeed to the plight of the Jews.

Following Arab riots in 1929 that left 133 Jews dead, Webb appointed Robert Shaw to head an investigation. Shaw found that the Arabs were to blame, but recommended nonetheless that the solution was to choke off Jewish emigration into Palestine in order to assuage Arab anger.

This scenario was enacted again the following decade in more ominous circumstances. The "Arab revolt" of 1936 to 1939 was led by the mufti of Jerusalem and apparently financed by Adolf Hitler's government. By the time it petered out, a few hundred Jews had died at Arab hands. Arab casualties were much higher, numbering thousands. Some of these were victims of Jewish retaliation but the large majority fell as the British suppressed the uprising or in Arab-on-Arab violence.

In response, London adjusted its policies. As the *Los Angeles Times* described it:

Just as Hitler's cruelties were becoming apparent to the world, the British issued a white paper that partially reneged on the Balfour declaration's promises. In deference to Arab feelings, the British established a limitation on Jewish immigration into Palestine. The Zionists were furious, but they were helpless to do anything about it.[8]

Even while the Arab revolt raged, some three dozen governments had convened at Evian in 1938 at the invitation of President Franklin Roosevelt. The first signs of Hitler's "final solution to the Jewish problem" were already visible, and the subject of the conference was the rescue of the imperiled Jews. The outcome was nil. The British government insisted that the possibility of haven in Palestine for European Jewry not even be discussed.

Germany's final defeat laid bare the full horror of the Holocaust, but even this did not soften London's attitude toward Zionism or the Jews. Labour's Clement Atlee had replaced Winston Churchill as prime minister, with Ernest Bevin as his foreign minister. Both men were anti-Semites, especially Bevin. (Or, as the British Labour historian, Kenneth O. Morgan, put it: "Bevin was not . . . anti-Semitic. But, without doubt, he was emotionally prejudiced against the Jews."[9])

Nonetheless, British policy was shaped less by prejudice than by recrudescent realism. London did not want to "fly in the face of the Arabs,"[10] explained Lord Halifax, Britain's ambassador in Washington.

The issue at hand was the fate of the Jewish survivors in European displaced persons camps. Their situation was desperate; and this steeled the determination of the Zionists, exemplified by the fictional Ari Ben Canaan, to bring them to Palestine. London's adamant refusal was exemplified by the fate of the *Exodus*, a real ship from which Uris took the title of his novel. Bound from France for Palestine with 4,500 refugees, it was intercepted by the Royal Navy, and its passengers were shipped back to Europe where they were incarcerated in the British occupation zone of Germany, under the watch, eerily, of "local" guards.

It was at this moment that a second figure stepped forward, as Arthur Balfour had, and placed idealism above realism in endorsing a Jewish state. This was U.S. President Harry S. Truman, who fumed that Attlee's policies lacked "all human and moral considerations."[11] Truman's decision to support the 1947 resolution of the UN General

Assembly that partitioned Palestine between Jews and Arabs, and to recognize the Jewish state almost as soon as it had declared its existence, tipped the scales on this historic issue.

While a senator in 1941, Truman had joined the American Palestine Committee, a pro-Zionist group. He claimed his interest in Palestine "went back to his childhood," write historians Allis and Ronald Radosh. "Raised as a Baptist, he had read the Bible 'at least a dozen times' before he was fifteen."[12] After the war, Truman received a report on the shockingly bad conditions in displaced persons camps housing European Jews who had managed to avert the genocide. Absorbing the grim details, he called their plight a matter of the "highest humanitarian importance" and fought with the British to allow them to go to Palestine.[13]

Roosevelt, too, had harbored Zionist sympathies. But Roosevelt had been warned sharply by the State Department that support for a Jewish homeland would compromise vital American interests with the Arabs. Roosevelt hoped he could square this circle through a personal meeting with King Ibn Saud of Saudi Arabia. But, as with Stalin at the wartime summit meetings, the president overestimated the effects of his own charm and powers of persuasion. Not only did Ibn Saud refuse to countenance a Jewish state in the Middle East, he opposed adamantly the entry of even a single additional Jew into Palestine. Following his meeting with the Saudi monarch, Roosevelt privately voiced his newfound conviction that "the project of a Jewish state in Palestine was, under present conditions, impossible of accomplishment."[14]

During the Roosevelt and Truman years, public opinion sympathized with the Jews and thus supported Zionist aims, insofar as it was aware of them. This, however, flew in the face of America's diplomats and generals. Government cables, revealed to a postwar commission examining the Palestine problem, showed that each time the White House had made promises to the Jews, the State Department hastened to tell Arab leaders to disregard them. And, after one Truman statement supporting further Jewish emigration to Palestine, senior American diplomat Loy Henderson went so far as to apologize to the British ambassador for the department's inability to control the president.[15]

Needless to say, Truman was a politician, and there were more Jews in America than in Britain or any other country, especially after the annihilation of European Jewry by Hitler. But to ascribe

Truman's actions to political considerations is unconvincing. He had a stronger reputation than any other president in modern times for doing what he thought was right rather than what was expedient. And his support for Zionism began when he represented Missouri, a state where Jewish influence was negligible.

Throughout his presidency "the State Department and Truman were at loggerheads" on Palestine, write the Radoshes.[16] The third of Truman's secretaries of state, General George C. Marshall, began as a visceral Zionist sympathizer with scant knowledge of the issue, but by the time the department's Middle East experts finished briefing him, he reversed his position completely. He became so adamant that once Truman decided to cast the American vote in favor of partition and to recognize Israel, he had to go to lengths to persuade Marshall not to resign in protest and oppose him publicly. This showed the toughness for which Truman was renowned, and which his predecessor did not share. David Niles, a White House aide who served both presidents, later wrote that he doubted Israel would have come into existence had Roosevelt lived out his fourth term.

Passage of the 1947 resolution in the UN General Assembly partitioning Palestine between Arabs and Jews required a two-thirds majority. The American decision influenced others but was not sufficient to ensure the outcome. Surprisingly, the Kremlin, never a friend to Zionism, decided also to support partition, calculating that the departure of the British from Palestine would enhance Soviet influence there. This constituted one of the rare instances when a state's calculus of *realpolitik* worked to the Jews' advantage.

In general, however, the UN vote was a moment when humanitarian considerations carried unusual weight in international deliberations. Apart from Truman's predispositions, several other factors contributed to the outcome that made the birth of Israel possible. The first was the Holocaust itself. Although authoritative reports had reached the outside world during the war, almost no one grasped the immensity of the crime until the war was over. Jewish communities had been pillaged many times in many places, and people on the outside who had heard reports of atrocities from Nazi-occupied Europe pictured pogroms, a sad but familiar spectacle. The unprecedented reality of murder as a mass-production industry was something no one other than the Nazis themselves had imagined.

When Allied forces liberated those camps whose traces the retreating Nazis had not managed to erase, they found half-dead prisoners, corpses stacked for burning, and the maniacal machinery of death. The shock reverberated around the globe over the next few years as the astounding details were gathered and publicized. Although knowledge of the Holocaust did not cleanse the world of anti-Semitism, it created a reservoir of sympathy for the Jews wider and deeper than they had known over the millennia.

In contrast, the role of Arab leaders during the war earned no goodwill among Western governments or publics. As the *Los Angeles Times* put it: "The Arabs, on the whole, sided with the Nazis with whom they shared common hatreds."[17] According to German historians Klaus-Michael Mallmann and Martin Cuppers, "Egypt's King Farouk sent [Hitler] a message in the spring of 1941 saying that 'he was filled with great admiration for the Führer and respect for the German people, whose victory over England he fervently wished for.'"[18] Saudi Arabia's King Ibn Saud declared that: "All Arabs and Mohammedans throughout the world have great respect for Germany, and this respect is increased by the battle that Germany is waging against the Jews, the archenemy of the Arabs."[19] Pro-Nazi military officers led by Rashid Ali Al-Gaylani seized Iraq in 1941, slaughtering two hundred Baghdadi Jews before their coup was put down by British forces. Gaylani and his co-conspirators enjoyed "widespread Arab Sympathy," notes Cruise O'Brien, while there was little such support for the Allied cause.[20]

Gaylani and the Mufti of Jerusalem, Haj Amin al-Husseini, who had come to Baghdad to aid the coup, escaped the Allied forces with the assistance of the Germans and Italians and made their way to Berlin.[21] There, after a personal audience with Hitler, the Mufti began broadcasts to the Middle East on German radio about the "common battle against the Jewish danger" that united the Muslims to Germany.[22]

The Mufti was the leader of the Palestinian Arabs and, by some estimates, the most popular figure in the Arab world, so his countless incendiary broadcasts against the Allies and the Jews amounted to a significant psychological warfare asset for the Axis. In addition, in 1943, he traveled to Yugoslavia where he recruited Muslim volunteers to create a division of the *Wafen SS*. In 1946, he escaped Allied captivity and possible trial as a war criminal, making his way to Cairo where he was welcomed as a hero.

In short, the Arabs had mostly supported the losing side in the world war, whereas the United Nations had been founded as a kind of victors' club. The very rubric, United Nations, had been the formal name that the alliance against the Axis had given itself, and it was now carried over to the new global body. And, indeed, the price of admission to the United Nation's founding conference was to declare war on the Axis. Thus, the history of Jewish persecution and of Arab collaboration helped tilt the General Assembly.

So, too, did the contrast between the two sides in their attitude toward compromise. Both camps were divided within themselves, but among the Jews the advocates of accepting half a loaf prevailed, whereas among the Arabs the absolutists reigned supreme. Golda Meyerson (later, Golda Meir), the Zionist representative at the United Nations, expressed disappointment that the proposed partition would deny Jerusalem to the Jews, but she embraced the plan nonetheless, hoping the United Nations would "improve" it.[23] In contrast, the Arab Higher Committee, which, with al-Husseini back at the helm, had regained its status as the voice of the Arabs of Palestine, was unyielding. The Arabs "would never allow a Jewish state to be established in one inch of Palestine," vowed the group's spokesman, warning that the effort to do so would lead "probably to a third world war."[24]

Sixty-four years later, Mahmoud Abbas, the president of the Palestinian Authority, conceded in an interview on Israeli television that this refusal of compromise "was our mistake. It was an Arab mistake as a whole."[25] There were many reasons for this mistake and for the contrast in the stands of the two parties. The key one was that the Jews were desperate for a state in Palestine even "the size of a table cloth," as David Ben Gurion famously put it, whereas the Arabs, including those of Palestine, had reached no consensus on what they wanted except that there be no Jewish state on even "one inch." Some envisioned an independent Arab Palestine, whereas others preferred to see the land absorbed into a "greater Syria" or an enlarged Hashemite Kingdom of Jordan. Still others yearned for a pan-Arab state or a pan-Muslim caliphate. When the war of 1948 ended, all of the West Bank, including Jerusalem, and the Gaza Strip were in Arab hands, but not a finger was raised to create a Palestinian Arab state. That was the Palestinian tragedy, or *Naqba*, as it is called today.

Over the ensuing years, the Arab world seethed with recriminations, sparking the overthrow of incumbent regimes in Egypt, Syria, and Iraq. International efforts to mediate the Arab–Israeli conflict proved futile, as Arab political discourse reverberated with the paramountcy of redeeming Arab honor, even while the strengthening Israeli state and army made this goal each day more unrealistic.

Then, with little warning, in the spring of 1967, the constant background noise of low-gauge confrontations and mutual threats swelled to a crescendo. For reasons that remain murky to this day, the Kremlin informed the Egyptian and Syrian governments falsely that Israeli forces were massing on Syria's border for an attack. Israel denied this, and UN and Egyptian officials saw for themselves that there was no truth in it. But the tension did not dissipate.

On May 15, following meetings between Egyptian and Syrian military leaders, Cairo declared an emergency, and tanks were seen rumbling through the streets of the capital. A day later Radio Cairo broadcast: "the existence of Israel has continued too long. We welcome the Israeli aggression. We welcome the battle we have long awaited. The peak hour has come. The battle has come in which we shall destroy Israel."[26]

Egyptian President Gamal Abdul Nasser demanded that the UN Emergency Force (UNEF) be withdrawn from the Sinai where it had been stationed as a buffer under the terms that ended the 1956 Sinai War. Much of the world was dismayed at the alacrity with which UN Secretary-General U Thant complied with this request, and some analysts speculated that Nasser may have counted on more resistance. But Nasser communicated directly with Yugoslavia's dictator, Josip Broz Tito, and India's president, Indira Gandhi. Their countries furnished the largest contingents of UNEF troops, and Nasser was close to both leaders, having collaborated with Tito and Gandhi's father, Jawaharlal Nehru, in founding the Non-Aligned Movement. They made clear to UN headquarters that their intention was to pull out their forces in compliance with Nasser's wishes, leaving U Thant few options.

On May 23, while Egyptian forces continued to pour into the Sinai, Nasser declared the Straits of Tiran closed to Israeli shipping. The Straits of Tiran are at the neck of the Gulf of Aqaba—a three-mile-wide waterway between Egypt and Saudi Arabia that leads to the port of Eilat, Israel's sole outlet to its south and east. Free passage through this channel had been internationally guaranteed, albeit without Egyptian concurrence, under the terms of Israel's withdrawal from the Sinai after the 1956 war. There was little question that the renewed blockade constituted an act of war. Mohamed Hassanein Heikal, editor of the leading Egyptian government newspaper, *Al-Ahram*, and a confidant of Nasser's, told his readers at the time, "an armed clash between [Egypt] and the Israeli enemy is inevitable."[27]

For his part, Nasser breathed fire. Addressing a trade union meeting on May 26, he declared:

> [I]f Israel embarks on aggression against Syria or Egypt the battle against Israel will be a general one . . . And our basic objective will be to destroy Israel. . . . I say such things because I am confident. I know what we have here in Egypt and what Syria has. I also know that other [Arab] states . . . will send . . . armored and infantry units. This is Arab power. This is the true resurrection of the Arab nation.[28]

Israeli leaders mostly tried to calm the situation. Levi Eshkol, Israel's prime minister, was known as an organization man, not an orator. When he addressed the Knesset on May 28, his words were so mild and delivered so fumblingly, that they "were conciliatory to the point of timidity," says historian Howard M. Sachar.[29] "We do not contemplate any military action," Eshkol insisted in words explicitly addressed to Egypt and Syria, appealing for "reciprocity" from them.[30] Cruise O'Brien speculates that these earnest assurances of peaceful intentions may have backfired in that they "seem to have suggested to Nasser that Israel was so anxious to avoid war that further risks could be taken."[31]*

While urging Israeli patience, Washington and London decried Egypt's action against freedom of navigation. Hoping to forestall a military response by Israel, they floated plans to organize an international flotilla to break the blockade. Although other governments agreed that freedom of the seas should be affirmed, few if any were willing to send ships into a potentially violent showdown. U.S. President Lyndon Johnson was strongly sympathetic to Israel, but he

---

*Not all Israeli utterances were pacific. Two weeks earlier, military chief of staff Yitzhak Rabin had reacted to some guerrilla actions emanating from Syria by threatening, "We may well have to act against centers of aggression and those who encourage it." For this bellicose outburst he was dressed down so severely by David Ben-Gurion, Israel's iconic first prime minister who was still active although he had been succeeded in office by Eshkol, that Rabin apparently had a brief nervous breakdown.

felt constrained by the mounting domestic and international protests against his escalation of the war in Vietnam.

On May 30, King Hussein of Jordan flew to Cairo. Israel's border with Jordan was by far its most vulnerable, directly abutting Israel's narrow midsection where most of its people lived. Before, Hussein had always distinguished himself as the most moderate of Arab rulers, the polar opposite of the inflammatory Nasser. In the heat of the moment, however, Hussein calculated that he could not resist the fervor of the "Arab street," so he opted to go all in. In Cairo he offered obeisance to Nasser and pledged unity against the Zionist enemy, going so far as to place his army under Egyptian command.

The tightening military encirclement of Israel was accompanied by a crescendo of blood-curdling threats. One Arab leader after another promised to "explode Zionist existence," or to "get rid of the Zionist cancer."[32] Ahmed Shuqairy, head of the Palestine Liberation Organization, vowed: "We will wipe Israel off the face of the map," adding the memorable fillip, "no Jew will remain alive."[33]

With Arab armies mobilized around them, Israeli leaders wanted to strike the first blow, believing that the advantage of surprise could compensate for their disadvantages of size and space. They waited as long as they felt they could for the American/British flotilla to materialize. But, with no sign of progress on that front, they launched their attack the morning of June 5, while claiming disingenuously that the Arabs had fired first. Within hours the Egyptian air force was destroyed, mostly on the ground, and the war's outcome had been determined.

During the three weeks of the prelude to war, the six days of fighting, and then the period of diplomatic jockeying that followed, Israel enjoyed broad if not unanimous support from the West. Washington and other Western governments were cautious, hoping to forestall the conflict, to bring it to a fast halt if and when the fighting started, and above all to avoid getting drawn directly into it. Still there was little doubt that most of them sympathized with Israel, a position fostered not only by sentiment but by the shrill anti-Western rhetoric of the Arabs and their close identity with the Soviet camp. That link seemed to tighten as the crisis intensified.

Public and elite opinion in the West showed little of the ambivalence or restraint evident in governmental reactions. Memories of the Holocaust, admiration for Israel's achievements, and its image as a diminutive David menaced by the Arab Goliath combined to create widespread support for the Jewish state.

In America, the Jewish community roused itself as never before. Donations poured in for Israel. Sampling the spirit of the giving, *The New York Times* offered this snapshot:

> "You have got it all now," said a brief letter containing a check for $25,000. The message was from a professor at the Jewish theological seminary who said he had gladly stripped himself of his worldly goods and sent the proceeds to the . . . Israel emergency fund. The owner of two gas stations . . . turned over the deeds . . . Other Jews walked in with the cash-surrender values of their life insurance policies. Still others, deeply moved by the Arab-Israeli war, sold real estate and securities and sent the money.[34]

Some donated themselves. During the run up to the war, many American Jewish students departed for Israel, hoping to replace Israeli workers in farms and factories who were mobilized to the front.[35] Others joined demonstrations. A rally in New York drew a crowd estimated variously at 45,000 to 125,000; one in Washington, from 7,000 to 35,000.[36]

A Louis Harris poll showed unsurprisingly that 99 percent of Jews sympathized with Israel. Among Christians, support was strong, too. About half of them said they had no strong feelings or were not sure. But those that did hold clear views were all but unanimously in favor of Israel. Among Protestants the ratio was 41 percent for Israel to 1 percent for the Arabs. Among Catholics it was 39 percent to zero. For Americans altogether, 41 percent sympathized with Israel but only 1 percent with the Arabs.[37] A Gallup poll yielded similar results: 55 percent said their sympathies lay with Israel against 4 percent supporting the Arab states. (The rest either answered "neither" or had no opinion.)[38]

As the crisis deepened a luminous group of intellectuals including Hannah Arendt, Ralph Ellison, Milton Friedman, Paul Samuelson, Lionel Trilling, and Robert Penn Warren signed a display ad in *The Washington Post*. "The issue can be stated with stark simplicity," it said. "Whether to let Israel perish, or to act to ensure its survival and to secure legality, morality, and peace in the area."[39] A similar declaration, calling on the US government to break the blockade of

Aqaba, was placed in *The New York Times* in the name of more than 3,700 academics.[40]

Another statement in this vein was issued by a group of prominent Christian religious leaders, including the famous theologian Reinhold Neibuhr and the Reverend Martin Luther King, Jr.[41] King was not the only civil rights leader to make himself heard. A Washington pro-Israel rally was addressed by Whitney M. Young, Jr., president of the National Urban League, and Bayard Rustin, the man who had conceived of and organized the landmark 1963 March on Washington.[42]

News organizations, too, embraced Israel. *The New York Times* editorially denounced Nasser as "crudely aggressive," a sentiment echoed by its star columnist, James Reston, who wrote: "the key issue has to be clearly defined . . . Nasser has committed an aggressive illegality." Humorist Russell Baker poured ridicule on the Arabs, going so far, in those days before the advent of "political correctness," as to make fun of "the Arab mind."[43] *TIME* carried stories with a pro-Israel slant several weeks running. "The real issue," it said, "is . . . Israel's . . . basic right to exist. Most of the world has accepted and acknowledged that right, but not the Arabs."[44] Reporting that "there was little doubt as to where the majority of Americans stood," the magazine offered a potpourri of illustrations such as: "in Chicago's Loop, Mayors Row restaurant changes the name of one of its dining rooms from 'Little Egypt' to the 'Tel Aviv room.'"[45]

Although the executive branch was cautious, worried about what actions might have to follow words, members of congress and senators were less so. When the State Department spokesman declared at the outset of fighting that the position of the United States was "neutral in thought, word, and deed," Senator Everett McKinley Dirksen, the minority leader, waxed indignant: "what's neutral? I call it 'snootral'—when you stick up your snoot at both sides." His colleague, Republican Senator Hugh Scott, condemned the administration's position as "very much confused." Democrats joined in the criticism, and *The New York Times* branded the neutrality declaration "grotesque."[46] Secretary of State Dean Rusk quickly issued a clarification, saying neutrality did not mean "indifference."[47]

Although support for Israel was bipartisan, Israel was above all a cause championed by liberals. In addition to civil rights leaders, AFL-CIO President George Meany warned that failure to defend Israel would imperil "the security of our country, of the entire free world."[48] So militant was labor's attitude that on the day the war broke out, "a labor rally for Israel almost turned into a riot . . . when some persons got the impression that one spectator was opposing a resolution pledging financial support for Israel," according to a report in *The New York Times*.[49]

John Kenneth Galbraith, the president of the leading liberal advocacy organization, Americans for Democratic Action, appeared on *Meet the Press* and declared that he would "absolutely" favor direct military intervention in defense of Israel. Like Galbraith, many of the strongest advocates of support for Israel were opponents of the Vietnam War. Senator Wayne Morse, who had cast one of only two votes against the Tonkin Gulf resolution that had originally authorized the war, called on the administration to unilaterally break Nasser's maritime blockade.[50] Senator Eugene McCarthy, who would become the champion of the Vietnam peace movement in the 1968 election, declared that the United States had "the legal and moral obligation" to take military action if Israel were attacked.[51] And Senator George McGovern, who would capture the Democratic presidential nomination as a peace candidate in 1972, said on the conclusion of the fighting that he hoped Israel "did not give up a foot of ground" until the Arabs made peace.[52]

The response in Europe to the Middle East crisis was very much like that in the United States. The British government under Labour Prime Minister Harold Wilson worked closely with the Johnson administration to end the Egyptian blockade but got nowhere. London's caution matched Washington's but so did the warm support of Israel displayed by the British public and opinion leaders.

Indeed, polls suggested that support for Israel among Britons was even marginally stronger than among Americans. A Gallup survey during the war found that 55 percent favored Israel, 2 percent favored the Arabs, with 43 percent favoring neither or having no opinion.[53] Editorials backing Israel appeared in *The Times*, *The Observer*, *The Guardian*, and *The Economist*.[54]

After Nasser closed the Straits, a rally in "solidarity with Israel" drew a crowd of ten thousand. They listened to Lord Janner pray to God to "protect the people of Israel [and] give them the strength to go to victory," then marched to the Israeli embassy.[55] Reuters reported a melee at Heathrow Airport as volunteers jockeyed for seats aboard a flight to Israel. *The Washington Post* reported that "some

5000 Britons have formally applied to go to Israel. . . . Roughly 15% are non-Jewish."[56]

In France, which had been Israel's closest ally, President Charles de Gaulle turned sharply against the Jewish state, but few followed him. According to Flora Lewis in the *Los Angeles Times*:

> By a count which cabinet ministers have leaked personally,
> there are no more than four of the 28 members of President
> Charles de Gaulle's government not opposed to his stand on
> Israel and the Middle East. At least half a dozen ministers have
> talked privately of resigning on the issue. Defense Minister
> Pierre Messmer did, taking it back only at the last minute.[57]

De Gaulle was defying public and elite opinion. Polls recorded that 56 percent of the French favored an Israeli victory whereas 2 percent backed the Arabs.[58] A support rally outside Israel's embassy in Paris outdid that in London, drawing twenty thousand.[59] According to the *Los Angeles Times*, "several thousand Frenchmen, only about half of them Jews, volunteered to serve as replacements for Israeli workers and farmers who were mobilized as reservists."[60]

France's most luminous literary couple, Jean-Paul Sartre and Simone de Beauvoir, led an intellectual outpouring of support for Israel that included artists like Pablo Picasso. "The press, virtually unanimous except for *L'Humanité*, the Communist newspaper, recited Israeli military victories with obvious relish under huge headlines," reported *The New York Times*.[61]

In West Germany, reported *The Guardian*,

> The . . . Government has been at pains to maintain a position
> of strict neutrality in the Middle East war, but the press has
> almost without exception championed the Israeli cause, more
> emphatically and more emotionally perhaps than have the
> newspapers of any other Western country. The Israeli embassy
> has been bombarded with offers of help, financial, humanitar-
> ian, and military, the last by young Germans volunteering to
> fight for Israel. Needless to say, they have been politely turned
> down.[62]

This nearly unanimous Western support made itself felt in the United Nations where, once the reality of Arab battlefield reverses became clear, Arab and Soviet bloc delegates began clamoring for an immediate cease-fire and a return to the *status quo ante*. This demand, which aimed to force Israel to relinquish its conquests while leaving in place the Aqaba blockade, was a tactical blunder. With each passing hour and day, Israel was consolidating victories on all three fronts, with territorial gains at the expense of Egypt, Jordan, and Syria. Because time worked in Israel's favor, its backers were in a position to insist that a Security Council cease-fire resolution be coupled not with a requirement for undoing the war's results but rather for an end to the Arab–Israeli conflict, itself.

Having staved off the explicit threat of annihilation by its neighbors, Israel now had two further war goals. The first was to trade its new material leverage over the Arabs for acceptance of its existence. The second was to adjust its borders—which were nothing but the 1948 armistice lines given legal standing—so as to be less vulnerable. At its center it was less than ten miles across. "Auschwitz borders," they were termed by Israel's usually restrained UN ambassador, Abba Eban.

The result was Security Council Resolution 242, introduced by the United Kingdom and backed by the United States, which called for "freedom of navigation through international waterways in the area," meaning Aqaba, "and respect for and acknowledgement of the sovereignty, territorial integrity and political independence of every State in the area and their right to live in peace." In its most crucial section, it specified "withdrawal of Israeli armed forces from territories occupied in the recent conflict." The Soviet delegate attempted to insert the word "the" before "territories," but was rebuffed. It was more than splitting hairs. The absence of "the" meant that Israel must withdraw but perhaps not from all of its conquests. Moreover, Resolution 242 also spoke of each state's right to "secure and recognized boundaries," opening the door to Israel's claim that its existing narrow borders were not secure.

The Arabs and the Soviets were compelled to accede to this resolution because, with Israeli forces triumphant on all fronts, the alliance of Western states and Israel held all the cards. A couple of weeks later, the Arab–Soviet forces attempted to recoup their diplomatic losses by taking the matter to the General Assembly. The Non-Aligned bloc sponsored a resolution that contradicted Security Council Resolution 242, but even with the Soviet and Arab blocs and the Non-Aligned (and de Gaulle's France), they could not gather the necessary two-thirds vote, so the stratagem failed.

Triumphant on the battlefield and in the diplomacy, Israel basked in the world's admiration and enjoyed a golden moment of peace and security. But the fruits of victory, however sweet, contained the seeds of bitter trials ahead.

Soviet enmity, which Israel had endured since a few years after the 1948 UN partition vote and the subsequent withdrawal of Britain from the area, grew fierce. Although hostile, the Kremlin had previously attached little importance to Israel. But the crushing defeat Israel had inflicted on a pair of Soviet clients armed with Soviet weapons was a huge blow to Moscow's prestige. In the Cold War contest for the allegiance of third world countries, the USSR had overnight suffered a steep slide in its appeal. And, to boot, the Soviet state no longer appeared all-powerful to its own downtrodden subjects, above all its Jews.

Natan Sharansky recalls:

> The Six-Day War had made an indelible impression on me as it did on most Soviet Jews, for, in addition to fighting for her life, Israel was defending our dignity. On the eve of the war, when Israel's destruction seemed almost inevitable, Soviet anti-Semites were jubilant. But a few days later even anti-Jewish jokes started to change, and throughout the country, in spite of pro-Arab propaganda, you could now see a grudging respect for Israel and for Jews. A basic eternal truth was returning to the Jews of Russia – that personal freedom wasn't something you could achieve through assimilation. It was available only by reclaiming your historical roots.[63]

The movement that stemmed from this, of which Sharansky was to become the living symbol, challenged the totalitarian grip of the Communists as never before. Lashing back, the Soviet propaganda machine went into overdrive in blackening the names of Israel and Zionism.

The Soviet backlash against Israel's triumph was mirrored in the West by de Gaulle. Perhaps because his stance on the war had evoked more dissent and criticism than he was accustomed to, or perhaps because Israel had ignored his stricture not to strike the first blow (and thus committed the "crime of *lèse-Gaullism*," Raymond Aron quipped), the French president lashed out furiously at the Jews. He is probably the only Western head of state to have done this since Hitler. He called them "an elite people, self-assured and domineering." His foreign minister, Maurice Couve de Murville, later explained implausibly that this was intended as a "tribute to their exceptional qualities,"[64] but Aron, probably the leading French political thinker of his age and a largely deracinated Jew, was moved to pen a short book protesting what he took as de Gaulle's deliberate reintroduction of anti-Semitism into French public discourse.[65]

Whatever bigotry de Gaulle exhibited, the motive for his reversal of France's alliance with Israel was not emotional but the coldest of *realpolitik*. The Arabs had numbers and oil. De Gaulle explained:

> In this region, where France has always been present and active, I naturally intend to re-establish our position. The political and strategic importance of the Nile, Euphrates, and Tigris basins, the Red Sea, and the Persian Gulf is all the greater now that, thanks to oil, it is coupled with an economic weight of the first order. Everything bids us to return to Cairo, Damascus, Amman, Bagdad, and Khartoum, as we stayed in Beirut, as friends and as partners.[66]

For the moment, de Gaulle was out of step with the rest of the West, but the other Europeans would soon begin to feel the same pulls he did. As Raymond Aron put it: "Once again, General DeGaulle realized before others which way the immediate future would go."[67]

Finally, Israel found itself in the awkward role of occupier. This was a label that the Arabs had placed on it since 1948, and on the Zionists even before that, in the belief that any Jewish sovereignty or even substantial settlement in Palestine was illegitimate. Thus, the six hundred thousand to eight hundred thousand Arabs who had fled or been chased from Palestine to surrounding countries in 1948 had been kept in camps rather than absorbed as Israel had absorbed the Jewish refugees from Arab lands. The purpose of this heartless policy was to dramatize the insistence that these people be returned to their homes in what had now become Israel. The "right of return" was an expression of the defeated Arab nations' determination to undo the outcome of the 1948 war.

Now, having vanquished Egypt, Syria, and Jordan yet again, Israel became overlord of millions of Arabs. As Israeli leaders imagined it, this situation would not last long, only until the neighboring countries agreed to grant them acceptance in return for most of the land captured in the Six Day War. But, in their humiliation, the Arabs were more determined than ever to defy Israel. So the temporary became increasingly permanent. And, as time passed, the once nebulous sense of national identity among Palestinians, the bulk of whom were now under Israeli rule, began to crystallize. Thus, not only did the Israelis occupy territory that the Arabs claimed as theirs, but they had become "occupiers" in a second, more fraught sense—standing between another people and its national aspirations.

two

The Arab Cause Becomes Palestinian (and "Progressive")

Israel would never again enjoy the degree of sympathy it experienced in 1967. The simplest reason was that Israel would never again seem so endangered. The devastating prowess demonstrated by Israel's fighting forces gave it an aura of invulnerability.

The implications of this new image were compounded by another transformation resulting from the war. Until 1967, Israel was pitted against the Arabs, who held an advantage in terms of population of roughly fifty to one, and in terms of territory of more than five hundred to one, as well as larger armies and more wealth and natural resources. The Six Day War, however, set in motion a redefinition of the conflict. No longer was it Israel versus the Arabs. Now it was Israel versus the homeless Palestinians. David had become Goliath.

The altered perspective that made Israel look big instead of small was accompanied by a shift in ideological appearances that was no less important. The Arab states were seen as autocratic and reactionary. But, the groups that came to speak for the Palestinians presented them as members of the world's "progressive" camp.

These twin transformations stemmed from the crystallization of the idea of a Palestinian nation in the second half of the twentieth century. The absence of a widespread sense of Palestinian nationhood before then may surprise those who came to the "Mideast conflict" in the 1970s or later, when Palestinian national aspirations came to be seen as the quintessence of the principle of self-determination. But, in historical context, it is easy to understand. Most of the countries of the Middle East, with Egypt the most notable exception, were modern creations—their borders drawn by colonial rulers— and the development of their national identities works in progress. And so it was with Palestine, except that there the process was strengthened by the presence of a hated enemy against whom the Palestinians could define themselves and make their cause sacred to their brother Arabs.

Traditionally, most of the people in the region identified themselves simply or primarily as Muslims. Indeed, strong traces of this legacy are still evident among Palestinians. As recently as 2011, according to the Palestinian press agency, WAFA, a survey revealed that when asked their first identity, 57 percent of Palestinians answered "Muslim," rather than "Palestinian," "Arab," or "human being."[1] Of course, by the same token, some people in the West might feel that Christianity is their first attachment, but it is likely that the proportion is much smaller. More to the point, "Christian" is a spiritual identity, not a political or ethnic one. For Islam, these two selves are not separable. When Palestinians were asked in the same poll to choose the political system best for themselves, a plurality of 40 percent favored an Islamic caliphate, whereas only 24 percent wanted "a system like one of the Arab countries" and 12 percent "a system like one of the European countries."

Beyond religion, another strong affinity that came before nationalism was pan-Arabism—the idea that all Arabs should form a single polity. This vision had germinated in the years after World War I in reaction to the high-handedness with which the Western powers carved up the Arab lands they had taken from Turkey. Pan-Arabism was central to the philosophy of the Baath movement that took power in Syria and Iraq in the 1960s. But its foremost proponent was Gamal Abdel Nasser, the most popular figure that the Arab world has known since the crusades.

Pan-Arabism was not so natural to Egypt, with its distinct and ancient national identity, as to the newly minted Arab countries. Nonetheless, it answered the burning need to restore dignity by creating a union strong enough to stand up to the West and to Israel. "Lift your head, brother, the days of humiliation are over," was one of the slogans of Nasser's revolution. As the *Cambridge History of Egypt* summarizes it:

> Arab unity, under Egyptian leadership, would guarantee victory over the Zionist enemy and the liberation of Arab land; [and] battling Israel was only the local facet of a struggle that set the Arabs in general, and particularly Egypt, against imperialism . . . and through which the connection with the third world was established.[2]

Although today there is not much left of this ideology, for the two decades bracketed by the 1948 and 1967 Arab–Israel wars, pan-Arabism was the dominant political idea of the Arab world. Given the salience of Muslim and Arab identities, Palestinian identity lagged far behind.

Palestine, after all, had never been a country. The name designated a portion of the Arab territory taken from the defeated Ottomans in World War I and given to the British to govern as a League of Nations "mandate," meaning they were not to treat it as a colony. The Balfour Declaration reflected an awareness of the Arab inhabitants without seeing them as a distinct nationality. Rather, it spoke of the Jewish people and "existing non-Jewish communities in Palestine." Likewise, a full generation later, the UN partition plan of 1947 referred to creating "Arab and Jewish states . . . in Palestine." The numerous other diplomatic documents of the preceding decades spoke in similar terms. Insofar as anyone referred to "Palestinians," the term simply meant those who dwelled in the territory called Palestine, Jews as well as Arabs, without any suggestion that these individuals constituted a distinct political or cultural community as is connoted by the word "nation."

It was Zionism, itself—made to seem real and threatening by the Balfour Declaration—that stimulated the Arabs of Palestine to search for their own identity. They first turned their gaze northward. Palestine had been connected with, or part of Syria, virtually since its earliest identity in the form of the second century Roman province called Syria Palaestina. "When Amir Faysal established a government in Damascus in October 1918, the Palestinian Arabs' aspirations focused on him," writes Ann Mosely Lesch, coauthor of a Rand Corporation study of Palestinian nationalism. "An all-Palestine Conference in February 1919 . . . supported the inclusion of Palestine in an independent Syria."[3]

Faysal's ouster by France was not fatal to his ambitions for a throne—he went on to become king of Iraq—but it eliminated this option for the Palestinians. So, in 1921, local Arab notables formed an alternative program to present to London. It sought cancelation of the Balfour Declaration, an end to Jewish immigration, restoration of Ottoman law, and agreement that "Palestine not . . . be separated from the neighboring Arab states."[4] It also called for the election of a representative government in Palestine, but this was less an expression of national identity than simply a demand for self-rule within the jurisdiction designated as "Palestine" by the reigning powers. The essential sensibility was not Palestinian, per se, but rather the feeling, as the Rand study puts it, "that Palestine is essentially Arab and that it should be governed by Arabs."[5]

The same sentiment motivated the Arab Higher Committee (AHC), which was formed in 1936 and led by Haj Amin al-Husseini, Grand Mufti of Jerusalem and president of the Supreme Muslim Council. Spearheading the Arab revolt against the Jews and British from 1936 to 1939, the AHC spoke in the name of the Arabs of Palestine but did not call itself "Palestinian."

During the 1948 war over the birth of Israel, al-Husseini declared the formation of a government of all Palestine. But Alain Gresh, former editor of *Le Monde Diplomatique* and a sympathetic authority on the Palestinian cause, observes that "this appears to have been much more an Egyptian maneuver intended to counter Hashemite designs [the Hashemites were the rulers of Transjordan] than a desire to nurture an embryo Palestinian government. This government was soon forgotten."[6]

Egypt came away from the 1948 war occupying Gaza, which had been part of Palestine. In the 1950s, tiring of al-Husseini and his AHC, Nasser directed the creation of some new Palestinian offices. But "Nasser was . . . concerned not with forming a provisional government . . . of a future independent state . . . only with creating a sort of Palestinian body [as] the spokesman for Cairo's policy," explains another French specialist, cited by Gresh, who adds: "At this time, the question of the Palestinian people and its self-determination and independent struggle was not an issue either for Nasser or the Arab Higher Committee. This view was, with some nuances, shared by the Palestinians themselves."[7]

This picture began to change in 1964 at the first Arab League summit meeting, convened in Cairo by Nasser, at which the decision was made to create the Palestine Liberation Organization (PLO). The PLO would eventually become the very embodiment of Palestinian national aspirations, but this is not how it began. As scholar Hussam Mohamed put it:

> Regardless of the claim that the creation of the Palestine Liberation Organization (PLO) in 1964 was necessary to fill a gap in the political life of the Palestinians, the new organization was the stepchild of inter-Arab rivalries and power politics. In

fact, it was President Nasser of Egypt who, during the 1964 Arab Summit Conference, recommended the creation of the PLO, and nominated [Ahmad] Shuqairy to be its first chairman.... The ... goals of the new Palestinian organization were simple: ... to cater more to the interests of certain Arab states than to those of the Palestinian people.[8]

Ahmad Shuqairy was born in Lebanon but his family home was in the ancient city of Acre on the Mediterranean coast just north of Haifa. His father, As'ad, was an Ottoman official, cool to the cause of Arab, much less Palestinian independence.[9] But, Ahmad made a career as an Arab spokesman. In the 1940s, he worked for al-Husseini's AHC until becoming, in 1949, a member of Syria's delegation to the United Nations. He followed that with seven years of service as assistant secretary-general of the Arab League and then several years back at the United Nations, this time representing Saudi Arabia until 1963, shortly before Nasser tabbed him to found the PLO.[10] In short, he was the very personification of pan-Arabism.

Shuqairy was a man of bombast who won few admirers. Conor Cruise O'Brien, who represented Ireland in the United Nations during Shuqairy's tenure there as the Saudi ambassador, preserves this memory:

All delegates are constrained in the General Assembly to become connoisseurs of windbags, and [Shuqairy] was, by common assent, the windbag's windbag. He used to begin his oratorical set piece each year with the words: "I am honored to address the members of the United Nations"—pause for effect—"all [x] of them." *X* always represented whatever the real current membership was, minus one. Israel was a non-nation.[11]

Years later, Yasser Arafat offered his take on Shuqairy to biographer Thomas Kiernan. "The appointment of [Shuqairy] to speak for the cause of liberation was a clear reflection of Nasser's contempt for our cause.... It was obvious from the beginning that the PLO was to be nothing but ... a tool of the Egyptians to keep us quiet."[12]

Shuqairy personally crafted the Palestinian National Charter adopted in 1964. Abdallah Frangi, a Palestinian leader, calls it a landmark "which for the first time formulated the ideas of a Palestinian identity."[13] Nonetheless, its "most striking feature" to Gresh was "the absence of all reference to any sovereignty either of the Palestinian people or of the PLO, or to a Palestinian state." Gresh attributes this in part to the pressures of Arab governments and in part to "Arab nationalism [which] was still heavily predominant."[14]

But Arab nationalism, or pan-Arabism, soon had the stuffing knocked out of it by Israel in the 1967 war. When, on the morrow of the defeat, Nasser tendered his resignation, crowds gathered in Egyptian cities—whether spontaneously or orchestrated by his henchmen, most likely some of each—to demand he remain in office, which he did until dying of a heart attack in 1970. By then he had lost much of his stature, and the pan-Arab philosophy that he had championed was moribund.

Its demise made room for individual nationalisms, especially that of the Palestinians. Such a movement already existed in embryonic form. In the 1950s, in Egypt, a group of students with Palestinian backgrounds had begun to forge a path different from the one laid down by Nasser and the other Arab rulers. They were angry at the manipulation of the Palestinian issue by the Arab governments that, with the partial exception of Jordan, refused to absorb the Palestinian refugees, preferring to keep them in UN-run camps as a symbol of the Arab cause. And yet these same governments seemed in no hurry to vindicate that cause by facing Israel on the battlefield. Thus, believing themselves to be the only ones who cared truly and deeply about Palestine, these young men formed tiny cells, determined to take the fight into their own hands.

In 1959, in Kuwait where many of them had migrated since its oil boom generated an abundance of jobs, several of these tiny groups came together to form the Palestinian Liberation Movement. Its initials, read backward, spelled the Arabic word for conquest: *Al Fatah*. They established a periodical, *Filastinuna*, meaning *Our Palestine*.[15] When the PLO was founded five years later under Nasser's aegis, Fatah viewed it as a rival.

Fatah's leader was a thirty-year-old activist who called himself Yasser Arafat. Born in Cairo in 1929, where his family had moved from Jerusalem a couple of years earlier, Arafat's full name was Abd al-Rahman Abd al-Rauf Arafat al-Qudwa al-Husseini. The nickname, Yasser, means "easygoing," which seems not entirely apt for a man who told his most credulous biographer, Alan Hart, that he worked "between 18 and 19 hours a day . . . 365 days a year."[16]

According to some biographers, he was a distant cousin on his mother's side of the Grand Mufti Haj Amin al-Husseini, whereas others say it was on his father's side, or not at all.[17] Whatever the exact relationship, most versions agree that during his political maturation Arafat was involved with Husseini and his AHC.[18]

This is a sensitive question because of al-Husseini's intimate alliance with Hitler, which has been amply documented despite the disingenuous claim of Arafat's deputy, Salah Khalaf, known as Abu Iyad, that "anyone who knew him personally, myself included, knew" al-Husseini was no "Nazi sympathizer."[19] But, however much Arafat may have looked up to al-Husseini, there is no evidence he shared the older man's proclivity for Nazism which was a spent force by the time Arafat came of age.

Rather, Arafat's own youthful affinity was with the Muslim Brotherhood. His biographers, Andrew Gowers and Tony Walker, write:

> Arafat was drawn to the Brotherhood's militant doctrines of anti-imperialism and national revival through Islam. It remains a moot point whether Arafat was actually a member or merely a sympathizer—he insists now that he was never a member—but he drew heavily on *Ikhwan* [Brotherhood] support in student elections at King Fouad I University . . . and subsequently in elections for the Palestinian Students' League.[20]

Gowers and Walker speculate that the time Arafat spent in an Egyptian jail in 1954 was part of a crackdown on the Brotherhood, which had helped Nasser to reach power but then fell out with him violently.[21] And they postulate that the connection between Arafat and the Brotherhood helped to bring support to Fatah from Saudi Arabia relatively early.[22] In a like vein, Arafat chose the *nom du guerre*, Abu Ammar who, he explained, had been "captured, tortured to force him to give up his faith and finally put to death by the infidels. . . . the first martyr of Islam whose name became the symbol of total fidelity to one's faith and beliefs in the Arab world."[23]

Yet, Arafat himself was apparently somewhat casual in observing the rituals of Islam. Arafat's fawning authorized biographer, Alan Hart, quotes Um Jihad, wife of Arafat's deputy, Abu Jihad, as explaining that Arafat "always prays in the morning and usually he gathers the fives times a day into one."[24] But, however observant he may have been, Arafat's connection to his religious roots was important to his success and that of Fatah. Other Palestinian armed groups tended to secularism. The Popular Front for the Liberation of Palestine (PFLP) and two of its splinters, the PFLP-General Command and the Popular Democratic Front for the Liberation of Palestine (PDFLP), were Marxist or Marxist-Leninist. The leaders of the PFLP and the PDFLP and a large share of the members of all three groups were Christians. Two other groups, As-Saiqa and the Arab Liberation Front, were closely tied, respectively, to the strenuously secular Baathist governments of Syria and Iraq. Within Fatah, some of Arafat's closest collaborators were also Marxists, but other leaders, including Arafat, were not. The genius of Fatah was that its only cause was Palestine. Individual members could lean left or right, but Fatah was a single-issue group. And Arafat's success as a leader owed much to the fact that he embodied this undeviating focus.

This is not to say that in these early years he or Fatah envisioned a Palestinian *state*. Rather, its original purpose was simply to build an independent Palestinian fighting organization to spearhead the Arab struggle. The pan-Arabists, they said, who claimed that Arab unity was the route to liberating Palestine had it backward: the liberation of Palestine would pave the way to Arab unity. The exact configuration of Arab rule over the area could be determined once the Zionist interlopers had been expelled.

Fatah's ambiguity about a Palestinian state was evident as late as 1968 when, having largely taken over the PLO, it reaffirmed the provision of the 1964 Palestinian National Covenant written by Shuqairy that said:

> The Palestinian people believe in Arab unity. In order to contribute their share toward the attainment of that objective, however, they must, at the present stage of their struggle, safeguard their Palestinian identity and develop their consciousness of that identity.[25]

Although the idea of Palestinian statehood still developed only gradually, Arafat's Fatah was more earnest and effective than Shuqairy's PLO at fostering a national identity. And Fatah's philosophy of guerrilla struggle gained salience even with Nasser after the Arabs' 1967 defeat.

At the Khartoum summit of Arab leaders convened in August 1967 to discuss a response to their military debacle, Shuqairy's star was in obvious descent. Although the war tarnished all Arab leaders, Shuqairy suffered particular humiliation for having forecasted, with characteristic bombast, that "no Jew will remain alive." Such statements, it was recognized in the postmortems, had deeply damaged the Arab cause.

"The PLO was not even mentioned in the . . . final communiqué," at Khartoum, observes the Israeli expert Moshe Shemesh, and "the *fidai* [guerrilla] organizations became undisputed rulers in the Palestinian arena."[26] They might have simply pushed the PLO aside but, instead, with Nasser's help, they took it over and made it their own. A few months after Khartoum and a day after meeting with one of Nasser's aides, Shuqairy submitted his resignation, to be replaced as chairman by Yahya Hamouda, a neutral figure.[27] During the course of 1968, Fatah and the other armed groups largely gained control of the various bodies of the PLO, and by 1969 Hamouda gave way to Arafat.

Leaving behind the bombast of Shuqairy as well as the pro-Nazi heritage of Haj Amin al-Husseini, the Arafat-led PLO rapidly won a place for itself in the diffuse global revolutionary Left. As early as 1962, Arafat and other top Fatah leaders had visited Algeria, whose successful guerrilla war for independence from France offered a model and inspiration. One of the group, Abu-Jihad (the *nom de guerre* of Khalil al-Wazir), stayed on to open the PLO's first foreign office.[28]

The Algerian example proved to be crucial. The independence movement there had triumphed more in the political plain than the battlefield. Mohammed Yazid, who had served as the new government's minister of information, shared the lessons with Fatah. Portray the enemy as not only Israel but also "world imperialism," he counseled, and "present the Palestinian struggle as a struggle for liberation like the others."[29]

"The others" meant Communists as well as various movements around the globe professing a less orthodox anti-capitalism or fighting to be free of colonial rule. It would be some years before Moscow would open its arms to Fatah, but the non-European Communists were more receptive. Algeria provided entrée to the most important of these regimes—China, North Vietnam, and Cuba. Arafat and Abu-Jihad visited China in 1964, and the latter went on to North Vietnam.[30]

Beijing began to provide material aid to Fatah, and the group issued a series of pamphlets titled, *The Chinese Experience, The Vietnamese Experience, The Cuban Experience*, etc.[31] The admiration of the

Fatah leaders seems to have been genuine. Abu Iyad relates that on one of several subsequent visits:

> I was extremely impressed by the Chinese people's dedication. They seemed totally devoted to labor—manual or intellectual— and spent their leisure time in simple and healthy activities. Their life-style seemed characterized by a Puritanism worthy of the most fundamentalist Islam. "The Prophet couldn't have done better than Mao Zedong," I remarked to Arafat.[32]

Abu Iyad also found Cuba intoxicating. The "Cuban intelligence" official who greeted him on arrival was a "wonderfully humorous man," and Fidel was a "veritable force of nature . . . plain-speaking . . . earthy and vibrant."[33] The most important model, however, was North Vietnam, which was accumulating sympathizers worldwide for its long-odds war against America. "The Vietnamese resistance . . . filled me with a sense of hope," said Abu Iyad. "Everything I was to see in North Vietnam was a source of enrichment and inspiration for me."[34]

Thus did Fatah (and the PLO under Fatah's leadership) master a lingo that lifted their struggle out of the reactionary Arab past and imbedded it instead in an international movement of "progressive" forces. A seven-point program adopted by Fatah's central committee in January 1969 declared: "The struggle of the Palestinian people, like that of the Vietnamese people and other peoples of Asia, Africa and Latin America, is part of the historic process of the liberation of the oppressed peoples from colonialism and imperialism."[35]

In contrast to Abu Iyad, who was held spellbound by every Communist state he visited, Arafat maintained his ties with the religious and conservative side of the Arab world, never squandering the patronage he assiduously cultivated of the Saudi royals or the other dynasties of the oil-favored Gulf. Nonetheless, he could channel *Das Kapital* and the holy *Koran* with equal conviction. "Our struggle is part and parcel of every struggle against imperialism, injustice and oppression in the world," he affirmed. "It is part of the world revolution which aims at establishing social justice and liberating mankind."[36]

So central was the Vietnamese model to the new persona of the Palestinian movement that forty-odd years later, long after the end

of the Cold War, and with Hanoi straining to import large elements
of free enterprise into its economy, Arafat's successor, Mahmoud
Abbas, was still singing the praises of Vietnam's Communist revolution. During a 2010 visit to that country he averred:

> [W]e are comrades in struggle and fighting, and our vision of the
> future is one. Historically, people have always linked Palestine
> and Vietnam, and to this day, when people mention the Palestin-
> ian struggle they recall the struggle of the Vietnamese people.
> We have both suffered occupation, colonialism and oppression,
> but you eventually prevailed, and we are certain that, thanks to
> your position and your support, we shall prevail as well.[37]

By 1968, with the PLO now in Fatah's hands, a new revolutionary
identity established, its relations blossoming with Beijing, Hanoi,
and Havana, and the whole arrangement blessed by Nasser, Arafat
found that Moscow was ready to open its arms. Nasser included him
in his entourage on a visit to the USSR, using a pseudonym identifying him as an Egyptian so as to conceal him from the West. That
year, the Soviet press began to liken Fatah to the heroic "partisans"
of World War II, and Moscow arranged for some of its East European
satellite states to supply it with weapons.[38] In 1969, the Kremlin formally recognized the PLO as a legitimate "national liberation movement," and Prime Minister Alexei Kosygin hailed its "just national
liberation and anti-imperialist struggle."[39]

More important even than the arms and training that the Soviet connection provided were the political benefits. "To recruit the
Soviet Union as a sponsor was undoubtedly a great coup for Arafat, because its worldwide propaganda services [were put] at his disposal," comments journalist David Pryce-Jones.[40] The Soviet Union's
state news agencies, like the newspaper *Pravda* and the news service
TASS, might have had little international credibility, but Moscow
nonetheless influenced discourse outside its own precincts through
a network of front groups and sympathizers and the contacts with
respectable journalists cultivated by Soviet personnel in many fields
and guises.

The strategy of embedding itself in the global revolutionary Left
inspired the PLO to adopt a new statement of the goals and purposes. This was unveiled by Abu Iyad at a Beirut press conference in
October 1968. "I announced," he wrote, "that our strategic objective
was to work toward the creation of a democratic state in which Ar-

abs and Jews would live together harmoniously as fully equal citizens in the whole of historic Palestine."[41]

The import of this new approach was explained by Arafat biographers Gowers and Walker:

> Gone, said Fatah, were the old chauvinist slogans about revenge and "throwing the Jews into the sea" that had been the stock and trade of Shukairy's generation of leaders . . . Instead, the Palestinians were now proposing to co-operate with those Jews who had been prepared to throw off the shackles of Zionism in building a completely new society.[42]

In a later interview with Gowers and Walker, Abu Iyad added this gloss: "In itself this was saying something revolutionary at the time as far as Arabs were concerned: that we were willing to live with the Jews in Palestine."[43]

Enduring the presence of some Jews, "revolutionary" though this idea may have been, did not imply acceptance of the existence of Israel. On the contrary, Fatah's manifesto of October 1968, explained: "Our struggle aspires to liberate the Jews themselves . . . [O]ur revolution, which believes in the freedom and dignity of men, considers first and foremost . . . the radical uprooting of Zionism and the liquidation of the conquest of the Zionist settlers in all forms." In other words, after the "liquidation" of Israel, the Jews could live on as a minority in Arab Palestine, where they could enjoy the same "dignified life . . . they had always lived under the auspices of the Arab state."[44]

And even this dubious honor was not offered to *all* the Jews of Israel, but only, according to the Palestinian covenant, those "Jews who had normally resided in Palestine until the beginning of the Zionist invasion." The "Zionist invasion" was defined in other Fatah documents as having commenced in 1917 with the Balfour Declaration. In other words, those who had arrived before 1917, and perhaps their descendants, could stay on as citizens of "democratic Palestine." The overwhelming majority of Israeli Jews would, however, have to leave. Boiled down, this differed little from Shuqairy's threat to drive them into the sea, but it sounded better.

Nor was this Arab state that the PLO envisioned intended to be "secular" although the phrase "democratic, secular state" came into circulation and was commonly attributed to the PLO. Gresh reports:

Contrary to a widespread notion, the idea of a democratic state is not associated with the idea of a secular state in Palestinian political thought. In fact, the idea of a secular state does not appear in any of the PLO's official texts of this period nor in those of Fatah or any other organization, although it can be found in one or two declarations.[45]

As Bernard Lewis catalogued at the time, the constitution of almost every Arab state, including those that had come under the rule of revolutionary parties professing "secular" ideologies, proclaimed Islam to be the "state religion" or the "religion of the state."[46]

The emphasis was on "democratic," but this was not meant in the sense in which the term is used in the West. The "democratic" countries after whom the PLO intended to model its state were the ones over which Abu Iyad gushed: the People's Republic of China, North Vietnam, and Cuba.

If the "democratic, secular state" was intended neither to be democratic nor secular, in the normal meaning of those terms, neither was it clear, for that matter, that it would long be a state. As late as 1971, Nabil Sha'ath, a top Fatah official, rebutted charges from left-wing groups within the PLO that Fatah had abandoned pan-Arabism, by reiterating Fatah's original view of the relation between the Palestinian and the broader Arab cause. "We see the Palestinian state as a step towards federation," he insisted.[47]

If there was, in short, more packaging than substance in the new vision that Arafat and his fellows were proffering; it nonetheless sufficed to put the Palestinian cause in good standing with the revolutionary Left. When, in 1969, some hundred-and-fifty young Europeans traveled to a Middle Eastern training camp to prepare themselves to enlist in revolutionary struggles, Palestinian liberation was among the designated causes.[48] That same year, a time of extreme radical agitation among Western youth, a bomb was planted in the communal hall of West Berlin's Jewish congregation. The authors of the act left a flyer decrying "the Left's continued paralysis in facing up to the theoretical implications of the Middle-East conflict, a paralysis for which German guilt feelings are responsible." It went on:

> We admittedly gassed Jews and therefore feel obliged to protect them from further threats of genocide. This kind of neurotic backward-looking anti-Fascism, obsessed as it is by past history,

totally disregards the non-justifiability of the State of Israel. True anti-Fascism consists in an explicit and unequivocal identification with the fighting *fedayeen*.[49]

Also that year the journal *Free Palestine* exulted: "[Al Fatah] has certainly been able to achieve a breakthrough in what used to be a Zionist domain: the Western leftist movements. Al Fatah has become to many synonymous with freedom fighting and an expression of struggle against oppression everywhere."[50]

Of course, the revolutionary Left occupied only a corner of the Western political scene. But, even if marginal, it was in much better odor than the fascist Right that had once constituted the European allies of the Arab leadership. Hitler's collaborator, al-Husseini, had continued to represent the Palestinian Arab cause into the 1960s, and the propaganda offices of Nasser's government employed several escaped officials of the Nazi regime. This may have explained some of the self-defeating over-the-top rhetoric that helped to put the Arabs at a disadvantage in the contest for international sympathy.

Now, however, a critical makeover had been achieved. No longer did Israel enjoy the public relations gift of opponents who were collaborators of Hitler and Goebbels; now they faced the comrades of such chic, romanticized figures as Ho Chi Minh and Che Guevara. Not only had David become Goliath, but on the other side the frog had become a prince.

This transformation reshaped the view of the conflict not only in the eyes of the international Left but to some extent in the mainstream. For example, *TIME*, whose reportage cum commentary had been warmly pro-Israel in 1967 to the point of endorsing the retention of territories Israel had captured, now ran a cover story on Al Fatah. The headline, "The Guerrilla Threat in the Middle East," sounded negative, but the body of the article was admiring:

> With the fanaticism and desperation of men who have nothing
> to lose, the fedayeen have taken the destiny of the Palestinians
> into their own hands. . . . In the aftermath of the Arab defeat,
> the fedayeen are today the only ones carrying the fight to Israel.
> The guerrillas provide an outlet for the fierce Arab resentment
> of Israel and give an awakened sense of pride to a people accus-
> tomed to decades of defeat, disillusionment and humiliation.
> In the process, the Arabs have come to idolize Mohammed

("Yasser") Arafat, a leader of El Fatah fedayeen who has emerged as the most visible spokesman for the commandos.[51]

In the battle for the hearts and minds of the rest of the world, the Arab side had taken, to borrow a phrase from the PLO's new hero, Chairman Mao, a great leap forward.

three

The Uses of Terrorism

The redefinition of the Middle East conflict from Arab–Israeli to Israeli–Palestinian sapped the sympathy Israel had enjoyed as an underdog since its founding. The emergence of Palestinian nationalism following the Six Day War transformed Israelis from "pioneers" into "colonizers." This furnished an ideological basis for supporting Israel's enemies that dovetailed with the enduring "realist" considerations that led diplomats and military brass of most countries at most times to tilt to the Arab side. Their instincts of self-interest were powerfully reinforced in the 1970s by new measures of intimidation brought to bear by the Arabs.

The intimidation took two forms: terrorism and oil. After Israel occupied the West Bank in 1967, Yasser Arafat himself led an effort to kindle guerrilla warfare there. But the small size of the territory and the nature of the terrain made it unsuitable for a guerrilla campaign. The Israeli army was strong and highly motivated, unlike the forces of many genuine colonialist armies whose morale was often low. And the population of the West Bank, which had forged ties with the Jordanian monarchy over the preceding two decades, was initially lukewarm to the Palestine Liberation Organization (PLO) cause.

So Fatah and the more radical Popular Front for the Liberation of Palestine (PLFP) and its various offshoots (all of these groups operating under the umbrella of the PLO) focused instead on small-scale infiltrations into Israel to kill random civilians and destroy property. In the various Arab uprisings of the 1920s and 1930s, invariably described as "glorious" in Arab discourse, women, children, and the elderly were targeted as freely as men capable of bearing arms.*

---

* And, indeed, much the same may be observed today in Syria, Iraq, Leb-

As Israel took steps to prevent infiltration, measures that were largely although not totally effective, the Arabs shifted their attacks to more vulnerable venues. The idea of striking Israelis outside of Israel was pioneered by the Marxist PLO faction, the PFLP. In July 1968, just a year after the Six Day War, a team of three PFLP commandoes hijacked an El Al flight en route from Rome to Tel Aviv and forced it to land in Algiers. Although the initial motive for such acts was simply to get at Israelis where they were less protected, the execution of terror abroad soon proved to have the considerable ancillary benefit of evoking an appeasement response from the nations that found themselves to be proxy battlegrounds.

Quite possibly, the idea of hijacking was borrowed from American radicals, several of whom had recently commandeered flights, demanding to be taken to Cuba. But the Arabs put some new twists on this form of protest. For the most part, the American radicals just wanted to get to Cuba because they idealized its political system. They used the method of air piracy because Americans were barred from travel to Cuba, and as a means of dramatization. The Arabs, in contrast, were hungry for violence. There was relatively little in this first PFLP hijacking, but the copilot was injured by the hijackers, one of whom then dipped his finger into the blood and tasted it, exulting, according to an account later given by an Italian priest aboard the plane, "It's good, the blood of Israel."[1] In subsequent actions, his comrades were to savor much more blood of Israelis and others.

A second innovation of Arab hijackers was to hold passengers and crew hostage, demanding the release of prisoners in Israel or elsewhere and sometimes also seeking ransom in cash. In the case of the hijacking to Algiers, the non-Israeli hostages were released promptly, but the Israelis were detained. After a few days the women and children among them were released, but a dozen Israeli men were held for forty days and "treated like war prisoners," in the words of the plane's pilot.[2] This means that they were held by the government of Algeria acting in shameless collusion with the hijackers. (This, too, contrasted with Cuba which, despite its enmity to Washington, did not abet hijackers except by allowing them to stay on Cuban soil.) Initially, Israel refused to bargain with Algeria. But eventually it ca-

---

anon, and elsewhere where Arabs are fighting other Arabs. A bomb in a market is a routine form of warfare.

pitulated and a deal was struck through the mediation of the Italian government in which two dozen Palestinian prisoners were released by Israel in exchange for the hostages and aircraft after thirty-nine days' captivity.

In response to the Algiers hijacking, El Al initiated security measures that foiled other hijackings, but the Palestinian tactic of terrorizing civilian aviation was just getting started. Five months later, two PFLP members raked an El Al jet preparing for takeoff in Athens with submachine guns, and one hurled incendiary grenades at the engines. The fire they ignited was put out, but one passenger died from his bullet wounds and a well-known Israeli actress, Hanna Maron, lost her leg.

Israeli Prime Minister Levi Eshkol sounded rattled as he denounced "insane terrorism," while Minister of Transportation Moshe Carmel struck a calmer, more ominous note. Noting that "members of the [PFLP] openly train in Lebanon," Carmel warned, as *The New York Times* summarized, that "Israel would not tolerate a situation in which El Al airliners were attacked and those of Arab countries could fly in peace and safety."[3] A few days later, Israeli commandos landed at the Beirut airport under cover of darkness and dynamited thirteen parked Arab airliners.

Israel's claim that the terrorists were aided and abetted by the various Arab governments was inarguable, but its choice of Lebanon as the target for retaliation was dubious given the weakness and relative moderation of the Beirut government. The UN Security Council passed a resolution denouncing Israel's action without mentioning the attacks that had provoked it. And French President de Gaulle, who, in 1967, had frozen a contract for the delivery of additional Mirage jet fighters to Israel, now seized the moment to claim a high-minded rationale for canceling it outright. Whatever the justice or wisdom of Israel's attack on Lebanese soil, the United Nation's unbalanced resolution was a harbinger of much that was to follow.

Two months later, February 1969, the Athens attack was repeated in Zurich, where four terrorists sprayed machine gun fire and tossed grenades at an El Al plane taxiing for takeoff. A pilot trainee was shot through the chest and died at the hospital. More would probably have been killed were it not for the heroics of Mordechai Rachamim, a twenty-two-year-old who had immigrated with his parents from Iraqi Kurdistan seventeen years before and was now a member of a squad of sky marshals that Israel had hastened to form in the wake of the Algiers hijacking.

Armed only with a twenty-two-caliber Beretta, deemed small enough that its bullets, if fired within an airplane, would pose little risk to the craft's integrity, Rachamim at first shot back at the attackers through a blown-out window in the cockpit. But the "horrifying realization" that a bullet or grenade to a fuel tank could immolate the entire plane impelled him to improvise more dramatic action.[4] He sprinted to the back of the now-stationary plane, and used an emergency exit to slide down to the tarmac, then scaled the perimeter fence and closed on the terrorists while finding cover behind mounds of snow plowed high along the road that paralleled the runway. When he got close he yelled at the gang to drop their weapons. Apparently not recognizing that he was alone and that his small pistol was no match for their two Kalashnikovs and grenades, one of the two gun-toters did as commanded. The other, apparently the leader, turned to confront Rachamim who shot him dead on the spot. Now out of ammunition, Rachamim rushed the other three terrorists in a rage. He seized one by the throat and began choking him, screaming "Why are you attacking civilians? Why won't you face me on the battlefield?" He stopped only when he felt the barrel of a gun pressing his back. It was a Swiss policeman, ordering him to desist.

Rachamim was taken into custody along with the three surviving terrorists, loaded into a police car where he was seated between two of them, none of the three in handcuffs. He was held for a month before being released on bail and allowed to fly to Israel after promising to return for trial on manslaughter charges,[5] which he did nine months later, winning acquittal.

With El Al increasingly well protected, the terrorists turned to non-Israeli carriers. In August 1969, a TWA flight from Los Angeles to Tel Aviv was commandeered over Italy by two hijackers, styling themselves the Che Guevara Brigade. One of them, a twenty-five-year-old woman who had once worked as a school teacher, was Leila Khaled. Petite, attractive, and given to posing with a Kalashnikov, she became something of an icon in the Marxist-Leninist world. At the time, the hijackers said they had targeted a US airline to protest America's sale of military aircraft to Israel. Later, in her autobiography, Khaled said, "Our minimum objective was the inscription of the name of Palestine on the memory of mankind."[6]

They forced the plane to land in Damascus where the crew and passengers executed an emergency evacuation before the "brigade" blew up the cockpit. Collaborating with the terrorists as the Algerian government had done, Syria held passengers and crew prisoner overnight, then released all but the six Israelis on board. Days later, four female Israelis were released. But the two men were held more than three months until Israel agreed to exchange thirteen Syrians in its custody.[7] The US State Department denied a leak that, in brokering the deal, Washington had promised Hafez al-Assad's government a seat on the UN Security Council,[8] but Syria was indeed soon elected to one of the rotating seats for the next two years, only the second time in the United Nations's history that the country had secured this position.

Only ten days after the TWA hijacking, grenades were tossed at the El Al offices in Brussels and the Israeli embassies in Bonn and The Hague. These caused injuries but no deaths. The PFLP released to the Lebanese press photos of four perpetrators who it said ranged in age between thirteen and sixteen, and whom it christened "Tiger Cubs," members of the front's Ho Chi Minh Division. It also warned in a press conference that it would no longer seek to avoid deaths among the nationals of other countries in its attacks on Israeli assets.[9]

As if to illustrate the point, two months later, November 1969, two men belonging to the Popular Struggle Front, an offshoot of the PFLP, threw a hand grenade into the El Al office in downtown Athens. Among the fourteen people injured none was Israeli. Hardest hit was the Natsos family, residents of a working class suburb of Athens who were migrating to Canada and happened to book El Al for one leg of their journey.

The father, Christos, was the only one to escape injury. "Why? Why?" he sobbed to journalists after his wife and two young sons were rushed to the hospital.[10] A few days later two-year-old George succumbed to his wounds while his five-year-old brother, Athanasios, was blinded, although surgeons held out hope they might restore vision to one of his eyes. The mother, Katina, was also seriously wounded. The two attackers arrested carried Jordanian passports. "If I ever meet a Jordanian, I am going to kill him," swore Christos after little George's death.[11]

February 1970 was a particularly bloody month. In Munich, three terrorists bombed and strafed an airport bus and a transit lounge holding passengers awaiting an El Al flight, causing one death and many injuries. Days later, a Swissair flight from Zurich to Tel Aviv was brought down by a bomb, killing all aboard, sixteen Israelis and thirty-one others. Yet another PFLP offshoot, the PFLP-General Command, claimed responsibility.

In July 1970, as the two men who had tossed the grenade that killed George Natsos and blinded his brother awaited sentencing, a team of six commandos, each carrying weapons, took over an Olympic Airways flight from Beirut to Athens. They commenced negotiations for the exchange of those on board for the seven Arab terrorists held in Greek prisons: the two killers of Natsos, as well as the two who had machine gunned the El Al flight in 1968, and three others whose plans to hijack a TWA flight had been aborted.

The Greek government agreed to the trade but insisted on the formality of first completing the process of sentencing the grenade-throwers. The government's official statement explained: "When the Greek laws will have been observed and the sense of justice will have been fulfilled by putting two of the Arabs on trial, the Government will hand them over to the International Red Cross."[12] Within a month, all seven terrorists were free.

Having succeeded in wreaking havoc at very little cost to themselves, the air terrorists were on a roll. Foreshadowing the terror spectacular mounted by al Qaeda decades later, the PFLP hit upon the idea of hijacking several jetliners simultaneously.

The plot was executed on September 6, 1970. A TWA flight from Frankfurt, a Swissair flight from Zurich, and El Al and Pan Am flights from Amsterdam were hijacked simultaneously. The first two were flown to a remote military airstrip in Jordan called Dawson's Field. The last was a jumbo jet unable to negotiate Dawson's short runway, so it was taken to Cairo.

The events aboard the El Al flight were the most dramatic, since El Al uniquely had begun carrying sky marshals. When the two hijackers made their move, the pilot put the plane into a sudden drop which succeeded in knocking them off their feet. Then a sky marshal shot and killed one hijacker, a Nicaraguan "Sandinista," while others overpowered his accomplice, a short woman who turned out to be none other than Leila Khaled, back again just a year after her first hijacking, having undergone plastic surgery to avoid recognition.

With one would-be hijacker dead and the other subdued, the pilot made an emergency landing in London. Almost at once, reportedly, he received orders to take off for home. Apparently, Israel was eager to interrogate Khaled rather than release her to Britain. But London would not allow the takeoff and took custody of Khaled. Three days later another PFLP commando hijacked a British Overseas Air Company flight and took it, too, to Dawson's Field, demanding the release of Khaled.

After a few days, the PFLP released most of its hostages, except crew members and Jews, and dynamited the three planes. This had unforeseen consequences in Jordan where Palestinians constituted the majority, their numbers augmented by King Hussein's policy, unique among Israel's neighbors, of granting citizenship to some of the refugees of 1948. The PLO had thus based itself in Jordan, where thousands of young fighters trained in camps around the country. As the movement gained momentum the PLO increasingly acted as if sovereign in Jordan, setting up road blocks throughout the capital, ignoring local laws, and disdaining Jordanian police and officials. King Hussein had tolerated these infringements on his sovereignty, but he could not allow them free rein to operate against Israel. A host country is always considered responsible for attacks emanating from its soil, and Hussein knew that Israel practiced severe retaliation.

More than once the king had come to the brink of expelling the PLO, but he dared not defy the other Arab states, especially Nasser's Egypt, which considered the Palestinian cause sacrosanct (except of course on their own territory). The use of a Jordanian airfield for hijacking operations and destruction of Western aircraft despite the king's firm alliance with the West was, however, a step too far—all the more so as one of the proclaimed goals of these highjackings was to destroy a new US peace initiative that Jordan had accepted, as had Israel and Egypt. This was the last straw. Only a week earlier King Hussein had escaped an attempt on his life, the second within three months' span, both attributable in all likelihood to the Palestinian bands.

Now, he unleashed his army against the Palestinian guerrillas and crushed them, surprising many who had overestimated the military prowess of the PLO. The fighting took a toll in civilians as well as combatants, with the number of Palestinians deaths estimated variously at two or three thousand. Nasser mediated an end to the onslaught at the price of the PLO's withdrawal from Jordan. A codicil to the deal secured the freedom of the remaining airline hostages in exchange for the release of seven terrorists from prisons in England, Germany, and Switzerland. These were Leila Khaled; the three who had attacked the Munich airport bus and lounge; and the three who had strafed and grenaded the El Al jet in Zurich and managed to escape Mordechai Rachamim's wrath.

Flight from Jordan proved to be the prelude to a new chapter in the history of the PLO. Until this point, all or virtually all of the attacks on civilian air travel had been the work of the PFLP and its offshoots. Fatah had held back from this particular tactic because, as the dominant group in the PLO, it felt answerable to the Arab states. Arafat's deputy Abu Iyad chafed at this self-restraint, complaining that Fatah had "compromised its revolutionary character" trading "militancy" for "respectability."[13]

His fretting proved premature. Although the PFLP's recklessness had pushed King Hussein too far and brought the whole PLO to disaster, it apparently convinced Fatah that it, too, needed to turn to international terror to compete with the PFLP for headlines and a reputation for revolutionary fervor. This impetus was reinforced by logistics. Expelled from Jordan, the PLO moved its headquarters and operational bases to Lebanon. There, it still had access to a border with Israel, but a shorter and more remote one that made infiltration more difficult, another factor arguing for action abroad.

Yet Arafat was reluctant to abandon all claim to the respectability his adroit phrasing of the Palestinian cause had won in the West. So he resurrected a tactic from the past. In 1965, when Fatah staged its first raids inside Israel, it took no credit. Instead, responsibility was claimed by al-Asifa, a fictional creation that was nothing but an alias for Fatah. Years later, Arafat explained his reasoning: "If al-Asifa succeeded, Fatah would then endorse" its actions. "If it did not succeed, then al-Asifa would take responsibility . . . and not Fatah."[14]

Fatah's new false front announced itself to the world in November 1971, just over a year after the expulsion from Jordan. Four men gunned down Jordanian Prime Minister Wasfi Tal, the executor of King Hussein's crackdown on the Palestinians, in the lobby of the Cairo Sheraton. Reenacting the bloodthirstiness of the first El Al hijacker, one of the killers knelt beside the body and lapped up Tal's blood. The PFLP at once issued a press release claiming credit, but the boast was false. It soon was established that the party behind the deed was a previously unheard of group calling itself Black September.

The next month the same group shot and wounded the Jordanian ambassador in London, and a few months later it mowed down five Jordanians in their sleep in Germany, claiming they were intelligence agents of some sort. Less spectacularly, Black September was apparently also responsible for several attacks on European oil and industrial facilities in 1971 and 1972.

So, by 1972, in addition to the PFLP and its offshoots, there was nominally a new major player in the international terror game. In February 1972, a team of three Arabs hijacked a Lufthansa plane and forced it to fly to Yemen, demanding release of those detained in Germany for the murder of the five Jordanians. One of the hostages was Joseph Kennedy III, the nineteen-year-old son of Robert F. Kennedy, assassinated four years earlier by the Palestinian, Sirhan Sirhan, whose release from jail in the United States had been a demand of earlier hijackers. In this case, however, the gunmen settled for a five-million-dollar cash ransom from Germany.

The year 1972 also marked the initiation of a new tactic, although it is not clear which of the terror groups was behind it. Arab men in Europe seduced local women then arranged trips in which the women could meet the young men's families in Palestine. In each case on some pretext, the Arabs convinced the women that they had to fly on separate flights and they loaded some small electronic device, a purported gift for the family back home, in the women's luggage. The "gift" contained a bomb. In February 1972, one such bomb detonated in an El Al cargo hold, but the damage was less than intended, and the pilot managed to return to Rome's airport and land the craft without casualties.

Early in May that year, Black September seized a Sabena flight to Tel Aviv where the four terrorists—two men, two women—demanded release of 315 Palestinians in exchange for the passengers and crew. The Israeli government commenced negotiations with them, but also organized a rescue operation. The hijackers were told that their demands would be met, and a team of mechanics in white overalls proceeded onto the tarmac to make the plane ready to fly to an Arab country. The "mechanics" were in truth an elite squad that stormed through the emergency doors, shooting the two males hijackers to death and taking prisoner the two females. The rescue team included two future prime ministers—Ehud Barak and Binyamin Netanyahu—as well as Mordechai Rachamim, the hero of the Zurich attack.

After this thwarted effort, the *Christian Science Monitor* reported that "Arab world opinion" expected "further and better-planned hijackings" and generally welcomed the prospect. "Photos of the Arab skyjackers were splashed through the press in Beirut and other Arab capitals, presented mainly as the pictures of 'heroes,'" the newspaper said.[15]

Two weeks later, these hopes were rewarded not by a hijacking but a new kind of attack on civil aviation. Three Japanese passengers disembarked from an Air France flight at Israel's Lod Airport carrying violin cases. From these, they extracted assault rifles and hand grenades and began killing anyone they could, taking twenty-six lives, seventeen of them Puerto Rican pilgrims. The trio had escaped closer scrutiny because they were not Arabs: they were members of the Japanese Red Army acting on behalf of the PFLP out of "revolutionary solidarity."

The pace of international terror attacks was accelerating. In September 1972, Munich hosted the summer Olympics which promised catharsis to two nations. For (West) Germany, the games signified a negation of the ugly past symbolized by the 1936 Berlin Olympics, a showcase for the Nazi regime. For Israel, the parade of Jewish athletes carrying the flag of Israel in the city so closely linked to Hitler seemed an affirmation of the mantra, *am Yisrael chai*, the Jewish people live.

But all of this was turned upside down when a team of eight armed Black September members stormed the residential block housing the Israeli team. Two athletes who fought back barehanded were killed on the spot, and nine were taken hostage. Spurning Israeli offers of help, Bavarian authorities planned a rescue operation in which the terrorists and hostages were first helicoptered to a military air base from which the terrorists were falsely informed that they would be allowed to fly with their prisoners to an Arab country. In fact, the Germans planned to attack them at the airport, using snipers and/or a special forces team that was stowed aboard the aircraft designated for the terrorists' supposed escape.

Astoundingly, members of the German special forces, as they waited for the terrorists and the hostages to be transferred from the Olympic village to the airport, *voted* to abort the mission on the grounds that they might be risking their own lives. Thus, the authorities had only the snipers to rely on, but there were fewer snipers than terrorists. The snipers opened fire as the terrorists alighted from the helicopters. Those who weren't instantly downed tossed hand grenades into the choppers where the nine bound Israeli hostages sat, mortally wounding all of them.

Five of the eight terrorists were killed in the gunfire, and the other three were taken into custody. But, not for long. A month later, a Lufthansa flight from Beirut to Frankfurt was hijacked and forced to divert to Zagreb, Yugoslavia. The hijackers demanded release of the three Olympics-massacre perpetrators, and the German government acquiesced at once, demanding only that the crew and eleven passengers be released simultaneously. It loaded the three onto a small executive jet and flew them to Zagreb where they boarded the hijacked plane. The hijackers, however, did not release their hostages but rather had the plane take off for Tripoli where the terrorists received a celebratory welcome. "The liberated heroes of the Munich [Olympics] operation and their liberators landed safely tonight," exulted Libyan radio.[16]

The Israeli government protested bitterly, but German Chancellor Willy Brandt defended his decision, saying, "The passengers and the crew were threatened with annihilation . . . I . . . saw no alternative but to yield to this ultimatum and avoid further senseless bloodshed."[17] Brandt's adamancy about avoiding "senseless bloodshed" left him vulnerable to terrorist blackmail. Fatah leader Abu Iyad observed contemptuously that "German authorities, moved by a sense of guilt or perhaps out of cowardice, were clearly anxious to have the captured fedayeen off their hands."[18]

This and the fact that the hijacked flight had carried, apart from the hijackers, only eleven passengers, all of them male, stimulated speculation that Bonn had been complicit in the entire episode. Author Aaron Klein put it:

> It was only a matter of time before a hijacked plane or some
> other extortionate measure would "force" the Germans to re-
> lease the three terrorists, who were, after all, putting German
> lives at risk. German, Palestinian, and Israeli sources contended
> that the hijacking . . . was coordinated, in advance, with German
> authorities. . . . When Ulrich Wagner, senior aide to the [Ger-
> man] interior minister Genscher, was asked point-blank and
> on camera what he thought of the alleged German-Palestinian
> scheme, he replied, "Yes, I think it's probably true."[19]

The operational commander of the Olympics killings, although not a direct participant, was Mohamed Daoud Oudeh, known as Abu Daoud. He found himself behind bars not long thereafter, albeit not for the Munich crime. Rather, he was arrested and condemned to death in Jordan for leading an infiltration of terrorists into Amman. This prompted Black September to mount "Operation Abu Daoud" to force his release.

It was staged not in Europe but in Khartoum where a team of eight gunmen took over a reception at the residence of the Saudi ambassador. A large number of hostages were taken and released gradually, the quarry being two American diplomats, Curtis Moore and Cleo Noel, who had rotated as Washington's chief representative in Sudan, and a Belgian diplomat, Guy Eid. The targeting of Eid remains unexplained. The terrorists said it was because he was Jewish, but he was not; and the name Eid, as they might have known, is actually Arab, reflecting the provenance of one of his forebears.

The hostage-takers demanded the release of various Palestinian prisoners in Israeli and Jordanian jails, along with Sirhan Sirhan and members of the German Red Army Faction, the so-called Baader-Meinhof gang. But they gradually scaled down their demands to just Abu Daoud. While negotiations with the Sudanese government were still under way, the PLO's Voice of Palestine broadcast this message: "Do what is required quickly because the blood of the martyrs is a revolution."[20] At this, the three diplomat hostages were taken to the basement of the building and, bound hand and foot, riddled with bullets by all eight terrorists.

Then, the radio station of Fatah broadcast further orders: "Your mission is over . . . Present yourselves to the Sudanese authorities with courage."[21] Fatah's leaders may have had a deal with Sudan's government or may have known that it would not dare impose any real punishment. The gunmen were taken into custody, tried, convicted, had their conviction upheld by the Sudanese Supreme Court, and then were released. They had not secured the freedom of Abu Daoud, but two months later he was included in a general amnesty of Palestinian prisoners, part of a bargain by King Hussein to restore himself to the good graces of Egypt and Syria.

Throughout the rest of 1973, the tempo of terror attacks in Europe continued unabated. In Cyprus, an El Al plane was fired upon and the building housing the Israeli ambassador was bombed. In Rome, an El Al employee was gunned down in the street, and two Arabs were arrested at Fiumicino Airport carrying revolvers and hand grenades. Two months later, five more were arrested with missiles preparing to down an EL Al flight. In Athens, a gunman tried to storm the El Al offices and, when thwarted, fled to a nearby hotel, taking seventeen hostages whom he traded for safe passage to Syria. Weeks later in that city, terrorists arrived too late to seize the El Al flight they had targeted, so they tossed their grenades and emptied their weapons randomly into a passenger lounge, killing three and wounding fifty-five. In Paris, six gunmen seized the Saudi embassy during a gathering, taking Arab and French hostages. They released the French in exchange for safe passage out of the country with their Arab hostages in tow.

As the toll of Palestinian terrorism mounted, the world repeatedly submitted, paying ransoms and releasing prisoners, and granting a miscellany of other demands. In this climate, terrorists never needed to fear capture. If arrested, they could be confident that new hostage-taking operations would follow to secure their freedom. In late 1973, *The New York Times* did a survey and concluded: "Although most Arab terrorists responsible for hijackings, kidnappings and the seizure and execution of hostages over the last few years have been captured or have given themselves up, few have suffered meaningful punishments." The paper listed thirty separate incidents, and in almost all cases reported that the guilty parties had been released. Author David A. Korn noted in his account of the Khartoum massacre that "in every case of Arab terrorism to that time, Arab and Western governments had let the killers go unpunished."[22] And, according to Aaron Klein, "a survey conducted by the Israeli Foreign Ministry found that 204 terrorists were convicted of terror-related felonies in countries outside the Middle East between 1968 and 1975; by late 1975, only three remained behind bars."[23]

The governments most compliant with the terrorists were those of the Arab states. Some of them gave enthusiastic support, reveling vicariously in the violence. Thus, Algeria and Syria held hostage Israeli passengers delivered to them by hijackers. Libyan dictator Muammar Qaddafi's support for Black September went beyond being its principal financial backer. Even before the three surviving Munich Olympics murderers were freed, he successfully demanded that the bodies of the five others killed by the German snipers be flown to Tripoli for heroes' burials.

Even the moderate Arab governments with scruples about targeting civil aviation and other noncombatants found it difficult to criticize anything the Palestinian groups did, no matter how egregious. Hussein of Jordan was the notable exception to this. His government was, for example, the only one in the Arab world to condemn the attack on the Munich Olympics; all the other Arab governments sent representatives to the funeral for the deceased perpetrators that Qaddafi staged in Libya.[24]

In addition to exhibiting an inability to distinguish ends and means in their support for the Palestinians, the Arab countries were plain scared. Sudan's president, Jaafar Nimeiry, explained his release of the murderers of American diplomats Curtis Moore and Cleo Noel, according to David Korn, on the grounds that, "Sudanese interests everywhere would be threatened if the Black September men were permanently jailed in the Sudan; Sudanese diplomatic missions abroad might be attacked and Sudanese diplomats killed."[25] Others showed the same fear. When a farewell ceremony was held in Khartoum for the widows of Moore and Noel, and the two deceased men in their coffins, the representatives of only two Arab states dared appear. The PLO leader Abu Iyad later chortled, "The Arab regimes didn't like us . . . but at least they feared us and took our opinions into account."[26]

A high point, in Iyad's rapturous telling, was the 1974 Arab summit in Rabat that confirmed the PLO's claim to be the "sole legitimate representative" of the Palestinian people, thus wresting from King Hussein of Jordan the right to speak for the West Bank:

> The meeting of the Arab Foreign Ministers Council, held in Rabat a few days before the summit, unfolded in a climate of terror. The Moroccan capital was alive with the most alarmist rumors: To listen to them, a veritable army of terrorists was preparing a whole series of attacks, indeed a massacre . . . The members of the PLO delegation participating in the working sessions of the council noted the extent to which the mounting anxiety influenced the attitude of the Arab ministers: even those known for their pro-Hussein bias were becoming ardent defenders of the PLO! The Rabat Summit was an outstanding victory for us. All the Arab heads of state, including King Hussein, adopted a series of resolutions in our favor.[27]

It seems clear that Abu Iyad, one of Arafat's two oldest colleagues and top aides, was the chief of Black September, and that blood-soaked group, at first mysterious in its origins, turned out to be nothing other than Fatah in disguise. Sudanese police investigating the Khartoum assassinations learned that, upon arrival in the country, the eight terrorists had been collected from the airport by the driver of the Fatah embassy. (Fatah enjoyed full diplomatic status in Sudan.) On the day of the operation, the terrorists had arrived at the Saudi facility in a Land Rover bearing the embassy's diplomatic plates, and they had secured entry to the reception by presenting the invitation that had been addressed to the Fatah embassy. The investigators discovered, too, that the Fatah ambassador had left the country just before the takeover was launched. On searching his office, they found written plans for the operation including sketches of the Saudi embassy. Arafat, himself, although he had been unreachable throughout the hostage drama, suddenly reemerged after the murders and negotiated the surrender of the killers. Once they were in custody, the PLO "privately . . . threatened reprisal if the Sudanese continued to hold them or put them on trial" even while it "publicly . . . continued to disavow the killings," according to David Korn's definitive account.[28]

The question of who was behind the Munich massacre yielded the same answer. In a preface to Abu Iyad's memoirs (which he co-authored), French journalist Eric Rouleau noted coyly that the CIA and the Mossad believe that Abu Iyad "organized" the Olympics attack. When Abu Daoud, the operational commander of that outrage, was held by the Jordanians, he broadcast a statement on radio. "There is no such thing as Black September. Fatah announces its own operations under this name. . . . Abu Iyad carries out special operations whose quality . . . is accentuated."[29] Helena Cobban, the pro-Palestinian journalist who claimed that the PLO/Black September relationship was a mere "flirtation," belittled Daoud's "confession" (she put the word in quote marks) on the grounds that he was in Jordanian custody.[30] But he was soon released and never changed his story. Three decades later, Abu Daoud gave an interview to the Associated Press in a Damascus hospital in which he actually added more telling details: "I remember Abu Iyad looked at me and said: 'Let's participate in the Olympics in our own way. Let's kidnap (Israeli) hostages and swap them for prisoners in Israel.'"[31]

Whereas the Arab states surrendered even more abjectly than Europeans to Palestinian terror, Israel, on the other hand, offered the greatest resistance. True, it bargained exchanges of Palestinian prisoners for Israeli hostages held by Algeria after the 1968 El Al hijacking and by Syria after the 1969 TWA hijacking. But its security measures prevented any successful El Al hijackings after the first one, and it mostly resisted releasing prisoners. It also fought back fiercely. After the Munich massacre, a special unit was created that attempted to track down everyone in the Palestinian chain of command who had had a hand in the operation. Almost all were then assassinated, as were other figures involved in the terror, such as Wadi Haddad, the operational mastermind of the PFLP's strikes.*

Israel's retaliation came at a cost to its relations with the West. When Israel assassinated Ali Hassan Salameh, one of the other Fatah officers in charge of the Olympics hostage-taking, the CIA was reportedly angered because Salameh had become their liaison with Fatah. Earlier, the murder in Norway of a waiter whom Israeli operatives mistook for Hassan Salameh precipitated anger that helped turn Norway into the European state arguably most hostile to Israel. And, the final act of retaliation for Munich, the gunning down of Abu Iyad's deputy, Atef Bseiso, in front of a Montparnasse hotel allegedly provoked French intelligence to tip off the PLO to some Israeli espionage assets.[32]

The American response to Palestinian terror was more muted. In November 1973, Secretary of State Henry Kissinger dispatched Vernon Walters, deputy director of the CIA, to a secret rendezvous with some PLO leaders in Rabat. Walters proffered the carrot of a United States–PLO dialogue while brandishing the stick of harsh reprisals. Kissinger notes suggestively that Walters "carried out his assignment with his characteristic swaggering efficiency and discretion."[33] Authors Andrew Gowers and Tony Walker quote Walters saying that he warned the PLO representatives: "I must tell you quite clearly that this killing of Americans has got to stop—or else . . . torrents of blood will flow, and not all of it will be American."[34] They add that this "blunt message astonished his listeners [who] had not expected to hear such a direct threat from an American official." Kissinger says that after this, "attacks on Americans—at least by Arafat's faction of the PLO—ceased."[35] It would be comforting to believe that America's bald threat sufficed to scare off the terrorists, but other versions claim that there was more of a quid pro quo, with America also agreeing not to act against the PLO.

---

* Israel did not get the mastermind of Munich, Abu Iyad. But poetic justice came many years later, after he had purportedly become a moderate ready to coexist with Israel: he was gunned down by the ultra-radical Abu Nidal Organization.

The strategy of the Europeans resembled that of the Arab states in placating the PLO. Historian Howard M. Sachar writes that Lufthansa "entered into detailed negotiations with several Arab guerrilla organizations to ensure the safety of its flights; even as France's Pompidou government negotiated a 'gentleman's agreement' with the PLO . . . to refrain from assaults on Air France."[36] Journalist Aaron Klein says that many Western European governments "reached secret agreements. France, Italy, and West Germany all bargained for their safety."[37] And Ibu Iyad himself boasts that "British authorities, like those of other European countries, avoid complications by not going to great lengths to apprehend Palestinian commandos."[38]

Such appeasement had a corrosive effect on the spirit of Europe, as almost always happens when people bow to threats and violence rather than finding the courage to stand up to them. A theme of several *The New York Times* editorials during this era of terrorism warned that "Arab states . . . suffer the greatest embarrassment and serious diplomatic damage from the insane escapades of the Palestinian extremists."[39] *The Times*'s point was common sense. The barbarism of Black September and the PFLP and their ilk was bound to disgust people and stain the Arab and Palestinian cause. Abu Iyad, however, disagreed. The Munich Olympics attack had "attain[ed some of] the operation's . . . objectives. World opinion was forced to take note of the Palestinian drama."[40] His gloating assessment was to prove more accurate.

four

The Power of Oil

If terrorism succeeded in placing the cause of Arab Palestine on the world's agenda, a second, less dramatic form of intimidation also helped to tip the balance of international support from Israel to the Arabs. It involved no bloodshed, but rather the lifeblood of the global economy: oil. On the second day of the 1967 Six Day War, as evidence of Israel's successful air campaign became undeniable, Arab boasts of victory were replaced by accusations that American, British, and even Australian aircraft were taking part in the bombing. Several Arab oil-exporting countries at once announced that they would withhold oil in retaliation. Almost overnight, a conference of Arab oil ministers convened in Baghdad to formalize the embargo.

But it was all to no effect, at least for the time being. In 1967, oil still traded in a buyer's market, and the United States, the main villain in this concocted story of outside military intervention, was pumping its own oil at less than full capacity. Simply by in-creasing domestic output and encouraging a few of the non-Arab oil-producing countries (notably Iran, which under the Shah was an ally of the United States as well as Israel) to increase theirs, Wash-ington was able to nullify the embargo.

The Arab oil weapon was not, however, an illusion, merely pre-mature. Global demand for petroleum products was growing faster than supply. Within a few years consumption in the United States began to exceed production. The country still contained reserves of coal and gas as well as other potential energy sources, but the do-mestic oil industry, now operating at full capacity, was not able to keep pace with usage. In early 1973, *The New York Times*, citing black-outs in Florida, brownouts the length of the eastern seaboard, and service station pumps run dry, reported that "energy had become a pressing political issue of national and international scope, a matter of concern and debate of 'crisis' magnitude."[1]

In April, President Richard Nixon sent a message to Congress announcing the lifting of "quotas," a system of tariffs on oil imports that had been designed to protect the market for domestic producers, and he proposed legislation designed to accelerate domestic energy output. "In the years immediately ahead, we must face up to the possibility of occasional energy shortages and some increase in energy prices," said Nixon, adding, "if present trends continue unchecked, we could face a genuine energy crisis."[2]

Although this proved to be an epic understatement, America's energy problems were nonetheless exceeded by those of other industrialized countries. Europe imported twice as much oil as the United States, and virtually all the oil Japan used had to come from foreign sources. The common concern about energy had been under discussion for months in the councils of the Organisation for Economic Co-operation and Development, the club of industrialized nations, without result.

Then, on October 6, not quite half a year after Nixon's message, a date which was also the Jewish holy day of Yom Kippur, the armies of Egypt and Syria took Israel by surprise with attacks across the Suez Canal and in the Golan Heights, routing the undermanned and overconfident defenders. For a few days, the Arab armies advanced; then, as Israeli reinforcements reached the front, the advance halted. For several more days of heavy fighting the outcome remained uncertain. The Soviet Union, apparently anticipating the war, rushed fresh supplies to its Arab clients.

A few days into the battle, a desperate Israeli Prime Minister Golda Meir woke her ambassador in Washington at 3 a.m., demanding that he deliver the following message to Kissinger at once:

> Tell him he must speak to the president. Tell him what he already knows—that huge military transports of Soviet aid are being supplied by sea and air to the Syrians and the Egyptians. Tell him that we're feverishly shopping around for foreign carriers to transport materiel to us, but they refuse. Tell him that European governments, notably the French and the British, have chosen to impose an arms embargo on us when we are fighting for our lives.[3]

She put the same plea into a personal letter to Nixon. In fact, during the preceding few days some arms had already been shipped in El Al passenger liners, but Israel needed much more than could be transferred this way. Arab oil producers had already let it be known that they would retaliate against anyone who came to Israel's assistance, and the threat resonated. All private airlines refused the use of their planes at any price. The government of West Germany stopped the transfer of American arms based on its soil. Secretary of Defense James Schlesinger told Kissinger, "If you want supplies there, we are going to have to use U.S. airlift all the way. There's no alternative."[4] Kissinger still reportedly hoped to keep the flights surreptitious which would have meant sharply limiting their number, but Nixon broke the logjam, insisting that the resupply effort go all out:

> It's got to be the works. . . . we are going to get blamed just as much for three planes as for 300 . . . Henry, I have no patience with the view that we send in a couple of planes . . . when we are going to make a move, it's going to cost us . . . out there. I don't think it's going to cost us a damn bit more to send in more.[5]

In the end, Nixon's rhetorical high-end of "three hundred" was surpassed. America's large transport craft, the C-141 and C-5, flew 566 missions with some twenty-two thousand tons of military hardware,[6] including tanks and even fighter planes, carried inside their cavernous fuselages.

These immense airplanes could not fly all the way from the United States to Israel without refueling. But America's North Atlantic Treaty Organization partners, despite their own dependence on America's steadfastness toward its allies, were so frightened by Arab threats to cut oil supplies that they refused to allow the US aircraft to refuel on their territory or even to fly over it. Finally, Portugal consented to the use of Lajes Airbase in the Azores as a stopover, after Nixon and Kissinger twisted the arm of dictator Marcelo Caetano. His regime, a relic of the tide of right-wing nationalism that had swept Europe in the 1930s, had traditionally been chilly toward Israel, and the two countries did not have full diplomatic relations. But, enmeshed in wars in Africa to hang onto its colonies, Lisbon was isolated and vulnerable. Kissinger sent Caetano a letter signed by Nixon, that, as Kissinger later described it, "threatened to leave Portugal to its fate in a hostile world"[7] if it failed to cooperate.

At virtually the same moment that Nixon was telling Kissinger to give Israel "the works," Shiekh Zaki Yamani, Saudi Arabia's oil minister, was warning Western executives with whom he was bargaining over prices that "if the United States overtly undertook to resupply Israel's fighting forces, Saudi Arabia would cut crude-oil production."[8]

Two days later, oil ministers gathered in Kuwait City to make good on such threats, but the political motives were hard to disentangle from economic ones. *The Sunday Times* reported: "the distinction between th[e] continuing attempt of *all* oil-producing countries to get more money for their oil, and the immediate attempt of the *Arab* oil producers to affect the outcome of the Yom Kippur War became steadily more blurred."[9] The Arabs wanted to target Israel's supporters, not their own. Oil, however, is fungible. Once you have sold your crude, how can you control where the refined products will end up? Compounding the Arabs' problem, Israel's chief supporter, the United States, was less reliant than most on imports.

The meeting settled on a 70 percent increase in the price of oil and a 5 percent cut in production. The final communiqué declared exemptions for "any friendly state which has extended or shall extend effective material assistance to the Arabs" and "any state which takes important measures against Israel."[10]

A day later, Saudi Arabia, the largest producer, announced that it would cut not 5 but 10 percent of its production. Moreover, reported *The New York Times*, "King Faisal's government said it would cut off all oil supplies to the United States if Washington continued its aid to the Israeli armed forces."[11] Two days later, Nixon having openly asked Congress for 2.2 billion dollars to fund the arms for Israel, Riyadh announced a total oil embargo of the United States, and it was joined in this by Kuwait, Qatar, Bahrain, and Dubai.

In addition to the United States, the Arab oil producers singled out Holland for a total embargo, although its transgressions were much less obvious than the massive airlift of arms to Israel that America was conducting. Indeed, no one was sure why Holland was targeted so severely. *The Economist* explained the general perplexity:

> The Dutch are charged with pursuing a consistently pro-Israeli policy — a policy that some Arabs believe stems from the cult created around the death of the young Dutch girl, Anne Frank, under the Nazi occupation. But there are few specific points to justify the total ban. The main one could be the report that the Dutch government was largely responsible for the fact that in

September 1972, the EEC council of ministers buried the pro-
Arab statement that had been passed to it by the European parliament. Other charges seem fairly innocuous, even if true: the
report, made in Israel and later denied by the Dutch that Holland was willing to replace Austrian transit facilities for Soviet
Jews and the supposed rudeness of a Dutch minister to a group
of Arab ambassadors who had come to protest about help going
to Israel during the October war.[12]

Whatever the reason behind targeting Holland, this heightened
the trial facing the European Economic Community (EEC; precur-
sor to the European Union). Ticklish enough was the question of
whether it would stand by the United States, which had rescued Europe from the devastation of World War II and still served as its
shield against Soviet imperialism. Doubly difficult was the test of
solidarity with one of its own.

Little more than two weeks following the announcement of the
Arab embargo, the foreign ministers of the EEC convened in Brussels
to formulate a response. There they adopted a statement on the Middle East that, according to *The Washington Post*, "was clearly aimed
at placating the Arab nations. . . . [It] seemed to indicate that the
Arab world is succeeding in placing pressure on Western Europe by
threatening oil boycotts."[13] The statement drew on UN resolutions,
but emphasized or augmented the portions that favored the Arab
argument at the expense of those reflecting the Israeli position. In
particular, it called for Israel to vacate the territories it had captured
in 1967 without negotiations or the border modifications clearly envisioned in Security Council Resolutions 242 and 338, which had
brought the wars of 1967 and 1973, respectively, to an end. It also affirmed without defining the "legitimate rights of the Palestinians,"
but did not call upon the Arabs to make peace with Israel.

"Publicly, spokesmen . . . denied that the statement was weighted
in favor of the Arab side," the *Post* story continued. "In private, however, EEC sources confirmed that the resolution was prompted by
fears of a cutoff in the oil flow to Europe . . . The aim, these sources
said, was to make a gesture of appeasement toward the Arabs sufficiently strong to avert a boycott."[14]

The *Post*'s interpretation was shared by virtually all other observers. *The Economist* was moved to ridicule:

The Nine [EEC members] decided on a brand new EEC spaniel policy. This new community policy for lying-on-your-back-and-wagging-your-feet-in-the-air has the following public rules. Any member state caught standing up to the Arab oil embargoes must immediately lie down on its back again, put out its tongue and wave its feet.[15]

The Guardian reported that "Egyptian diplomats . . . were hugely cheered by Europe's new policy"[16] while Israel's Golda Meir prevailed upon the Socialist International to convene an emergency meeting so that she could confront her long-time comrades serving in European governments about what she saw as a betrayal.

Holland's situation was also on the agenda. According to *The Guardian*,

> The Foreign Ministers, after more than two hours behind closed doors, failed to respond to Dutch and West German calls for "Community solidarity" when it came to the specific issue of ensuring the free flow of oil throughout the EEC.
>
> Britain and France want to avoid at all costs giving the impression that they are willing to come to the aid of their Dutch partners, who are already threatened by the Arab boycott.[17]

British Prime Minister Edward Heath, facing a possible strike by coal miners, almost outdid the French government in pandering to the Arabs, getting Britain classified as "friendly" by the oil producers, who promised to continue deliveries to the United Kingdom at pre-embargo levels. However, this was easier said than done. It was not governments that bought, sold, and delivered oil but rather oil companies, and they had their own interests not to mention contractual obligations. In the face of cuts by the producers, their safest move was to spread the shortage equally among their customers.

In *The Prize*, Daniel Yergin describes a meeting at Chequers, the prime minister's country estate to which Heath summoned the chairmen of British Petroleum (BP) and Shell. The Shell chairman, Sir Frank McFadzean, made short work of Heath's attempt to strong-arm him by reminding the prime minister that while the British own 40 percent of Shell, the Dutch owned 60 percent. So Heath leaned his full weight against Sir Eric Drake of BP, pointing out that the British government owned 51 percent of the company. But Drake argued that the company was obligated by law to treat all shareholders alike, and further, that the British government, by the terms of its original purchase into the business, was pledged not to intervene in BP's management. If Heath directed him to deliver a fixed amount of oil to Britain and to cut off Holland, he would obey, he said, but only if the order were in writing. "You know perfectly well that I can't put it in writing," fumed Heath, because such an open directive would have sounded the death knell of his larger foreign policy goal of bringing Britain into the European Community.[18] There the matter ended.

The Dutch also had a card to play. Although they imported oil, they exported natural gas in relatively large quantities to several other European countries. At a follow-up meeting a month later, the implicit quid pro quo was made explicit, "no oil, no gas."[19] Quietly, then, Holland's fellow Europeans acquiesced as the oil companies delivered the same reduced quantities of refined products to the Dutch as to everyone else.

Although the Arab embargo of Holland was thus blunted, the Dutch nonetheless retreated from their pro-Israel inclinations and supported the EEC's Brussels declaration. *The Economist* explained: "the Dutch want to give French and British diplomacy in the Middle East—making use of the Nine's loaded document in favour of the Arab cause—its chance." The magazine added: "this puts a heavy load on the French and British gamble that appeasement and diplomacy will do the trick."[20] Nor was this the end of Holland's backdown. By the end of the year, a new policy was in place. Scholar Roy Licklider describes it:

> Since 1974, the Dutch government has pursued its Middle Eastern policy strictly within the framework of European Political Cooperation. This marks a major change from its earlier policy. Within the confidential discussions of the EPC process, the Netherlands reportedly remains more likely to support Israel than most other members. However, in public statements, United Nations votes, and similar activities the Dutch government stands by the decisions reached by the Community. It will differ publicly from its allies only if at least one other country does so as well: it is not prepared to be isolated on a Middle Eastern issue.[21]

Capping it off, Holland, which alone among the Europeans had its embassy in Jerusalem, moved it to Tel Aviv. (Jerusalem is Israel's capital but because its legal status remains disputed most nations keep their embassies in Tel Aviv.) Later that month, November 1973, at a summit in Algiers, the Arab states exulted: "The diplomatic isolation of Israel has today become a reality. It is significant in this respect that certain European governments, which traditionally have been won over to the Israeli viewpoint, are beginning to wonder about the foundations of an adventurous policy which has raised grave risks for international peace and cooperation." [22]

Only a day before, Arab radicals from an obscure Palestinian group commandeered a jumbo jet belonging to KLM, the Dutch national airline, and forced it to fly to Libya, whose mercurial dictator, Muammar Qaddafi, remained avid for terror tactics. The PLO's Arafat, however, denounced the escapade. This time he seemed more sincere than when he had distanced himself from Black September. If so, the reason is not hard to fathom. The Arab governments were fully embracing the PLO, and they were wielding a club even more intimidating to the West than terrorism. Why create a distraction?

Simultaneously with the Algiers summit, French President Georges Pompidou and German Chancellor Willy Brandt held a mini summit of their own. Pompidou sold Brandt on the idea of developing European relations with the Arabs independently of Washington. Pompidou, it appears, had already reached out on this subject to none other than Qaddafi. According to Saled A. al-Mani, the dean of King Saud University in Riyadh and a specialist in this subject, "The Euro-Arab Dialogue (EAD) was conceived initially by the French and the idea was explored in contact with Libya prior to the outbreak of the 1973 war."[23] In November 1973, while much of this other diplomacy was taking place, the French newspaper *Le Monde* held a conference on cooperation between Europe and the Arab world in which various government officials from the two sides participated "unofficially," including notably Qaddafi.

Why was France engaging with such a bad actor? In part, probably, because it had historical ties to the country, and in part because Libya was a major oil producer. But also, perhaps, because Qaddafi's very extremism made him anathema to Washington, and one of Paris's goals was to distance itself from the United States. Indeed, only four months after Qaddafi had seized power, France had agreed to sell his government one hundred fighter planes, even while it continued to embargo arms sales to Israel.[24] In announcing this deal, French officials claimed that Libya had given a commitment not to use this aircraft against Israel or to transfer it to fellow Arab states that would do so. But against whom else would the planes be deployed? And how could Libya's assurance about their use be enforced?

With the Arab states expressing appreciation for the "kiss blown from afar," as one Arab official described the EEC's Brussels declaration[25] (and at the same time demanding further diplomatic concessions), the EEC held a summit in Copenhagen just weeks later, on December 14 and 15, 1973. The meeting had one extremely unusual feature, as Kissinger recounts sarcastically:

> A group of Arab foreign ministers appeared "unexpectedly" to lobby for pressure on Israel. If the accounts given to us were to be believed, it must have been the first time in history that a delegation of foreign ministers appeared uninvited at the summit meeting of a continent to which they did not belong.[26]

Kissinger suspected that French Foreign Minister Michel Jobert had orchestrated the "surprise" with the acquiescence of others. At that strange summit, says Kissinger, "The EC strengthened its November 6 declaration [tilting to the Arab position] now in public opposition to the main thrust of our diplomacy." He was referring to two issues: peace-making and oil. Kissinger had begun to mediate disengagement agreements between Israeli forces and those of Egypt and Syria. On the Egyptian front, this entailed the first ever direct talks between Israeli and Egyptian military officials, which may have planted the seed that blossomed a few years later in a peace treaty. By echoing Arab demands for Israeli withdrawal without any conditions, the Europeans impeded that diplomacy.

In addition, Kissinger had initiated discussions with other Western states about how to parry the bullying tactics of the oil cartel. This objective, in his view,

> reflected not only economic analysis but—even more—political, indeed moral, conviction. The industrial democracies could not permit themselves to be turned into panicked, paralyzed bystanders while the oil producers played fast and loose with the internal cohesion of their societies. . . . It [was] intolerable that

countries of 40 million [could] blackmail 800 million in the industrial world.[27]

In his eyes, the oil consumers were not defenseless; they possessed weapons of their own. The oil-exporting states produced very little else and depended on imports for their manufactured goods and even for food. The game of cartels and embargoes could be played two ways. To be sure, tit-for-tat was dangerous, but in a contest with the oil states the West held a trump card: overwhelming military superiority. The European impulse, however, was to placate the oil producers rather than confront them. As Kissinger understood it, "The dialogue with the Arabs was . . . being urged by France explicitly as an alternative to a unified consumer challenge to the oil producers."[28]

That strange December 1973 summit, with its unusual guests, formalized this approach by laying the foundation stone for an apparatus called the Euro–Arab Dialogue (EAD). Its "practical consequence," said Kissinger, "could only be to institutionalize the Atlantic differences."[29] The EAD established a permanent headquarters in Paris, assembled a staff of 350, and held regular conclaves of officials, experts, and even of an "inter-parliamentary group." By taking part in the latter, the duly elected representatives of European states lent legitimacy to Arab "parliaments" that were not freely chosen by their citizens but rather window dressing for absolute monarchies and harsh dictatorships. The first such confab met, fittingly, in Damascus, seat of one the world's most repressive regimes.

Europe's obeisance was rewarded—to a degree. Ten days after the Copenhagen summit, the oil producers met again in Kuwait and decided to reverse in part their reductions of shipments to Europe and some other countries. The producers had pledged in October to cut production by 5 percent per month, although "friendly" countries, including all of Europe except Holland, were supposedly exempt. Now they announced a 10 percent *increase* in shipments to friendly countries to make up for any recent cuts.

Whatever the actual production level (which often deviated in practice from official pronouncements), the real news out of Kuwait was another massive price hike, more than doubling the already-raised price. This, according to *The New York Times*, yielded a net increase of 470 percent within the span of a year.[30] Europe could now have, more or less, all the oil it wanted—but at a crippling cost. The industrial countries were thrown into a recession that lasted most of the 1970s. And the oil-importing countries of the developing world suffered even more sharply, despite come crocodile tears from the producers and some crumbs of foreign aid from the wealthy Arab states.

In the wake of this devastating action, Kissinger tried anew to rally the consumers, but he found that they still had "no stomach for a concerted diplomacy, believing that the attempt to join forces would 'provoke' the producers into retaliation."[31] In an early 1974 tour of European capitals, he writes, "every minister I consulted was still terrified of possible confrontation with the producers."[32]

Fear, no doubt, was plentiful, but there was also an undertone of backbiting. Europeans often resented their dependence on the United States in the Cold War, and this resentment may have been reinforced by Kissinger's relentless efforts to summon them to a fight with the oil producers for which they lacked the courage. The ill-feeling showed when American mediation between Israeli and Egyptian forces began to succeed, thus garnering gratitude to Washington from Arab governments. As Kissinger tells it, certain Europeans seemed disappointed rather than pleased at this prospect of US–Arab rapprochement:

> We were being told that some of our allies were asking for preferential treatment from the Arabs for having disavowed our policy. The United States, so the alleged argument ran, must not be rewarded even should our diplomacy make progress. The embargo against us should be kept in force for several months or else the European and Japanese dissociation from our policy would be seen to have been pointless.[33]

The one country whose timorousness toward the Arabs was most strongly tinctured with spite toward the United States was France. At moments French leaders stressed their country's helplessness. Pompidou had told Kissinger, "You only rely on the Arabs for about a tenth of your consumption. We are entirely dependent upon them."[34] Pompidou was succeeded in 1974 by Valery Giscard D'Estaing, and Giscard sounded an even more pathetic note. "Europe is in decline," he pronounced at a news conference. "It is going down in relation to others who are going up. . . . It is the revenge on Europe for the 19th century,"[35] an apparent reference to colonialism.

Yet, under each of these French leaders, Paris's posture of weakness was evident only toward the Arabs, not toward the United States for which it always seemed to have out the knife. Kissinger claims that Pompidou's foreign minister, Jobert, toured Arab capitals to "mount a direct challenge to American policy" on oil and that he even "egged on the Arab radicals to oppose the American mediation" between Israel and its neighbors.[36] When his turn came, Giscard denounced American "domination"[37] among the oil consumers, and his foreign minister, Jean Sauvagnargues, went so far as to justify the Arab embargo against the United States by saying the oil producers resented Washington's "policy of the big stick."[38]

Europe was far from alone in squirming as it stared into the barrel of the oil weapon. Japan was especially vulnerable because of its extreme dependence on energy imports. Since World War II, Japan had struck a low profile outside of its neighborhood, although its voting record in the United Nations tilted more than most other industrial states toward the Arabs. Therefore, writes scholar Roy Licklider:

> Japan was surprised to be a target of the oil weapon. Initially the Japanese government reiterated its previous [pro-Arab] position, but it became clear that this was not sufficient. On November 6 [1973], the government issued a statement remarkably similar to the EC Brussels statement of the same day. However, this was also unsuccessful; the next day the Saudi and Kuwaiti governments declared Japan a "nonfriendly" country, and on November 18 the EC countries were exempted from the 5 percent December cuts while the Japanese pointedly were not, causing something of a panic in the Japanese government.
>
> Japan was apparently asked (1) to break diplomatic relations with Israel, (2) to sever all economic ties with Israel, (3) to provide military assistance to the Arabs, and (4) to pressure the United States to alter its policy toward the Arab-Israeli dispute. On November 22 Japan responded with a new statement, asserting that Israel should withdraw from all of the 1967 territories (thus going beyond both 242 and the November 6 EEC statement), advocating Palestinian self-determination, and threatening to reconsider its policy toward Israel if Israel refused to accept these preconditions. Japan also announced the

first of several visits to the Arab Middle East by high-ranking government officials in which large sums of foreign aid were promised.[39]

Tokyo did not go so far as to meet the four conditions Licklider enumerates, but apparently it went far enough. Japan's new position, writes Daniel Yergin, constituted its "first major split on foreign policy with the United States in the postwar era. Such an action was hardly to be undertaken lightly, as the U.S.-Japan alliance was the basis of Japanese foreign policy."[40] The Arabs were appeased sufficiently to exempt Japan from further delivery reductions and then to include it with Europe and the Philippines in the 10-percent increase announced in late December.[41]

The Arab oil weapon was also deployed to great effect against Africa. In 1958, Golda Meir, then Israel's foreign minister, visited Ghana a year after it had become the first European colony of sub-Saharan Africa to achieve independence. Within the year, a Division of International Cooperation had been established within Israel's foreign ministry. Over the next decade-plus, more than 1,500 Israelis served in Peace Corps-like missions, sharing expertise in Africa while some 9,000 Africans traveled to Israel for training, mostly at the Afro-Asian institute set up by Histadrut, the labor organization that largely dominated Israel.[42] Israel believed its own post-colonial development experience offered useful lessons for other newly independent states. In exchange, Israel hoped to win friends and perhaps establish a backdoor to its Arab neighbors. In addition, assisting the poor newborn states of Africa appealed to the idealism of Israel's socialist leaders and mirrored the special bond between Jews and blacks evident in the US civil rights movement.

The ties thus forged, however, could not withstand Arab oil power. A few African states had broken ties with Israel after the 1967 war. Now, in 1973, most of the rest followed suit—in all, thirty out of thirty-three black-ruled states.[43] In return for this cooperation, the Arabs wielded the oil weapon against the continent's remaining bastions of white rule, adding South Africa, Rhodesia, and Portugal (which still ruled Mozambique, Angola, and Guinea-Bissau) to the short of list of countries subjected to a total embargo.

Although the vast majority of the countries affected surrendered to the oil weapon, the embargo was brought to an end in 1974 thanks to the prowess of the Israeli army, the adroitness of Kissinger's diplomacy, and the vision of Egypt's President Anwar Sadat. Israel had been bloodied badly in the early days of the 1973 war, but in the end it had turned the tables and seized territory deeper into Egypt and Syria than it had held from 1967, far enough even to menace their capitals. Shuttling between the sides over many weeks, Kissinger negotiated separation-of-forces agreements based on Israeli pull-backs. But, at critical moments in the talks, he insisted to his Arab interlocutors that he would not continue his mediation while the United States remained under embargo by the Arabs. Sadat had been the principal initiator of the embargo, just as he was of the war. Although Egypt exports no oil of its own, Sadat had taken the lead in convincing Saudi Arabia and the other Arab producers to use this leverage. Now, to get the separation agreement he believed would salvage Egypt's accomplishment in the war, namely, a restoration of the sense of honor it had lost in the one-sided shellacking it took from Israel in 1967, he urged an end to the embargo. And so it was done.

The effects lingered, however. The dramatic rise in oil prices gener-ated a massive transfer of wealth from the consumers to the suppli-ers, suppressing economic growth in the wealthy importing countries and setting back the development of the poorer ones. The effects were not overcome until the 1980s. The embargo's political consequences endured still longer, indeed they never dissipated. "The oil weapon had finally been successfully used," writes Yergin, "with an impact not merely convincing, but overwhelming, and far greater than even its proponents might have dared to expect. It had recast the alignments and geopolitics of both the Middle East and the entire world."[44] He adds: "those who seemed to control oil prices were regarded as the new masters of the global economy" and "the security of access to oil [had become] a strategic concern of the first order."[45] With this achieved, the weapon "could be resheathed. But the threat would remain."[46]

It was frightening enough to cause a permanent readjustment of the balance of political influence between Israel and the Arabs.

five

The Arabs Take Over
the United Nations

There was dancing in the aisles as the tote board at the UN General Assembly made clear the outcome of the vote. The date was October 25, 1971. The issue was the expulsion of the anti-Communist Republic of China from the world organization, in favor of the People's Republic of China. The real butt of the gloating celebration was not Taiwan, but Washington, as was made clear by the taunts from the rostrum, such as the Iraqi ambassador's jibe that America, if it wanted so badly to keep Taiwan in the United Nations, should give up its own seat to the island. US ambassador George H. W. Bush commented afterward: "There was an ugly mood in there . . . an emotional release at seeing the U.S. get kicked around."[1]

The United Nations had been an American invention and, during the organization's first two decades, Washington largely had had its way there. But the balance of sentiment had shifted markedly as the size of the United Nations had grown. From 1958 to 1968, the number of member states climbed from 82 to 126. Most of the newly admitted were former colonies that had recently won their independence.

In its early decades the United Nations had been divided by the Cold War, but as more states were admitted a third bloc made its presence felt, the Non-Aligned Movement (NAM), which soon overshadowed both the Western and Soviet camps. The superpowers still possessed vetoes in the Security Council, but in all other UN bodies, the NAM held sway.

The NAM had been founded in the 1950s under the leadership of India's President Jawaharlal Nehru, Egypt's Gamal Abdel Nasser, and Yugoslavia's Josip Broz Tito. Its avowed purpose was to carve out some political space free from domination by the superpowers, but the movement did not position itself equidistant from East and West. The leitmotif of the NAM was anticolonialism, a cause that Communists embraced and that put the West in the dock. Thus, the movement was "non-aligned" far more emphatically with the West than with the communist world. Indeed, although the Soviet Union was not welcome, other communist states, some of them Soviet-allied such as Cuba and Vietnam, played leading roles in the NAM. So did the People's Republic of China (PRC).

No country in the world was more flamboyantly hostile to America than the PRC, which was fond of ridiculing America as a "paper tiger." For its part, Washington still recognized the Republic of China government, the Kuomintang, which had fled to Taiwan in 1949, as the legitimate representative of the whole country. Thanks to US influence that regime had continued to represent China at the United Nations long after it had ceded the mainland. For two decades, America had successfully parried moves to seat Beijing's government in place of Taiwan's, but by 1971 Washington was fighting a rearguard action. Its final gambit was to propose seating both Chinas. The Beijing authorities insisted, however, on being recognized *in place of*, not in addition to, and their demand was upheld by the required two-thirds of the General Assembly: seventy-three to thirty-five.

Dominance of the United Nations had slipped from America's grasp forever, and now was held by the third world, sometimes in alliance with the Communists. The new anti-Western, anti-American *zeitgeist* of the United Nations, with many Arab and other Muslim states represented in NAM, reshaped the body's stance toward the Middle East. Almost overnight, it became the principal instrument to legitimize and solemnize the advantages that the Arabs had gained since 1967 by bringing Palestinian national claims to the fore and by intimidating others through terrorism and the oil embargo. The Arab offensive in the United Nations was reinforced and envenomed by Moscow, which was humiliated and even felt in a sense threatened by Israel's victories over Soviet-armed client states in 1967 and 1973. "Anti-Sovietism is the profession of Zionists," complained *Pravda*.[2]

Thus, in September 1974, the Arab states proposed to put the question of Palestine on the agenda of the General Assembly as an item distinct from the larger question of the Middle East, and in October the General Assembly voted to invite the Palestine Liberation Organization (PLO) to send a spokesperson to take part in the deliberations. No one who was not a representative of a government except the Pope (and even he was the head of a quasi-state, the Vatican) had ever before been granted such a privilege, but the vote was overwhelming, 105 to 4, with only the United States, Israel, and two Latin American governments opposed.

Not a single European or other major industrial state joined America in resisting this extraordinary move. Most of them abstained, although a handful voted with the majority. Daniel Patrick Moynihan, the US ambassador, assessed the atmosphere this way:

> The West generally, and Japan particularly, had entered a time of prolonged economic difficulty consequent upon the decision of the Arab nations, which were also Israel's enemies, to quintuple the price of energy. It would be predicted that the Europeans would somehow begin to blame the Israelis for this, while for certain the Japanese would want to stay aloof. . . . Whether Israel was responsible, Israel surely would be blamed: openly by some, privately by most. Israel would be *regretted*.[3] (Emphasis in original.)

The PLO had proved adept at playing on European fears. Harris Schoenberg, an author who represented the nongovernmental organization (NGO) B'nai B'rith, the Jewish fraternal association, at the United Nations, interviewed various European delegates who told him that "PLO spokesmen had undertaken to halt and actively seek to prevent further Arab aerial piracy and terrorist attacks in countries other than Israel if permitted to participate in the General Assembly debate."[4] Ironically, at the very time that Arab representatives in New York were putting it about that the PLO would be domesticated by inclusion in UN affairs, the PLO itself was busy in Rabat, Morocco, creating, in the boastful words of Abu Iyad, a "climate of terror" that induced the Arab League summit meeting there to declare it the "sole legitimate representative" of the Palestinians.[5]

The hollowness of these vague promises of moderation was personified by the chief security aide accompanying Arafat to the United Nations: none other than Ali Hassan Salameh, the commander of the Munich Olympics massacre. Underscoring it further was Arafat's decision to arrive at the United Nations wearing a holstered pistol. Bringing the weapon into the UN building was a breach of the rules, but Arafat was not stopped. Reportedly, he was induced to leave the gun in the keeping of Secretary General Kurt Waldheim while delivering his address, but, in an eerie display of bravado, he made the holster around his midriff conspicuous during the speech.

In his peroration, Arafat warned: "I have come bearing an olive branch and a freedom-fighter's gun. Do not let the olive branch fall from my hand." Some reports of the speech, focusing on this final passage, suggested that he was offering Israel a choice of peace or war. But this was far from what he meant, as the assembled delegates must have understood. They heard him proclaim the necessity of getting at the "historical roots" of the issue, namely "the Jewish invasion of Palestine [that] began in 1881," and to address it with a "radical . . . antidote," rather than "a slavish obeisance to the present." The locution may have been tortured but its meaning was inescapable: The "present" to which Arafat wished to banish "obeisance" was the very existence of Israel.

"We live in a time of glorious change," he exulted. "An old world order is crumbling before our eyes, as imperialism, colonialism, neo-colonialism and racism, the chief form of which is Zionism, ineluctably perish." He pledged his "resolve to build a new world . . . a world free of colonialism, imperialism, neo-colonialism and racism in each of its instances, including Zionism."

Far from entertaining peace with "the Zionist entity" (whose name he studiously refused to utter), Arafat proffered his wilted olive branch only to Jewish individuals willing to live in a liberated Palestine under Arab rule after the dissolution of Israel. To Israel, he offered neither compromise nor any quarter whatsoever. His threat, "do not let the olive branch fall from my hand," uttered twice in succession for emphasis as he wagged his finger in warning, was not directed to Israel but to the Jewish people. He left unspoken what lay in store for them should they spurn his offer, but could it be far from his predecessor Ahmed Shuqairy's vision that "no Jew will be left alive"?[6]

This bloodthirsty harangue was greeted in the temple of nations with a standing ovation the likes of which had perhaps never been heard there before. The ugly mood that Ambassador Bush had noted during the ouster of Taiwan was no momentary phenomenon. An alliance of communist and third world states was after the scalps of its chosen enemies, and the United States, drained by Vietnam, could offer only token resistance.

Besides Taiwan, the most vulnerable of the targets of this ruling coalition was South Africa. To the black-majority states of Africa, South Africa's formal system of racial hierarchy and oppression was an insufferable insult, never mind that the world was replete with more violent abuses and regimes more repressive. In 1974, Pretoria's credentials were rejected by the General Assembly, which meant that the country "was effectively expelled," wrote America's then-ambassador to the United Nations, Daniel Patrick Moynihan.[7] This violated the UN Charter which left decisions about membership to the Security Council, but few nations were willing speak up for due process lest they appear equivocal about South Africa's odious racial system.

The next year, the foreign ministers of the Organization of the Islamic Conference (OIC) determined to have Israel expelled in the same way. The PLO lined up support for this move at a meeting of the African states while training its sights on a ministerial meeting of the NAM scheduled for Lima a month later, August 1975.

Looking ahead, Moynihan judged that "the real decision would be made" at this meeting that would precede the General Assembly by a month."[8] In anticipation, Washington pulled out all the stops. Secretary of State Kissinger delivered a major speech on the subject with a thinly veiled warning that the United States might turn its back on the United Nations if this road were taken. Referring to the OIC's proposal as well as resolutions that challenged the participation of South Africa and Israel in some of the United Nations' other constituent bodies, he said:

> If the U.N. begins to depart from its Charter, where suspension and expulsion are clearly specified prerogatives of the Security Council, we fear for the integrity and the survival of the General Assembly itself, and no less for that of the specialized agencies. Those who seek to manipulate U.N. membership by procedural abuse may well inherit an empty shell. We are determined to oppose tendencies which in our view will undermine irreparably the effectiveness of the United Nations.[9]

Then he added the bluntest and most telling salvo: "It is the smaller members of the organization who would lose the most. They are more in need of the U.N. than the larger powers such as the United States which can prosper within or outside the institution."[10] Left unsaid was the fact that Washington provided the largest share of the United Nations's budget.

Undeterred, the Organization of African Unity was on the verge of adopting a resolution calling for Israel's expulsion when an unexpected dissent was registered by none other than Egyptian President Anwar Sadat. Sadat's argument was that "Israel must be present at the United Nations if it is expected to comply with its resolutions."[11] This made it sound as if his goal was to hold Israel's feet to the fire. But something more subtle seems to have been at work. Having expelled Soviet advisors in 1972, restored Egyptian pride by besting Israel in the opening rounds of the war of 1973, and negotiated a separation of forces agreement through Kissinger's good offices in 1974, Sadat was following a trajectory that would eventually lead to his historic visit to Jerusalem in 1977 and the Egypt–Israel peace treaty of 1979. In short, he seems to have opted for peace, whereas the Arab drive to expel Israel from the United Nations was an act of political warfare.

In addition to Washington's hard line and Sadat's defection, the anti-Israel campaign was slowed by NAM's own loss of elan. At the Lima conference, allies of Moscow and Beijing turned on each other as did oil producers and consumers, and these stumbles were capped off by a Peruvian coup that overthrew the host government in the midst of the conference. The move to expel Israel from the General Assembly fizzled.

But any sighs of relief in Jerusalem would have been premature. Its enemies soon ginned up an alternative measure that did Israel almost as much damage: a resolution of the General Assembly echoing Arafat (and soviet propagandists) in declaring Zionism to be "a form of racism." As Moynihan pointed out, the United Nations was predicated on the equal legitimacy of all political systems, however odious. It mattered not a whit how repressive a regime was or whether it starved or slaughtered its own subjects. Only one thing was declared unacceptable: racism. To label Zionism a form of racism was to declare Israel inherently illegitimate, regardless of its borders or behavior.

The Welsh journalist and academic Goronwy Rees, who had written much about pre-war Germany and who had returned there in 1945 as a British intelligence officer, observed the critical vote in the UN's Third Committee to recommend the resolution to the General Assembly. He described the spirit of the occasion:

There were ghosts haunting the Third Committee that day; the ghosts of Hitler and Goebbels and Julius Streicher, grin-

ning with delight to hear, not only Israel, but Jews as such denounced in language which would have provoked hysterical ap-
plause at any Nuremberg rally. . . . And there were other ghosts
also at the debate: the ghosts of the 6,000,000 dead in Dachau
and Sachsenhausen and other extermination camps, listening
to the same voices which had cheered and jeered and abused
them as they made their way to the gas chambers. For the fundamental thesis advanced by the supporters of the resolution,
and approved by the majority . . . was that to be a Jew, and to be
proud of it, and to be determined to preserve the right to be a
Jew, is to be an enemy of the human race.[12]

In addition to the atavistic hatred that Rees observed, there
were also practical, one might say Machiavellian, motives in play,
in Moynihan's analysis. "The Soviets were using the Zionism resolution . . . to attack Israel—and to intimidate Egypt," he wrote. "Israel
and Egypt, with American sponsorship, were moving toward something like peace. The Soviets, especially after having been expelled
from Egypt, would not have it."[13]

Moynihan reports that following the vote he "rose and walked
over to [Israel's ambassador, Chaim] Herzon and embraced him.
'Fuck 'em!' I said."[14] That was a warm gesture of solidarity, but also
a confession of despair in the face of an immovable wall of unreason.

Moynihan later mused that "our principal tactical mistake
was not to understand the willingness of the Arabs simply to buy
themselves a majority."[15] But on this point he is not convincing.
The Arabs certainly had used their oil wealth to buy political influence, and indeed do it to this day. There were even open references
by some of those present to the use of "blandishments," meaning
material inducements, in the course of rounding up votes for the
Zionism-is-racism resolution. Nonetheless, the margin was deci-
sive: seventy-two to thirty-five with thirty-two abstentions. More
than bribery, it reflected what the Soviets used to like to call the
"correlation of forces." In the United Nations at that time, the combined weight of the Arabs, the Islamic Conference states, the NAM,
and the Soviet bloc was overwhelming.

The resolution equating Zionism and racism was the most egregious but far from the only General Assembly declaration against
Israel. A year after the 1967 war, the body voted to establish a Special Committee to Investigate Israeli Practices Affecting the Hu-

man Rights of the Population of the Occupied Territories. Those territories had been seized from Baathist Syria, Nasser's Egypt, and the Hashemite Kingdom of Jordan—a totalitarian state, a semi-totalitarian one, and an absolute monarchy. Needless to say, the citizens of these three states had never before known their human rights to be acknowledged either by their governments or by the General Assembly, which was itself composed preponderantly of dictatorships.

To double-down on the hypocrisy, the committee tasked with this "investigation" was composed of three member states: Ceylon, which enjoyed a relatively democratic system; Yugoslavia, a communist regime; and Somalia, a member of the Arab League ruled by one of the most ferocious tyrants of the day, General Mohamed Siad Barre. And, as was to become standard in UN actions regarding Israel, in the same resolution mandating an "investigation," the General Assembly spelled out its conclusions in advance, declaring its "grave concern at the violation of human rights in Arab territories occupied by Israel" for which it warned Israel of "grave consequences resulting from the disregard of fundamental freedoms and human rights in occupied territories."

In the ensuing years, the Arab states, confident of commanding overwhelming majorities in the General Assembly, would reiterate this resolution and add new ones. In 1982, the body declared that Israel "is not a peace-loving Member state and that it has not carried out its obligations under the Charter."[16] Since the Charter itself specifies that "membership . . . is open to all . . . peace-loving states which accept the obligations contained in the . . . Charter," this kept alive the threat to expel Israel. Moreover, it called for an international campaign against that country, exhorting "all Member States to cease forthwith . . . all dealings with Israel in order totally to isolate it in all fields." It even called upon "all States to put an end to the flow to Israel of human resources," thereby stamping the United Nations's imprimatur on the practice of the Soviet Union and other European communist regimes of denying freedom of emigration.

This language was adopted again and again throughout the 1980s, but the fever cooled a little with the end of the Cold War and the disappearance of the Soviet Union which also led to the rescinding of the resolution equating Zionism with racism in 1991. Although the fierceness of anti-Israel declarations diminished, their number did not. Moynihan had written of his perplexed discovery upon becoming ambassador to the world body that Israel was "the center of the political life of the United Nations."[17] This did not change with the Soviet demise and has not changed since. Every year the General Assembly votes on anywhere from seventy-odd to one hundred-odd resolutions, apart from meaningless consensus resolutions on administrative matters and the like. Between fifteen and twenty of these votes pertain to Israel, all in a pejorative way.

Variously, they affirm the rights and sovereignty of the Palestinian people, denounce Israel's actions in Jerusalem and the Golan Heights, take Israel to task for alleged violations of international law and of human rights, and so on. It need hardly be added that these are almost never balanced within their own texts or in other motions by any word of criticism of the Palestinians or the Arab states. That censure of Israel accounts for one-fifth to one-quarter of all motions passed by the General Assembly seems bizarre, all the more so considering that, given the diplomatic minuet danced in the organization, it is rare for states to be singled out for criticism. Very few of the world's most repressive or blood-soaked regimes have received even a single rebuke from this august chamber. Another way of parsing the numbers is this: of all General Assembly resolutions that criticize a particular country, three-quarters apply to Israel.

Ordinarily, the only "no" votes cast amidst this annual blizzard of condemnations come from Israel itself, as well as the United States, and one or more of the four tiny pacific island states (Micronesia, Nauru, Palau, and the Marshall Islands) which are closely tied to the United States. (In 2010, the oil-exporting sheikhdoms of the Persian Gulf offered these barely populated nations a sum of one hundred million dollars in aid, ostensibly to help them develop alternative energy sources, more likely in the hope of altering their voting habits.[18]) Even the governments of Europe do not bother to oppose the anti-Israel resolutions, mostly abstaining, presumably on the grounds that these are nothing more than exercises in which the nonaligned nations "let off steam." Rosemary Righter, an editor of *The Times* (London), put it:

> [Washington's] insistence on defending "mere words" appears to most European diplomats arrogant and doomed to failure. This difference of perspective has been at times so marked as to give the impression that "European policy," insofar as there is such a thing, is largely about mitigating the excesses in UN forums of Europe's embarrassing friend, the United States.[19]

The view that General Assembly resolutions amount only to empty rhetoric is true insofar as there are no enforcement mechanisms. But this ignores the fact that third world countries, lacking the military, economic, and political power of the large industrial states, attach greater importance to the United Nations and are therefore more likely to be influenced by its declarations. It ignores, too, the consequences of relentless recitation of UN declarations in the discourse of the Arab world where they reinforce the conviction that all right lies on the Arab side and that Israel is irredeemably evil, an outlook that impedes compromise and peace.

Perhaps most malicious of the General Assembly's positions is its insistence on sanctifying violence and even terrorism—so long as it is carried out in the name of an approved cause. This stance, which contradicts the UN Charter, originated in the struggles for African independence and then was carried over to the Arab–Israeli conflict. In the 1960s, the General Assembly passed several resolutions regarding Portugal's colonies and the white-ruled states of southern Africa, affirming "the legitimacy of the struggle of the colonial peoples to exercise their right to self-determination and independence."[20] In 1970, an important codicil was added, the phrase "by all the necessary means at their disposal."[21]

In the 1970s, the PLO, backed by the Arab states and the Islamic Conference, was to cite this phrase as sanctioning its deliberate attacks on civilians. Referring to Palestinian airline hijacking, Secretary General U Thant demurred. "A criminal act is judged by its criminal character and not for its political significance," he said.[22] However, Arafat, in his speech to the General Assembly, claimed the diametric opposite. "The difference between the revolutionary and the terrorist lies in the reason for which each fights," he said. "Whoever stands by a just cause . . . cannot possibly be called [a] terrorist."

In the years and decades that followed, Arafat's position won hands down over U Thant's. Just a week after Arafat's appearance before it, the General Assembly affirmed "the right of the Palestinian people to regain its rights by all means,"[23] although an apparent qualification in the text left the meaning somewhat blurred.* Any ambiguity was wiped away in a 1982 resolution that lumped the Palestinian case together with lingering cases of white rule in south-

---

* It asserted "the right of the Palestinian people to regain its rights by all means in accordance with the purposes and principles of the Charter of the United Nations."

ern Africa and affirmed "the legitimacy of the struggle of peoples against foreign occupation by all available means, including armed struggle."[24] Because the Palestinians were engaged neither in conventional nor even, for the most part, guerrilla war with Israel, but rather in a campaign of bombings and murders aimed at civilian targets, this is what was meant by "armed struggle."

This endorsement was repeated and invoked in various other UN resolutions over the ensuing decades until the attacks on America of 9/11 brought new urgency to the issue of terrorism. Then-Secretary General Kofi Annan, using words that echoed U Thant's,* urged the adoption of a general treaty against terrorism, but the Islamic Conference would have none of it, insisting, as *The Washington Post* reported, "that anti-Israeli militants be exempted."[25] The Pakistani ambassador explained the Islamic states' reasoning. "We ought not, in our desire to confront terrorism, erode the principle of the legitimacy of national resistance that we have upheld for 50 years."[26] Thus, Annan's efforts were thwarted, and on the tenth anniversary of 9/11, his successor, Ban Ki Moon, lamented that the United Nations still had not been able to adopt a treaty against terrorism.

As if the General Assembly's topsy-turvy stance on terrorism were not enough, the UN Commission on Human Rights went even further, affirming that Palestinian terrorism (i.e., "resist[ing] Israeli occupation" by "all available means, including armed struggle") was not only "legitimate" but something more exalted: a means of "fulfilling . . . one of the goals and purposes of the United Nations."[27]

This was only a particularly tangy sample of the fare that was invariably on the Commission's menu regarding Israel. Year after year, the governments that most egregiously abused or repressed their citizens would escape without a word of censure. Indeed many of them—the People's Republic of China, the Soviet Union, Cuba, Saudi Arabia, Libya, Syria, and others of their ilk—sat as members of the council. Occasionally, a dictatorship that had become politically isolated, such as, say, Burma's, would suffer the indignity of a single diplomatically worded resolution chiding it for misdeeds.

---

* "The right to resist occupation . . . cannot include the right to deliberately kill or maim civilians," he wrote in his report of March 21, 2005, to the General Assembly, titled *In Larger Freedom, Toward Development, Security and Human Rights for All.*

Meanwhile, at every session, some five to eight separate resolutions would excoriate Israel.

This bias also infused other UN activities in the name of human rights. The UN's 2001 World Conference Against Racism in Durban was so extreme in its anti-Israel focus and tone that Secretary of State Colin Powell ordered the US delegation to leave. The actions of Hutus toward Tutsis or Turks toward Kurds or Russians toward Chechens or Serbs toward Albanians or scores of other cases of intergroup conflict might also have been on the agenda. But not a single one was. When a resolution decrying bigotry was adopted, a proposal to include anti-Semitism on the list of proscribed prejudices was turned aside.

All of this transpired in the deliberations of governmental representatives, but the evident bias was as nothing compared to the goings on at the parallel session of officially recognized NGOs, which was also part of the official UN program. Congressman Tom Lantos, one of the American delegates, described the scene:

> Each day, [Palestinian and Islamist] groups organized anti-Israeli and anti-Semitic rallies around the meetings, attracting thousands. One flyer which was widely distributed showed a photograph of Hitler and the question "What if I had won?" The answer: "There would be NO Israel." At a press conference held by Jewish NGOs to discuss their concerns . . . an accredited NGO, the Arab Lawyers Union, distributed a booklet filled with anti-Semitic caricatures frighteningly like those seen in the Nazi hate literature printed in the 1930s.[28]

Eventually, the hypocrisy that had become the hallmark of the Commission on Human Rights alarmed Secretary General Kofi Annan who lamented that it "casts a shadow on the reputation of the United Nations system as a whole."[29] At Annan's initiative, the Commission was replaced in 2006 by the Human Rights Council. It was designed with somewhat different rules of selection intended to make the body more faithful to its mission than its predecessor. But these hopes were to be disappointed badly on all counts. Most of the world's worst abusers never have suffered even mild rebuke by the council whereas Israel continued to be lacerated, chastised as often as the rest of the countries combined. At every meeting, the council hears reports from UN officials and discusses broad themes like "racism," but its official agenda always includes two items that are country-specific: one on the "human rights situation in Palestine and other occupied Arab territories" and one on all of the rest of the world. Exemplifying its double standards, in 2007, the council mandated a follow-up conference to the 2001 Durban confab against racism and selected Muammar Qaddafi's government in Libya to chair the preparatory committee.

To top this off, the council has a special rapporteur on "Israel's violations . . . in the Palestinian territories." He is Richard Falk, a professor emeritus of international law at Princeton, who describes himself as "harshly critical of Israel's policies"[30] and who put "support for the Palestinian Solidarity Movement" at the top of his "Manifesto for Revolutionary Emancipation."[31]

In bringing a sharp-edged ideological sensibility to his work as special rapporteur for the Human Rights Council, Falk is not unique. The council's Special Rapporteur on the Right to Food, Jean Ziegler, a Swiss sociologist and activist, concentrated primarily on castigating Israel for allegedly depriving the people of Gaza of nourishment, although he also found time to denounce the "imperialist dictatorship" that rules the United States for "genocide" of Cubans by means of its embargo.

For his Israel- (and America-) bashing, Ziegler was awarded the 2002 Muammar Al-Qaddafi International Prize for Human Rights along with several other recipients, including the convicted French Holocaust-denier Roger Garaudy. Ziegler claims he declined the honor on the grounds of his "responsibilities at the United Nations," although it is unlikely he was embarrassed by it, since he had been one of a group of self-described "intellectuals and progressive militants" who gathered in Tripoli in 1989 to announce the creation of the prize. At the time, Ziegler explained that its purpose was to counterbalance the Nobel Prize, which, he said, constituted a "perpetual humiliation to the Third World." Besides Ziegler and Garaudy, other winners of the Libyan government–funded prize included Fidel Castro, a female leader of Saddam Hussein's Ba'ath Party, "the stone-throwing children of Palestine," and even one American: Louis Farrakhan.

The obsessive focus on Israel that occupies the General Assembly and the Human Rights Council also seeps into other UN activities where it would seem not at all germane. For example, the UN Commission on the Status of Women holds an annual meeting, and each year in addition to general statements of principles and intentions, it passes a total of one resolution addressed to the situation of women in a particular country or place, namely, Palestine. One observer noted the irony that during the war in Darfur, this resolution had been sponsored by Sudan whose government was at that moment employing mass rape as a tactic.[32]

Although it is true that most UN bodies are devoid of practical power and cannot enforce their resolutions, this endless drumbeat, from one body to the next, from one corner of the world to another, singling out Israel as the pariah among nations, ineluctably shapes the political environment in which Israel must live, trade, defend itself, and pursue peace with its neighbors. Moreover to dismiss the United Nations (apart from the Security Council which holds certain powers of enforcement) as a feckless "talk shop" is to overlook those of its actions that do indeed have practical consequences.

One was the creation in 1975 of the Committee for the Exercise of the Inalienable Rights of the Palestinian People with a mandate to help the Palestinians to achieve their larger goals. For some Palestinians today that means a state alongside Israel, but in 1975 it meant a state *in place of* Israel—and for some today it still means that.

Twenty member states were appointed to this committee of which almost all were predisposed to favor this annihilationist goal: eighteen had voted in favor of the resolution equating Zionism and racism and sixteen refused to have diplomatic relations with Israel. The PLO, which was of course not a member of the United Nations and was still drenched in the blood of terrorism, was nonetheless appointed a member of the drafting committee that wrote the larger committee's first report.

This report emphasized that all Palestinian refugees from 1948 and after had an "absolute" and "inalienable right to return to their homes."[33] It made clear that the importance of this right was not humanitarian but political, to wit, "the exercise of the individual right of the Palestinian to return to his homeland was a *condition sine qua non* for the exercise by this people of its rights to self-determination, national independence and sovereignty" rights that required "full implementation."[34] The language was a little dense, but its implications were clear. A people can exercise "self-determination" and "sovereignty" within a given territory only by ruling that territory. The point in this case was that all "Palestine," apparently including Israel, belonged by right to the Palestinian Arabs. Not a word was to be found in the twenty-three-page document of any right possessed by Israelis or Jews.

This report was not a culmination of the committee's work but only a starting point. Unlike most UN committees, this one was given a staff, which grew by 1979 into a special division within the UN Secretariat, the Division of Palestinian Rights. Once again, the disproportionate attention to Palestine was egregious. Within the UN's Department of Political Affairs, there is a single division for Asia and the Pacific, another for the Americas and Europe, another for West Asia and the Middle East, and another for Palestinian Rights. With some two dozen employees and a budget of millions of dollars, this office has functioned for more than three decades as a permanent, round-the-clock boiler room for anti-Israel propaganda and organizing.

Exemplifying its approach to the issue, in 1990 the Division published a book-length study titled *The Origins and Evolution of the Palestine Problem 1917–1988*.[35] It explains that "the Balfour Declaration . . . can be considered the root of the problem of Palestine." The Balfour Declaration was, of course, the statement of the British government during World War I that endorsed a homeland for the Jews in Palestine. This was codified in the peace treaty placing Palestine under British trusteeship with a mandate from the League of Nations. But this UN study informs readers that "several authorities of international law . . . have questioned the validity of the Mandate." Apart from the fact that the bona fides of these "authorities" are dubious,* the essence of this argument is that Israel had no right to exist.

This book is just one of "over 30,000 text documents" in a collection called UNISPAL, the United Nations Information System on the Question of Palestine, which functions as a vast data base for pro-Palestinian/anti-Israel advocacy. But this is only a small part of the activity of the Division of Palestinian Rights. Its larger project is to promote anti-Israel activism.

Toward this end, it sponsors an annual day of "solidarity with the Palestinian people," observed at UN offices worldwide on the anniversary of the United Nations's 1947 resolution proposing to

---

* The principal such "authority" that it quotes is Professor Henry Cattan whom it neglects to mention represented Haj Amin al-Husseini's Arab Higher Committee before the General Assembly in 1947 and 1948.

partition Palestine into Jewish and Arab states, which is treated as a tragedy because it brought a Jewish state into being. The spirit of the occasion was expressed, for example, in the highlight of the 2011 commemoration at the UN's New York headquarters (others were held in Geneva and Vienna), a screening of the film, *La Terre Parle Arabe*. According to its publicity materials, this documentary reveals that "well before the Balfour Declaration . . . Zionist leaders" plotted to "transfer . . . the Palestinians out of their land [by] all possible means."[36] Surely it must be unique for the United Nations to sponsor and fund a worldwide commemoration designed to lament one of the organization's own decisions.

In May each year, the committee joins in yet another ritual lamentation of Israel's existence, the annual observance of Naqba Day—the anniversary of Israel's statehood which is commemorated as a "catastrophe" (i.e., *naqba*) by the Palestinians.

Perhaps more important than these observances are the committee's quarterly conferences, each one in a different city, bringing together as many as four to five hundred participants (at UN expense). They include officials of governments hostile to Israel but more importantly international representatives of nongovernmental groups and local activists. According to the committee's website, more than one thousand NGOs are accredited to it. Each year, one of the meetings focuses on civil society, and in 2004 it endorsed a boycott of Israeli goods. The 2005 gathering went further, concluding with a ringing "Call to Action" that said:

> [W]e urge international, national and regional social movements, organizations and coalitions to support the unified call of Palestinian civil society for a global campaign of boycotts, divestment and sanctions (BDS) to pressure Israel to end the occupation and fully comply with international law and all relevant United Nations resolutions. We have identified the coming year to mobilize for and inaugurate this BDS campaign. We call on our partner organizations to intensify all our activities, focusing on the BDS campaign so that together we will end the Occupation.[37]

This appeal was reiterated in subsequent years, thus putting the prestige of the United Nations as well as millions of dollars in resources behind the global campaign to ostracize and materially damage Israel. For example, the Division of Palestinian Rights

maintains a website where NGOs from every part of the world pub-
licize their BDS and other activities.

The United Nations has its largest direct impact on the conflict
between Israel and the Palestinians and other Arabs through the
operation the United Nations Relief and Works Agency (UNRWA).
UNRWA was created at US initiative in 1949. Its original purpose,
as conceived by the Americans, was to provide temporary succor to
those who were uprooted by the war of Israel's birth. At almost the
same time, another UN agency was created, the High Commissioner
for Refugees (UNHCR), designed to assist persons who remained
displaced from World War II. Although both UNRWA and the High
Commissioner were created as short-term projects, both have endured ever since.

There is, however, a critical difference. Over the decades, the High
Commissioner has moved on from one group of refugees to another,
helping them to rebuild their lives, either through repatriation or
resettlement. After dealing successfully with the refugees from
World War II, the UNHCR's next concern was Hungarians fleeing
the Soviet invasion of their country in 1956. Then came the spillover
from Algeria's war of independence, and then other crises in Asia,
Latin America, sub-Saharan Africa, and eventually even back to Europe with the Balkan crisis of the 1990s.[38]

UNRWA's work, in contrast, has focused on a single population for more than sixty years and is supported more lavishly. The
UNHCR has a staff of 7,685, serving some 33.9 million "people of
concern,"[39] whereas UNRWA reports it has a staff of 30,000 serving
5 million,[40] in other words, four times as many staff for one-seventh
as many beneficiaries. The essential reason for these differences is
that according to its statue, "the work of the High Commissioner
shall be of an entirely non-political character; it shall be humanitarian and social." But the work of UNRWA is wholly political, and
only incidentally humanitarian. According to the United Nations's
history of its refugee work:

> Arab states insisted that Palestinian refugees receiving UNRWA
> assistance should be excluded from UNHCR's mandate. . . .
> Arab states were concerned lest the individual refugee defini-
> tion . . . undermine the position of Palestinians, whose rights
> as a group to return had been recognized in General Assembly
> resolutions.[41]

The General Assembly resolution creating the UNHCR called on all states to "promot[e] the assimilation of refugees, especially by facilitating their naturalization."[42] The Arab states, except for Jordan, ignored this injunction precisely because they wished Israel to disappear and therefore insisted that all Arabs who had fled or been expelled must be repatriated. They insistently pointed to an earlier General Assembly resolution specifying that "refugees wishing to return to their homes and live at peace with their neighbors should be permitted to do so at the earliest practicable date."[43]

Not only did the Arab states thus wish to pick and choose among General Assembly resolutions, but their insistence that Resolution 194 conferred a "right of return" ignored its qualifying phrase "wishing . . . to live at peace with their neighbors." There was of course no "practicable" way that Israel or anyone else could sort individuals by this criterion in the absence of an overall reconciliation between Jews and Arabs. In any event, the Arabs themselves insisted that the refugees be treated not as individuals but "as a group," and that group was not prepared to make peace with Israel, thus rendering Resolution 194 moot.

The Arabs' view that the refugee question was political rather than humanitarian prevented UNRWA from concentrating resources on those most in need. Such efforts met objections from the Arab host countries and Palestinian leaders. They insisted that the refugees were entitled to the benefits offered by UNRWA regardless of individual circumstance.

James G. Lindsay, the former general counsel of UNRWA, notes that, "it was clear from the beginning that rations were not desperately needed by all UNRWA beneficiaries—some refugees, for example, sold or 'rented' their ration cards to merchants, who . . . resold them on the open market." Yet, when donors pressed for a more focused use of their largesse, "the refugees, including UNRWA local staff, insisted that general distribution of rations continue, viewing the program as a guarantor of recipients' well being, as 'an acquired right,' and as a reflection of the international community's political commitment to them."[44]

The same point is underscored by the living arrangements of the Palestinians served by UNRWA. In the early years these were camps, mostly of tents. Later the "camps" became small shanty towns or poor neighborhoods. But according to UNRWA, by 2011 only 1.4 million of the 5 million Palestinians registered with it live in these "camps." The rest—nearly three-fourths—"live in and around the cities and towns of the host countries, and in the West Bank and the Gaza Strip."[45] Nonetheless, they receive rations, medical care, education, and other services from the United Nations.

This points to the question: by what token are these five million refugees? Statistically, it is unlikely that more than 5 percent of them, perhaps less, were alive in 1948. UNRWA's answer is that not only are those who fled their homes "refugees," but so are their descendants, now comprising three or even four additional generations. Nowhere else in the world are refugees counted in this manner. The standard English and French dictionaries define "refugee" as the person who has fled; none mention progeny or perpetuity. More importantly, the Convention Relating to the Status of Refugees, the governing international law on this question, defines "refugee" as "any person who," for various specified reasons, "is . . . outside the country of *his former habitual residence*." (Emphasis added.) It, too, says nothing of descendants.

The sole reason why these five million—or 95 percent of them— are treated as "refugees" is to keep alive the Palestinian "right of return" which means the end of Israel.* Were it not for this dream, the Palestinian case would have been among the easiest to solve of the world's many refugee problems since the surrounding countries that could absorb them share language, faith, and culture with the Palestinians. Resettlement would have been far easier, for example, than Israel's integration of an equivalent number of Jews fleeing or expelled from the Arab countries at the same time, whose language was not Hebrew but Arabic.

The conclusion is inescapable. By its countless one-sided resolutions and numerous "investigations" of Israel with predetermined results; by providing a global infrastructure for the movement to boycott, divest from, and sanction Israel; and by UNRWA, which sustains the idea of the "right of return," the United Nations has served systematically to challenge Israel's legitimacy and weaken its global position. This is the crucible of Israel's demonization.

---

* Were the Palestinians (and the Arab states) prepared to make peace with Israel, it might not be difficult to fulfill the terms of the much-trumpeted Resolution 194. Of course, in most cases, the homes that were left no longer exist. But if some of the Palestinian senior citizens who were among the 1948 refugees wanted to live out their days in or near the locales of their childhood, it is hard to see why some such arrangement could not be made.

Six

Europe's Socialists
Go Third World

The United Nations's tilt against Israel reflected simple math. The numerical advantage of the Arab and Muslim states, reinforced by the communist world and the Non-Aligned Movement (NAM), made an overwhelming majority. Still, despite the raw numbers, Israel retained some weighty support. In addition to the United States, one other bastion on which Israel could count was the Socialist International. But, in the 1970s, one European leader took upon himself the mission of reversing Israel's privileged standing with the socialists. He was Bruno Kreisky, the chancellor of Austria, vice president of the International, and one of the most memorable European politicians of his era.

The International was an agglomeration of moderate Leftist parties that were influential and sometimes even dominant in Europe and a few other countries—for example, the British and Australian Labour parties, the German and Swedish Social Democrats, the French Socialists, and the like. Historically, these parties had been firmly pro-Western in the Cold War. Indeed, the idea of the North Atlantic Treaty Organization (NATO) had first been conceived by Ernest Bevin, foreign minister in Britain's Labour Party government.

The movement's warmth toward Israel was not based primarily on geopolitics but on that country's socialist achievements. Among the world's democracies, no country was molded more decisively by socialist ideas than Israel, which was governed for its first three decades by the Labor Party whose philosophy had dominated the Zionist movement prior to statehood. All land and much else was owned by the state or by the national labor federation which was the leading force in Israel's economy and politics. To top it off, the *kibbutzim*, communes practicing the purest socialism, even collective child-rearing, constituted the emblem of the country. As a kind of socialist model, Israel enjoyed great prestige within the halls of the Socialist International.

Kreisky, however, although highly idealistic in his own attachment to socialist philosophy, reacted against Israel's esteemed standing in terms that were paradoxically tinged with *realpolitik*. "The European parties were one-sidedly pro-Israeli, and I considered this short-sighted and dangerous," he later recalled. "Time and again I drew attention to this problem."[1] By influencing the Socialist International, Kreisky aimed to gain leverage toward a wider goal. "I set out to change [the] attitude on the part of the Western world" whose sympathy for Jews as a consequence of the Holocaust was, in his view "exploited by those in power in Israel in the most brutal fashion."[2]

Remarkably, Kreisky was himself of Jewish lineage, born in 1911 to a well-to-do secular Viennese family. But he apparently felt nothing for this heritage—at least nothing positive. At age nineteen or twenty, he had taken the trouble to have his name stricken from the official list of Austrian Jews.[3] A few years earlier he had become a devoted member of the Social Democratic Party, a disciple of Otto Bauer's, the chief theoretician of Austrian Marxism to whom Kreisky says he "felt bound . . . from the start with every fiber of my political being."[4]

It is easy to trace a direct descent from Marx to Bauer to Kreisky—all three Germanic and of Jewish parentage who turned their backs on this heritage. Marx had penned a vitriolic monograph, *On the Jewish Question*, which described the Jews as the incarnation of capitalism. "Money is the jealous god of Israel," he wrote, adding: "the emancipation of the Jews is the emancipation of mankind from Judaism." Citing this essay as his foundational text, Bauer had updated the analysis less acerbically. "The Jew [is] the mediator of commodity circulation and the circulation of monetary capital,"[5] he put it, but he foresaw that the concentration of capital would reduce many Jews to workers. "Only then will the misery particular to the Jews disappear, and they will be left with the shared misery of the proletariat, which they will struggle against and triumph over, shoulder to shoulder with their Aryan colleagues."[6] With these mentors, the young and affluent Kreisky made himself over as best he could from a Jew to a proletarian, spurning the socialist students' organization for the young workers' movement so as to participate more directly in the class struggle.

This framework shaped his attitude toward his Nazi fellow-prisoners when, in the mid-1930s, he served time for subversive activities under the authoritarian regime of Kurt Schuschnigg, which repressed challenges to the Austrian state from radicals, left and right. Kreisky's biographer, H. Pierre Secher, writes that political discourse among these factions was "rarely . . . hostile." On the contrary:

> There was a well-founded solidarity among the political [prison-ers], directed against the despised "clerico-fascist" government.
> . . . Ideologically, the distinction between "*Sozis*" [Socialists and] Commies on the one hand and Nazis on the other, was probably only the internationalism of the Marxists and the nationalism of the Nazis. In every other respect they agreed on the evils of capitalism. Even the primary connection by the Nazis of capital-ism with the Jews did not necessarily encounter heated critical opposition from the Socialists.[7]

Kreisky formed a bond with his Nazi cellmate, Sepp Weninger. Once, Kreisky was cornered by guards while in possession of a note he was attempting to smuggle out for Weninger. Rather than trying to save his own hide by surrendering the note, Kreisky took the risk of swallowing it before his captors could see, earning his cellmate's special gratitude. When Germany absorbed Austria into the Third Reich, Weninger remembered his debt.

Arrested by the new authorities, Kreisky sent an audacious letter to the Gestapo, somehow supposing that its officers would nurture a certain sympathy for him. He wrote:

> I [have] decided to direct my request directly to the Gestapo since I believe that organization now consists largely of former illegals; I am prepared to provide you any time with the names of currently prominent, well-known members of the NSDAP [Nazi Party] who can testify that during my time as [a] prisoner I have always shown solidarity toward my National Socialist prison mates.[8]

It is unlikely this appeal melted hearts at Gestapo headquar-ters, but Weninger, now a functionary, used his influence to enable

Kreisky to flee to Sweden instead of being sent to a concentration camp. After the war, on learning that Weninger was being tried by the Allies for summary executions of Austrian militia members under his command and for abusing Jews and prisoners of war, Kreisky "lost no time in intervening for his former cellmate," reports Secher, but was unable to save him from execution.[9]

It is possible to understand why in the 1930s Kreisky, like many other socialists who were steeped in Marxism and viewed capitalists as the true enemies, might have seen Nazis as merely misguided revolutionaries. Back then, it was hard to know what exactly to make of Hitlerian rhetoric. But it is much harder to fathom how Kreisky could have clung to such a view after the war. He could not have been unaware of the Holocaust since most of his immediate relatives had been murdered in it. Yet he hastened to aid Weninger even though Weninger was charged with, among other bloody deeds, at least marginal participation in the destruction of the Jews. Perhaps this was blind loyalty, but it foreshadowed the controversial stance toward Nazis that was to become a hallmark of Kreisky's career.

Devoting himself in the postwar decades to resurrecting the Austrian Socialist Party, Kreisky rose to become foreign minister in the 1960s and then to lead the party in national elections. The socialists lost in 1966 when the leader of the rival People's Party campaigned as a "true Austrian" in implicit contrast to Kreisky's Jewish roots. But, in 1970, for the first time, the socialists won a plurality of seats. Rather than form a coalition, Kreisky opted to lead a minority government after securing the agreement of Friedrich Peter, leader of the Freedom Party, not to oppose him. The Freedom Party was an odd mix. It traced its roots in part to traditional liberalism, that is, belief in free enterprise, but it also was a magnet for former Nazis, a body of voters proportionately larger in Austria than in Germany itself. Austria's leading political scientist, Anton Pelinka, put it bluntly. The Freedom Party, he said, was "founded by former Nazis for former Nazis."[10]

Kreisky's 1970 cabinet appointments sparked contention when the famous Austrian Nazi-hunter, Simon Wiesenthal, revealed that no fewer than four of the eleven ministers were former Nazis. The Minister of Agriculture Hans Ollinger had been a member of a *Waffen-SS* unit guilty of war crimes, although it was subsequently shown that he had left that service for the regular army quite early in the war and had been acquitted of wrongdoing by the Allied Commission. When Ollinger nonetheless soon resigned his post, Kreisky replaced him with another former Nazi.

Kreisky argued that no one, including those who had been Nazis, should be condemned for past political positions unless he or she could be shown to have committed a crime. He lashed out furiously at Wiesenthal calling him a "Jewish fascist," according to an interview published in a Dutch paper, adding: "Wiesenthal . . . is a reactionary and they do exist among us Jews, just as there are among us Jews also murderers and whores."[11]*

Kreisky's conflict with Wiesenthal intensified in connection with Austria's 1975 national election. The run-up featured speculation (and apparently secret negotiations) about a possible coalition between Kreisky's socialists and Peter's Freedom Party. When the votes were counted, the socialists had a majority by themselves, obviating such a deal. But, just after the election, Wiesenthal released records showing that Peter had served as a sergeant in an *Einsatzgruppen* brigade whose sole mission was the extermination of civilians in occupied territory, in particular, Jews.

In response, Peter acknowledged having belonged to the unit, although he had previously obscured this, but he denied having been present when any of its ten thousand victims were killed. Kreisky responded with rage—not at Peter, but at Wiesenthal. He launched into a campaign of vilification, accusing Wiesenthal of "mafia methods" and "spying," and he even encouraged a parliamentary investigation of Wiesenthal's activities rather than those of Peter.

The reasons for his rage may have included protectiveness toward Peter with whom he appears to have been close and who spoke of Kreisky as something of a mentor or model, despite their party differences. In addition, Kreisky was jealous of Austria's international image, and he charged Wiesenthal with making a "living from telling the world that Austria is anti-Semitic."[12]

The reverse side of Kreisky's lack of Jewish identity was Austrian chauvinism. He lamented "the breakup of the old empire" after World War I,[13] speaking wistfully of it as a "huge melting pot,"[14] apparently deaf to the incongruity between this view and his anticolonial stance toward the third world.

---

* Kreisky later denied having used the word "fascist," which mattered little in light of the rest of the quote and also because he used the expression "Jewish fascist" on other occasions.

This ardent patriotism led him to deny Austria's responsibility for its part in Hitler's Reich despite the fact that Austrians were present in greater proportions than Germans in the Nazi Party, in the SS, and in carrying out the Holocaust,[15] a painful reality that was finally acknowledged by Kreisky's successor, Franz Vranitzky.[16] Gunter Bischof, a historian in other respects sympathetic to Kreisky, writes: "Kreisky's approach towards . . . Austrians' role in World War II . . . was as strangely uncritical and superficial as that of his predecessors. Kreisky never publicly questioned the mythology of the 'rape' of Austria in 1938 and Austria's 'victim' ideology."[17]

The dramatic contrast between Kreisky's rejection of the Jewish component of his background and his embrace of the Austrian component was illustrated most poignantly in the "irony" noted by Secher that Kreisky, while still in Sweden at war's end, had:

> [W]ork[ed] day and night to obtain the release of and favored treatment for former members of the German *Wehrmacht*, even *Waffen-SS*, of allegedly "Austrian origin" at the very same time when those whose "Jewish origins" he shared roamed Europe by the tens of thousands in search of food and shelter.[18]

Kreisky's vendetta against Simon Wiesenthal culminated in the accusation that this famous scourge of former Nazis had himself been a Nazi collaborator. "I understand that at that time he wanted to save his life, but he has no moral authority to point an accusing finger at others," said Kreisky.[19] The evidence on which Kreisky based this allegation had come from the intelligence service of communist Poland. Wiesenthal sued for libel but, after the intervention of some mutual friends, he withdrew his suit when Kreisky publicly retracted the accusation. A decade later, having left office, Kreisky repeated the charge and Wiesenthal renewed his legal action, winning the largest libel award in Austrian history to that point.[20]

While acknowledging his "Jewish origins," Kreisky was antagonistic to the idea of a "Jewish people." Having removed himself as a young man from the roll of the Jewish community, he had his children listed as Protestant in their school registration and, according to his biographer, did not have his son circumcised.[21] He viewed Judaism as nothing more than a religion, and he himself was an adamant nonbeliever. To sharpen his point in an interview with *Der*

Spiegel, he added provocatively that if the Jews did constitute a people "they are a wretched people."[22]*

Der Spiegel commented that "Lately, Austria's chancellor hardly misses an opportunity to detract, through fits of anger, from his image as a superior statesman."[23] The scholars Andrei Markovitz and Anson Rabinbach note, however, that Kreisky's antics and his "apparent personal dislike of Jews" were no domestic liability: "Kreisky's personal prejudice happened to be superb politics in a country where well into the 1970s more than 70 percent of the population still harbored anti-Jewish sentiments."[24]

Whether the motive was political or psychological, Kreisky seemed to relish using his Jewish lineage as a shield allowing him to take on the Jewish world with a fierce pleasure that would have been impossible for a gentile politician. Explaining his attack on Wiesenthal he boasted: "So far no one has dared to talk back to this man because everyone was afraid that Mr. Wiesenthal would say, well, this is because you were perhaps a Nazi. . . . It is necessary that someone say: now, look, Mr. Wiesenthal, that has gone far enough."[25] More consequentially, he adopted a similar approach in his relations with Israel, quipping once that he was "the only politician whom Golda Meir could not intimidate." This alluded to his campaign to reverse Europe's pro-Israel stance.

Mrs. Meir was prime minister of Israel in September 1973 when a pair of Palestinian "commandos" turned their hijacking skills on a train rather than a plane and seized hostages. The train had crossed from Czechoslovakia into Austria, and among its passengers were dozens of Jews emigrating to Israel.

The Six Day War had ignited a Zionist movement within the USSR despite that country's tradition of denying its citizens the right to leave. After struggle and sacrifice, Jews had pried ajar the gates, and in 1971 the number allowed to depart had for the first time exceeded ten thousand. To well-wishers of freedom everywhere this was a portentous crack in the façade of totalitarianism. To Zionists, it promised an immense step toward the dream of reuniting the Jewish people in their ancestral home. To Arabs, and especially

---

* He used the word *mieses* which has been translated as "wretched" in most accounts. Others have rendered it as "lousy," "ugly," "unattractive," "repulsive."

to Palestinians, it threatened a more populous and therefore more formidable Israel.

The Lebanese newspaper, *Al Hayat*, called the train hijacking "the most effective commando action since Munich," meaning the 1972 attack on the Olympics.[26] The hijackers demanded that Austria cease allowing the transit of Soviet Jews, and they wanted free passage out of Austria with their hostages. Kreisky offered to meet them halfway. He agreed to let them fly to Libya albeit without the hostages, and he promised to shut down Schonau Castle, the processing center for the Jewish emigrants.

Kreisky's decision "won front-page headlines and acclaim from Cairo to Baghdad," reported *The New York Times*.[27] Newspapers in countries of the Soviet bloc joined in the praise of Kreisky. But he was condemned in Israel and the West, especially the United States where the Senate passed a resolution expressing dismay and President Richard Nixon deplored "giv[ing] in to international blackmail by terrorist groups."[28] Golda Meir made a hasty visit to Vienna where, after an extremely chilly meeting—according to her aide, the Chancellor did not so much as step out from behind his desk to greet her—Kreisky declared himself unmoved and she refused to speak to the press.[29]

Kreisky struck a defiant posture toward these protests. "The worst thing in this matter would be to put pressure on us," he warned.[30] A day later, he added: "We certainly won't allow ourselves to be intimidated,"[31] apparently missing the irony that what others were decrying was precisely his decision to be intimidated by the terrorists.

In memoirs, Kreisky claims he never intended to impede the flow of Soviet Jews to Israel, and his biographer, Secher, makes a similar case. In the end, another Austrian facility replaced Schonau. But it is doubtful this was Kreisky's original intent since in closing Schonau he insisted that other countries share the "burden" of providing passage, although this was not logistically feasible. The hijackers certainly believed they had extracted a pledge to obstruct Jewish emigration, not just to change the facilities.

The Schonau controversy was eclipsed by the eruption of the Yom Kippur War only days later, and with it the imposition of the Arab oil embargo. When the smoke had cleared, Meir sought a meeting of the Socialist International at which she confronted the party leaders, eight of whom were then heading governments: "Not one inch of your territory was put at our disposal for refueling the planes that saved us from destruction." Kissinger had bemoaned the Europeans' noncooperation with the American airlift as a betrayal of the spirit of the NATO alliance.[32] Meir's complaint was on moral grounds and on the presumed obligation of international solidarity among socialists. Amazingly, no one replied, and in the silence Meir reports that a voice behind her said: "Of course they can't talk. Their throats are choked with oil."[33]

Although the situation was an embarrassment to most of the socialists, Kreisky saw it as a welcome opportunity. "We cannot ignore the political consequences of our clear dependence upon essential reserves vital to Europe's energy economy," he wrote later. "As a result of the shock of the oil crisis I achieved a breakthrough with the Socialist International."[34]

The breakthrough consisted of a decision to create a fact-finding mission to the Middle East under Kreisky's chairmanship. It is unlikely its real purpose was to find facts. The Arab–Israeli conflict was neither new nor obscure; all of these leaders and their parties had been dealing with it since its inception. So it is hard to understand what "facts" they may have lacked. Had they nonetheless wanted a genuine probe of the subject they would have chosen someone to lead it who was neutral, whereas Kreisky, who had proposed the mission, had already carved out a position as the one leader of the International least friendly to Israel. His role, then, was to run interference for the others as they shifted away from their longstanding support for Israel in deference to their newly felt need to win Arab favor. That Kreisky was of Jewish background was a bonus. By allowing him to lead the way, they shielded themselves against charges of anti-Semitism.

Kreisky led the "fact-finders" on tours of the region in 1974, 1975, and 1976; then in 1977 he issued a report. It contained an introduction with his byline while its body was unsigned, presumably issued by the participants as a group, but the entire document bore Kreisky's imprint. It blamed the lack of peace in the Middle East squarely on Israel although not a single Arab state had yet expressed any willingness to accept Israel's existence nor had the Arab League altered its 1967 summit resolution, pledging "no peace . . . , no recognition . . . , no negotiations." Nonetheless, the report concluded airily that "Israel would be totally unchallenged in her existence" if only she would "take into account developments in the Arab world and adjust . . . her future political aspirations to this area."[35]

This report was never adopted by a congress or governing body, not even formally debated. But it was released publicly by Kreisky and thereafter was seen widely as the International's most definitive statement on the Middle East.

The "fact-finders" had met with Yasser Arafat on their first trip to the region, and their report called for recognition of the Palestine Liberation Organization (PLO). Two years later, in 1979, Kreisky took a further step, this time in tandem with West German Chancellor Willy Brandt. Brandt was now also the president of the International and had set an agenda of realigning the socialists away from the United States and toward partnership with the global "South." Carl Gershman, who participated in the International as the leader of Social Democrats, USA, wrote that Brandt and Kreisky sought to "refashion democratic socialism into an international movement aligned with anti-Western revolutionary movements in the Third World."[36] Toward this end, Kreisky hosted Arafat in Vienna in July 1979 for talks with Brandt and himself on behalf of the International.

Arafat, who arrived in battle fatigues directly from Bulgaria where he was inspecting PLO "commandos" in training, was welcomed at the airport by Kreisky and members of his cabinet and was treated with all the honors reserved for a visiting head of state from a friendly country, including a banquet in his honor attended by Brandt. The three leaders issued a joint communiqué blasting Israel, and at a concluding press conference, Kreisky likened the Palestinians' situation to his own Swedish exile during World War II, thus embracing the PLO's claim, as Gershman put it, that its "campaign against Israel [was] analogous to the European resistance against the Nazis."[37]

This summit with Arafat paved the way for a shift in Europe's relations with the PLO. Until then, Western Europe generally mirrored US policy that made diplomatic contact with the PLO conditional on its willingness to accept Israel's existence and to renounce terror. Now, however, Europe began to open its arms to the PLO in the hope that moderation would come later. Two months after his welcome by Kreisky in Vienna, Arafat was received on an official visit to Spain, then two months after that, to Portugal. In March 1980, Kreisky announced that Austria was granting diplomatic recognition to the PLO, rare status for an organization that is not a state. No other Western government had yet done this, but more were to follow. Then in June, the European Economic Community (forerunner of the European Union) issued a declaration on the Middle East endorsing the "legitimate rights of the Palestinian people," implicitly recognizing the PLO, demanding Israeli withdrawal from the territories occupied in 1967, and rejecting Israel's unification of Jerusalem.

Just as he led the way in shifting the stance of European governments on the Middle East, so Kresiky was in the vanguard in the transformation of the socialist world. The Socialist International had once described itself as *democratic* socialist, with an emphasis on the adjective. But, with the rise of the third world, the members of this organization felt increasingly embarrassed at belonging to a club of the white skinned and prosperous. In atonement, they began to admit various parties in the developing countries if they preached socialism even without practicing democracy, such as Nicaragua's Sandinista Liberation Front. Eventually, too, the International admitted Arafat's party, Fatah, which had never even given lip service to democracy in the Western sense. Meanwhile, Israel's Labor Party, once the most accomplished member of the International, was dropped from the rolls for nonpayment of dues.

In later years, after Israel itself recognized the PLO in the 1993 Oslo Accords, Kreisky was credited by his admirers (and himself) with having been ahead of the curve. But at Oslo, the PLO made a historic change: it agreed to accept Israel and live in peace with it, renouncing violence. To recognize the PLO once it had done this was entirely different from recognizing it and granting it legitimacy while it was still sworn to Israel's destruction and practicing terrorism. Had Israel and the United States followed Kreisky's position, that is, had they not insisted that they would deal with the PLO *only* if it made the concessions that it finally did at Oslo, who knows if it would ever have signed on for compromise and a peaceful solution?

It is true that Israelis on the whole were slow to accept the reality of a Palestinian people. They argued that this idea had been ginned up by the Arabs in their campaign against the existence of Israel, which was true but not the whole story. Nationhood is largely a subjective thing, and once the sense of national identity spread and deepened among Palestinians their peoplehood became real. Ironically, while Kreisky had no doubts that the Palestinians were a nation, he repeatedly denied that the Jews were. "It has been established by science," he declaimed, "that there is no Jewish people but rather a religious community."[38] And "there is not a Jewish race any more than there is a Roman Catholic race or an Islamic race."[39]

In referring to "science" Kreisky was alluding to a theory, since discredited by genetic research, that European Jews were descended from Asiatic tribes and not from the Israelites driven into exile by the Romans. He went on to compound this farrago with a crackpot corollary of his own devising, venturing that the true descendants of the Jews of biblical times were the contemporary Palestinians, analogous to the *conversos* of the Spanish Inquisition.[40]

In crediting the nationhood of the Palestinians but not the Jews, Kreisky exhibited a double standard that infused his approach to the Middle East. He despised one Israeli leader after another often in overtly anti-Semitic terms. In Meir he noted mannerisms "so characteristic of Jews from Eastern Europe."[41] Menachem Begin, he said, was a "political grocer . . . a little Polish lawyer," adding, "they think in such a warped way, these Eastern [European] Jews."[42] Kreisky accused Begin's successor, Itzhak Shamir, of being so cynical as to welcome anti-Semitism because "it makes Israel the last and only refuge of the Jews."[43]

In contrast, he developed an abiding affection for Arafat and he found Egypt's Anwar Sadat "impressive, fascinating, elegant, open, prophetic."[44] Sadat, of course, won many admirers thanks to his bold initiative of peacemaking with Israel. But this was precisely the part of Sadat's record that Kreisky did *not* like, and he denigrated the Camp David Accords that Sadat entered into with Begin. Kreisky was angered by Arafat's celebration of Sadat's assassination, but soon forgave him and resumed their friendship. In addition, Kreisky courted Libya's Muammar Qaddafi, hosting him for a four-day state visit in March 1982, and later praising Libya's "advances in water management and . . . remarkable development projects."[45] He also expressed admiration for Syria's Hafez al-Assad, whom he called "an outstanding personality . . . very 'European.'"[46] While several times lambasting Israelis and other Zionists as "fascists," he never criticized Assad's ideology, Baathism, which, founded at the height of Axis power in Europe, borrowed unabashedly from authentic fascism.

In his memoirs, Kreisky justified his relentless animus toward Israel:

What is happening presently in Israel is so abominable and re-
pugnant that it is really difficult for me to remain calm about it.
And why should I? I have always utterly detested violence and
injustice and have combated them wherever they appeared, and
I feel it to be a moral duty to take the same attitude towards
Jews who commit or defend such wrongdoing.[47]

This bit of self-admiration was, if not a plain lie then delusional.
Arafat, Assad, and Qaddafi committed grave abuses of their own
citizens, and each was also was stained with the blood of other Arabs, not to mention Israelis, but there is no record of Kreisky's having "combated" or voiced "detest[ation]" of any of this. At bottom,
Kreisky nursed, as he admits in his memoirs, a "critical attitude
towards the existence of the state of Israel."[48] This followed naturally from his heavy investment—intellectual, and perhaps also
psychological—in the proposition that the idea of a "Jewish people"
was a myth.

Bruno Kreisky may be seen as one of the ancestors of the Jews
who now served in the front ranks of the hate-Israel movement,
using their ethnic "authenticity" to lend weight to their attacks on
the Jewish state. But few have matched the impact of Kreisky who
stands alongside de Gaulle as the foremost leaders in undoing Europe's sympathy for Israel and its people.

seven

Edward Said Conquers Academia for Palestine

For half a century following the Bolshevik seizure of power in Russia, the global Left divided into two main camps, communism and social democracy, each of them a mighty political force ruling numerous countries and shaping national destinies. Except for a brief moment in the late 1940s, communist regimes and movements were hostile to Israel, whereas Social Democrats supported the Jewish state overwhelmingly, until Bruno Kreisky and the Arab oil weapon appeared on the scene. But, in the 1960s, the New Left became dominant among the postwar generation coming of age in the United States and Europe. In time it was to lend great weight to anti-Israel sentiment in the Western world including the United States, where the New Left achieved a cultural power far greater than older leftist currents had exerted.

In contrast to the Communists and Social Democrats who focused on the working class, the New Left appealed to students and the college-educated. Its ideology was amorphous and grew constantly more radical until the movement imploded. Street protests lost their kick, and its constituent groups splintered over what to do next, with the remnants devolving into terrorist bands like the Weathermen in the United States or the Baader-Meinhof gang in Germany or the Red Brigades in Italy. Even at the height of its popularity, the New Left never produced a political party that could compete for power. But the movement shaped the sensibilities of a generation, and as that cohort came to fill the ranks of college faculty, it transformed the intellectual atmosphere of academe.

The students who had taken over campuses physically through sit-ins and class boycotts grew up to be teachers who took over in a more profound way by reshaping the curriculum. The books and ideas that for generations were regarded as the backbone of Western civilization were now systematically "deconstructed." Moses and Jesus, Plato and Aristotle, Augustine and Aquinas, Shakespeare and Tolstoy, Locke and Burke, Hamilton and Jefferson were exposed as but so many "dead white males" whose principal importance was to perpetuate the hegemony of their race, class, and gender. At long last, their victims' day had come, and the study of their oppression and resistance replaced the traditional "canon" on the front stage of higher education.

The young professoriate was steered by new stars, and one of the brightest in their firmament was an American of Palestinian origin, Edward W. Said. Raised in Cairo, the scion of a prosperous businessman, Said had been sent to an elite New England prep school at fifteeen, then to Princeton. After graduate studies at Harvard, he began to teach literary criticism, rising to the award of an endowed chair at Columbia by the time he was forty and later to the rank of university professor, Columbia's highest faculty title.

This honor consecrated his standing as one of America's most influential intellectuals. According to a 2005 search on the utility "Syllabus finder," Said's works were assigned as reading in 868 courses in American colleges and universities (counting only courses whose syllabi were available online). These ranged across literary criticism, politics, anthropology, Middle East studies, and other disciplines including post-colonial studies, a field widely credited with having grown out of Said's work that examines the ongoing effects of colonialism. More than forty books have been published about him. A few are critical, but most, such as *The Cambridge Introduction to Edward Said*,[1] published seven years after his death of leukemia in 2003, are adulatory. Georgetown University, UCLA, and other schools offer entire courses about him. According to the Social Sciences Citation Index, he remains one of the most cited authors in the humanities. A 2001 review for *The Guardian* called him "arguably the most influential intellectual of our time,"[2] and Nobel laureate Nadine Gordimer cast him in an even wider frame, placing Said in 1999 "among the truly important intellects of our century."[3]

The springboard that launched Said to such fame was *Orientalism*, published in 1978 when he was forty-three. It expressed perfectly the temper of the intellectual times. Said's objective was to expose the evil worm at the core of Western civilization, namely, its inability to define itself except against an imagined "other." That "other" was the Oriental, a figure "to be feared . . . or to be controlled."[4] Ergo, Said claimed that "every European, in what he could say about the Orient, was . . . a racist, an imperialist, and almost totally ethnocentric."[5] Elsewhere in the text he made clear that what was true for Europeans held equally for Americans.[6]

This echoed a theme of 1960s radicalism which was forged in the movements against Jim Crow and against America's war in Vietnam, namely that the Caucasian race was the scourge of humanity. Rather than shout this accusation from a soap box, as the activists had done, Said delivered it with an erudition that awed readers into admiring assent. The names of abstruse contemporary theoreticians and obscure long-ago academicians rolled off pages strewn with words that sent readers scurrying to their dictionaries. Never mind that some of these words ("paradeutic") were made up or that some were misused ("eschatological" where "scatological" was intended); never mind that some of the citations were pretentious ("the names of Levi-Strauss, Gramsci and Michel Foucault drop with a dull thud," commented historian J. H. Plumb, reviewing *Orientalism* for *The New York Times*"[7]); and others were erroneous (attributing to the famous historian Jacob Burckhart a book by the little-known travel writer, John Lewis Burckhart)—never mind any of this, the important point that evoked frissons of pleasure and excitement was that here was a "person of color" delivering a withering condemnation of the white man and, so to speak, beating him at his own high-falutin' game.

Said reveled in his status as the model of the new-age academic unfettered by the traditional canon. But, in contrast to many academics riding the updrafts of "deconstructionism" and "post-modernism," he was more than just an intellectual on the make. He was also a man with a cause. A year after the appearance of *Orientalism*, Said published *The Question of Palestine*. Fifteen years earlier, the Palestine Liberation Organization (PLO) had been founded in the effort to crystallize a distinctive Palestinian identity. The introduction of that identity to the world had mostly taken the form of spectacular acts of terror whose purpose was in large measure to draw attention to Palestinian grievances. Now, Columbia University's Parr Professor of English and Comparative Literature gave the Palestinian cause a dramatically different face both in his own persona and in his characterization of the positions of the PLO.

This was something Said could speak of with apparent authority as a member of the Palestinian National Council, the nominal governing body of the PLO. Declaring himself "horrified" by airplane hijackings and the like, Said assured his readers that the PLO had, since the early 1970s, "avoided and condemned terror."[8] And asserting his own belief in a Palestinian state alongside—rather than in place of—Israel, he claimed that the PLO had often "stated its willingness to accept a Palestinian state on the West Bank and Gaza."[9] PLO leader Yasser Arafat, said Said, was "a much misunderstood and maligned political personality."[10]

The net effect swept up *New York Times* reviewer, Christopher Lehmann-Haupt, who wrote: "So logically and eloquently does Professor Said make [his] case, that one momentarily forgets the many countervailing arguments posed by the Israelis."[11] *The Question of Palestine* established Said as "the most persuasive voice in the West for Palestinian self-determination," as a writer in *The Guardian* put it.[12] Upon Said's death, Alexander Cockburn lamented that "the Palestinians will never know a greater polemical champion."[13]

These two books—*Orientalism* and *The Question of Palestine*— each of which was followed by various sequels and elaborations, established the twin pillars of Said's career as the avenging voice of the Palestinians against Israel, and more broadly of the Arabs, Muslims, and other "Orientals" against the West as a whole. For the Palestinian cause, the acquisition of an American avatar of Said's skills and stature was a great boon. But arguably the ideas he put across in *Orientalism* were even more important to the pro-Arab/anti-Israel cause, albeit by indirection, than his direct role as a Palestinian advocate.

In the Leftist worldview, politics was at its core a contest between the forces of good and evil or of progress and reaction. To the Old Left this meant the struggle of the proletariat against the bourgeoisie. But to the New Left, of which Said was an avatar, the lines of conflict were demographic: young against old, female against male, and above all black against white. The Marxist notion of class struggle had never resonated in America, which lacked Europe's history of hereditary social position. Race was a different matter. For Europe, colonialism and imperialism were the original sins. But in America the victimization of blacks through slavery and segregation was the running sore, the great stain on the nation's honor, the excruciating counterpoint to the proclaimed ideals of the founding fathers.

Said rolled American racism and European colonialism into one ball of wax: white oppression of darker-skinned peoples. He was not the only thinker to have forged this amalgam, but he made a unique contribution in portraying "Orientals" as the epitome of the dark-skinned; Muslims as the representative Orientals; Arabs as the essential Muslims; and, finally, Palestinians as the ultimate Arabs. Abracadabra, Israel, in conflict with the Palestinians, was transformed from a redemptive refuge from two thousand years of persecution to the very embodiment of white supremacy.

The engineer of this transfiguration was himself an unlikely personification of the wretched of the earth. His father, who called himself William, had emigrated to America in 1911, served in World War I, and been naturalized a US citizen. Reluctantly yielding to his aging mother's entreaties, he returned to the Middle East in the 1920s and settled in Cairo where he made his fortune in business and created a family by marrying a younger woman, Hilda, who shared his Protestant faith. Edward, whose skin tone would have raised few eyebrows at a Klu Klux Klan meeting, was told he was named after the Prince of Wales. He and his four siblings—Rosemary, Grace, Jean, and Joyce—were reared in the church and in opulence, with a box at the opera, membership in country clubs, piano lessons, and education entirely at British and American primary and secondary schools in Cairo. Said felt "proud of my mother for conversing in Arabic, since she alone of the entire social group to which we belonged knew the language well." The rest were more fluent in English or French. "The families close to us all had their own staff of drivers, gardeners, maids, washerwomen and an ironing man," recalled Said. "We felt as if they were our possessions." In what may have been a harbinger of the revolutionary consciousness he was to develop as an adult, young Edward, although "brought up not to be too familiar with the servants, which meant not talking to or joking with them . . . found this . . . an irresistible rule to break."[14] And, too, despite affluence, his life was no bed of roses: during his first year at prep school he was "unfairly" relegated to the *junior* varsity tennis team.

If his social class made Said a strange specimen of the oppressed, his persona as symbol of Palestine was curious in other ways. From the time he came into the public eye, Said had presented himself as an "exile,"[15] having been born and raised in Jerusalem until forced from there at age twelve by the Jews. A sympathetic writer in *The Guardian* put it: "His evocation of his own experience of exile has led many of his readers in the west to see him as the embodiment of the Palestinian tragedy."[16] Indeed, he wrote and narrated a 1998 BBC documentary, *In Search of Palestine*, which presented his personal story as a microcosm of the ordeal of his people.

But in 1999, *Commentary* published an investigative article by Justus Reid Weiner presenting evidence that Said had largely falsified his background.[17] A welter of documents showed that, until he moved to the United States to attend prep school in 1951 and never left, Said had resided his entire life in Cairo, not Palestine. A few months after the article, Said published his autobiography which confirmed Weiner's findings, without acknowledging or making any attempt to explain the earlier contrary claims that he had put about widely and had asserted in print. (Said apparently got wind that Weiner was requesting interviews with his relatives and acquaintances over a three-year period, and Weiner speculates that Said may have decided to put a more truthful version on the record.)

In reaction to the exposé, Said and several of his supporters unleashed a ferocious assault on Weiner. Said sneered that "because he is relatively unknown, Weiner tries to make a name for himself by attacking a better known person's reputation."[18] And eleven ideological soul mates of Said's, styling themselves The Arab-Jewish Peace Group, cosigned a letter to the editor that likened Weiner's article to "deny[ing] the Holocaust."[19]

But Said's response only served to confirm that he was devoid of honesty. Apart from the personal invective, Said tried both to refute Weiner's proofs that he had not grown up in Palestine and also to insist that he, himself, had never overstated his Palestinian background. These two points were in tension with each other, but Said squared this circle by asserting that in his soon-to-be-published autobiography, he would "scrupulously record the facts of my early life spent between Jerusalem, Cairo and Dhour Al-Shweir (Lebanon)." However, his autobiography did not in fact describe a life divided among three locales. Rather, it revealed that until moving to the United States his home had always been in Cairo, with summers spent in Dhour Al-Shweir where his mother's family lived. His wealthy father liked to travel, and thus there were also sojourns to Alexandria, to various other sites in Lebanon, to the United States, and some to Jerusalem.

The autobiography mentions only three significant stays in Jerusalem while implying there were occasional other visits. The first, of course, was the time of his birth. The reason Said gives for this visit echoes with irony. He writes that his mother "had already given birth to a male child . . . in a Cairo hospital, where he developed an infection and died. . . . As a radical alternative to another hospital disaster, my parents traveled to Jerusalem [where] I was delivered at home by a Jewish midwife."[20] Zionists sometimes point out that the Arab population of Palestine increased as Jews immigrated and brought modernization. Edward's birth seems to exemplify this dynamic.

The next extended stay he mentions came six or seven years later: "During the first part of the war we spent more time than usual in Palestine. In 1942 we rented a summer house in Ramallah . . . and did not return to Cairo until November [after the Allies' October victory at el-Alamein]."[21] Said explains that during the months that the German forces were advancing, "as an American in Egypt, my father must have thought he was targeted for an unpleasant fate."[22] What the autobiography does not explain about that summer is why they rented and why in Ramallah.

Much of the debate between Weiner and Said revolved around the house in which Said was born and which viewers of his BBC documentary were given to understand was the home where he had grown up. Weiner showed from tax and land registry documents that the house never belonged to Said's father but rather to his aunt. In his rebuttal, Said had written: "the family house was indeed a family house in the Arab sense,"[23] meaning that in the eyes of the extended family it belonged to them all even if the official records showed it to be the property only of Edward's aunt and her offspring. No outsider, of course, can know what was in the minds of the Saids, but it is noteworthy that when they fled to the safety of Palestine to escape from Rommel's feared approach on Cairo, Edward's family did not take up residence in the beautiful house in Jerusalem they allegedly co-owned. (It is also hard to fathom why, if that house was really theirs, Edward's birth certificate, which gave the family's home address in Cairo, left blank the separate space for a local address.)

Then, according to the autobiography, five years after their Ramallah summer, Said and his family "spent most of 1947 in Palestine," the only visit of such length. While there, he writes, "I missed several months of CSAC [Cairo School for American Children] and was enrolled at Saint George's School in Jerusalem,"[24] an episode that in addition to the issue of the ownership of the house had been central to Weiner's expose and Said's retort.

Until he published the autobiography and was forced to do some damage control, Said, in cultivating the image that he had grown up in Palestine, had given the impression that he had received his pre-secondary education at Saint George's. *Current Biography Yearbook*, in an entry that he, himself, had approved, said: "Edward Said attended St. George's, an Anglican preparatory school, where his extracurricular activities included riding, boxing, gymnastics, and playing the piano." And his own BBC documentary included substantial footage of the place, with Said as narrator wandering its halls and reminiscing, then thumbing through an old registry book, pausing over one student's photo and saying softly, "I remember him very clearly from my time." Neither viewers of Said's BBC film nor readers of *Current Biography* could have gathered that his "time" at Saint George's was brief and temporary and that he in fact resided in Cairo where he had gotten all but a few months of his schooling.

In his exposé, Weiner reported discovering that there was no record of Said in Saint George's registry books and that the one boy whose photo Said picked out on camera denied, for his part, having any recollection of Said. In response, Said stormed: "[Weiner] says that I didn't attend St. George's School. This is an outright lie." But this in itself was an outright lie, and Said's display of indignation was a diversionary tactic. Weiner in fact had been careful to allow that his discoveries did not "gainsay the possibility of the young Said's having been now and then a temporary student at St. George's while on visits to his Jerusalem cousins." This turned out to have hit the nail on the head, as Said acknowledged in his autobiography. The issue was not whether Said had ever attended Saint George's but whether his days there constituted the whole of his boyhood, as he had made people believe.

Thus, the entry for him in *Current Biography Yearbook*, which by its rules had to have been approved by him, said: "In December 1947, the Said family left Jerusalem and settled in Cairo, Egypt." And Janny Scott, the experienced *New York Times* reporter who profiled him for the paper's Sunday magazine section, wrote after interviewing him: "Mr. Said was born in Jerusalem and spent the first twelve years of his life there" until he and his family "fled" in 1947.

Said's cynical *modus operandi* was to stop short, where possible, of telling an outright lie while deliberately leaving a false impression. Even so, he did not always avoid crossing the line or dancing so close to it that whether his words should be labeled a lie or merely a deception amounted to a difference without a distinction. "I have never claimed to have been made a refugee, but rather that my extended family . . . in fact was," he wrote in response to Weiner. But what was a reader supposed to have inferred from his book, *The Pen and the Sword*, where he had spoken of his "recollections of . . . the first twelve or thirteen years of my life before I left Palestine"?[25] Or from the article in the *London Review of Books*, where he had written: "I was born in Jerusalem and spent most of my formative years there and, after 1948, when my entire family became refugees, in Egypt"?[26] Would one in a thousand have guessed that his parents had made their home in Cairo since years before Edward was born?

It may be that Said, as he claimed, "scrupulously" recounted his life in his autobiography where at last the true facts of his education and residence emerge, causing a friendly reviewer in *The Independent* to record his surprise: "The impression gained by most readers of Said's earlier autobiographical writings is that Jerusalem was his home until the age of twelve, when the family was forced to leave. Certainly this has been my perception—and I have read almost everything that Said has ever published."[27] But does finally telling his story truthfully wipe away twenty years of lying about it? In the end, Said downplayed the matter. In a late interview with *The New York Times* he said: "I don't think it's that important, in any case. . . . I never have represented my case as the issue to be treated. I've represented the case of my people."[28]

But how can the truthfulness or mendacity of a scholar and public intellectual not be important? This was not a matter of something unrelated to his work like, say, misstating his golf handicap or concealing an infidelity. He was the one who had chosen to concoct a false biography precisely in order to represent the case of his people. More importantly, the same disingenuous and misleading methods that he employed in presenting his life story also form the backbone of all his work, beginning with the most influential, *Orientalism*.

The central idea of this book is that Western imperial conquest of Asia and North Africa was inextricably entwined with Western study and depiction of the native societies, which universally misrepresented and denigrated them. This served not only to justify but also to facilitate their subjugation. Said explained: "Knowledge of subject races or Orientals is what makes their management easy and profitable; knowledge gives power, more power requires more knowledge, and so on in an increasingly profitable dialectic of information and control."[29]

The archetype of those who provided this knowledge was the "Orientalist," a formal designation for scholars, most of them Europeans, whose specialties were the languages, culture, history, and sociology of societies of the Middle East and the Indian subcontinent. However, Said defined the term far more inclusively to include "anyone who teaches, writes about, or researches the Orient."[30] He explained further that he used the term "Orientalism" even more broadly to mean any of three things. First it meant any Orientalist in his expansive definition, that is, any Westerner who said (or otherwise expressed) anything about the Orient. Second, it connoted "a style of thought based upon a . . . distinction made between 'the Orient' and 'the Occident.'"[31] And, third, it was "the corporate institution for dealing with the Orient . . . by making statements about it, authorizing views of it, describing it, by teaching it, settling it, ruling over it."[32] In sum, he said, Orientalism is a "Western style for dominating, restructuring, and having authority over the Orient."[33]

Orientalism, he said, embodied "dogmas" that "exist . . . in their purest form today in studies of the Arabs and Islam." He identified the four "principal" ones as these:

> [O]ne is the absolute and systematic difference between the West, which is rational, developed, humane, superior, and the Orient, which is aberrant, undeveloped, inferior. Another dogma is that abstractions about the Orient . . . are always preferable to direct evidence drawn from modern Oriental realities. A third dogma is that the Orient is eternal, uniform, and incapable of defining itself. . . . A fourth dogma is that the Orient is at bottom something either to be feared . . . or to be controlled.[34]

Initial reviews of the book, often by specialists, were mixed, but it took on a power all its own in the "postmodern" university, eventually being translated into more than three dozen languages and becoming one of the most influential and widely assigned texts of the latter part of the twentieth century.

Critics pointed out a variety of errors in *Orientalism*, starting with bloopers that suggested Said's grasp of Middle Eastern history was shaky. Said had written that "Britain and France dominated the

Eastern Mediterranean from about the end of the seventeenth century on," whereas for another two hundred years it was the Ottomans who ruled that area. He had written that the Muslim conquest
of Turkey preceded that of North Africa but in reality it followed by
about four hundred years.* And he had referred to British "colonial
administrators" of Pakistan, whereas Pakistan was formed in the
wake of decolonization.

More serious still was his lack of scruple in the use of sources.
Anthropologist Daniel Martin Varisco observes that "one of Said's
rhetorical means for a polemical end is to partially . . . quote a phrase
while judiciously neglecting words that would qualify and at times
refute what the phrase alone might imply."[35] For example, Said
quotes Bernard Lewis saying: "The Western doctrine of the right
to resist bad government is alien to Islamic thought." Said is trying
to portray Lewis, the consummate Orientalist, as contemptuous of
Islam. But Varisco points out that Lewis's next sentence, omitted
by Said, is this: "Instead there is an Islamic doctrine of the duty to
resist impious government, which in early times was of crucial historical significance." Taken together, the two sentences seem to be
saying that the Islamic view is different from the Western, but ultimately analogous. This is the opposite of the spin Said put on it. To

---

* These two errors were first pointed out by Bernard Lewis, evoking an astonishing response from Said. Most scholars caught in Said's embarrassing
position would respond, "I regret my mistake, but it does not invalidate my
larger point," or words to that effect. Said, however, acknowledged no error
and instead tore into Lewis: "Far from dating the rise of Orientalism from
the late eighteenth century [as Lewis said Said had done], I specifically date
it from 1312 (pp.49–50)." Said went on contemptuously: "Having mistaken
the fourteenth century for the eighteenth, Lewis is scarcely in a position
to fault my sense of history." But Lewis's error in misreading Said's book is
not comparable Said's error in inverting well-known events; and the one
would not cancel out the other. In fact, however, Lewis had *not* misread Said;
rather, Said was simply lying about his own book. On pages 49 and 50, Said
writes, "Orientalism is considered to have commenced its formal existence
with the decision of the Church Council of Vienna in 1312 to establish a
series of chairs." Far from accepting this dating, Said goes to explain its
dubiousness. Meanwhile on page 3 of *Orientalism*, in the course of setting
out his own definition of the term, Said explains that he "tak[es] the late
eighteenth century as a very rough starting point" for Orientalism. Here,
as throughout the book, Said's meaning is less than crystalline, but Lewis's
presentation of what it says about the dating of Orientalism was much truer
to the text than was Said's.

make this worse, Said followed his misleadingly abridged quote with the assertion that Lewis saw this doctrinal difference as leading to "defeatism" and "quietism" in Islam. But Varisco notes that these two words, each isolated in quote marks by Said, were torn from other parts of Lewis's essay where he was summarizing the thought of two ancient Islamic thinkers, and in context they conveyed nothing of what Said led his readers to believe.

Lewis was Said's favorite target for reasons that, as we shall see, had entirely to do with contemporary politics, not scholarship. But Varisco's intervention on this point can scarcely be born of political motivation for he makes clear that, on ideological matters, his own views fall closer to Said's than Lewis's. Even so, he is offended by Said's duplicitous method. Likewise, Varisco shares Said's low esteem for the writings of Sania Hamady, an Arab-American who wrote critically of Arabs, but again Varisco objects to Said's method. Said offers two quotes from Hamady that put her in a bad light, but both times, says Varisco, the quotes are taken from passages where Hamady is merely summarizing someone else's view, not giving her own.[36] In the same vein, John Rodenbeck, the professor of comparative literature at the American University of Cairo, in assessing Said's treatment of the nineteenth century Orientalist Edward Lane, finds that "persistent misconstruction and misquotation of Lane's words are so clearly willful that they suggest . . . bad faith."[37]

Said's misleading use of quotes shows the problem with his work in microcosm: it fundamentally misrepresents his subject. Varisco challenges Said's first alleged "dogma" of Orientalism that ascribes all virtue to the West and its opposite to the Orient. He says that Said is describing "a stereotype that at the time of his writing would have been similarly rejected by the vast majority of those [Said] lumps together as Orientalists."[38] And the British writer, Robert Irwin, whose book, *Dangerous Knowledge*, offers a thorough history of Orientalism and also a rebuttal of Said, notes that historically "there has been a marked tendency for Orientalists to be anti-imperialists, as their enthusiasm for Arab or Persian or Turkish culture often went hand in hand with a dislike of seeing those people defeated and dominated by the Italians, Russians, British or French."[39] (Like Varisco, Irwin makes clear that he is no opponent of Said's political position, but is offended by his travesty of scholarship.)

These points are intuitively obvious to anyone familiar with academicians: they usually develop affinity with their subjects.

Moreover, Said's sallies to the contrary are spurious. "None of the Orientalists I write about seems ever to have intended an Oriental as a reader," he declaims. But Irwin retorts: "So why on earth did Hamilton Gibb [a prominent Orientalist harshly criticized by Said] write articles in Arabic? [And w]hat about "all the Western contributors to *Muslim World* and *Islamic Culture*, both periodicals with a largely Muslim Indian readership."[40]

This is but a small instance of a large methodological problem that invalidates Said's work entirely, namely, his selectivity with evidence. Said made clear that his indictment was aimed not at this or that individual but at "Orientalists," per se, which, as we have seen, was a category in which he included all Westerners who said anything about the Orient. Thus, he wrote "all academic knowledge about India and Egypt is somehow tinged and impressed with, violated by, the gross political fact of empire."[41] And: "Even the most imaginative writers . . . were constrained in what they could either experience of or say about the Orient."[42] And: "No one writing, thinking, or acting on the Orient could do so without taking account of the limitations on thought and action imposed by Orientalism."[43]

One might hazard a guess at why Said chose to paint with such a broad brush. Had he asserted merely that *some* Westerners wrote pejoratively or condescendingly or misleadingly about the East while others did not, his argument would have lost much of its punch and excitement. It would have demanded clarification about the relative numbers or weight of the two groups, about variations within the groups, about reciprocal attitudes among Easterners toward the West. Above all, it would have begged the question: so what? Was it news that some individuals favored their own societies over others? (Surely not to Said, who reports in his autobiography that his mother's family harbored "an embattled, even belligerent, sense of what it meant to be Christian in a Muslim part of the world . . . [a] hostility toward Islam."[44])

But the only way Said could make his generalized indictment seem plausible was to select whatever examples fit it and leave out the rest. When challenged on his omissions, Said replied that he was under no obligation to include "every Orientalist who ever lived."[45] But this was a dodge. It was his choice to condemn Orientalists as such, not merely this one or that one. Even so, the critics never chastised him for failing to be exhaustive, but rather for dealing at length with insignificant figures who expressed the ideas that he wanted to pillory and omitting others of higher standing whose writings contradicted his analysis.

Thus Said referred repeatedly to the unabashed nineteenth century racial theorist, the Comte de Gobineau, the object of much criticism by writers before Said. Irwin says about him:

> Gobineau's work in the field of ancient languages had the sort of importance for Oriental studies that attempts to patent perpetual motion machines have had for the history of science. Far from being part of an Orientalist genealogy he was both the first and the last to pursue this peculiar line of inquiry.[46]

The two Orientalist figures in addition to Gobineau given greatest space by Said are the Briton, Edward Lane, whom Rodenbeck accuses Said of distorting and misquoting, and the Frenchman, Ernest Renan, of whom Varisco says:

> The focus on Renan as an archetypical Orientalist is telling in large part because it is very much Said's unique choice. In an endnote Said acknowledges that Renan is mentioned only in passing by Schwab, one of his most important sources on French Orientalism. Renan is rarely cited by Orientalist scholars; when this happens, the French author is usually disparaged.[47]

On the other hand, Said ignores almost entirely Ignaz Goldziher who was arguably the most important Orientalist of them all. Ibn Warraq writes that "as early as 1889, [Goldziher] was recognized as the founder of a new field of scholarship—Arabic and Islamic studies."[48] The twentieth century Dutch scholar, Jacques Waardenburg, whose 1963 book about Orientalism Said, himself, praises as "a very valuable and intelligent study,"[49] wrote: "It is no exaggeration to say that Goldziher had created Islamology in the full sense of the term."[50] To top it off Goldziher had penned a "searching critique" of Renan, anticipating Said by a century. (This was only one of countless cases in which one Orientalist challenged the work of another, all of them omitted by Said because they would undercut his depiction of a "guild" with a uniform "discourse.")

In *Orientalism*, Said's only substantive reference to Goldziher comes in a paragraph treating an anthology to which Golziher had contributed, about which Said concludes: "their Orientalist consensus on Islam: latent inferiority."[51] In rendering this generalization, Said does not quote Goldziher, whose attitude was in fact the diametric opposite. During his time in Arab countries, Goldziher, despite being an identifying Jew, wrote in his diary:

> I truly entered into the spirit of Islam to such an extent that ultimately I became inwardly convinced that I myself was a Muslim, and judiciously discovered that this was the only religion which, even in its doctrinal and official formulation, can satisfy philosophic minds. My ideal was to elevate Judaism to a similar rational level.[52]

Toward the beginning of *Orientalism*, Said concedes he has omitted German Orientalists from his study, and includes Goldziher's name on a list of examples (although Goldziher was Hungarian). Said says that he "reproach[es]" himself for the omissions but explains them on the grounds that "no close partnership developed between Orientalists and a protracted, sustained *national* interest in the Orient,"[53] meaning that Germany practiced little imperialism in the Middle East and South Asia. This in itself cuts a gaping hole in Said's thesis, namely his claim, to quote it again, that "all academic knowledge about India and Egypt is somehow tinged and impressed with, violated by, the gross political fact of Empire." Germany, as he says, had no such empire, and nonetheless the writings of the German Orientalists were not different, as a group, than those of the French or British. Nor does Said claim they were. He merely sweeps them under the rug.

This is not all. The most fundamental point of Orientalism is, to repeat, that "every European, in what he could say about the Orient, was . . . a racist, an imperialist, and almost totally ethnocentric." Even to allow Said some wiggle room that he does not request, namely to discount the word "every" as a deliberate exaggeration, his point is that the prevailing slant of the Orientalists toward their subject was pejorative. How would a conscientious scholar test or prove such a proposition?

The answer in broad terms would be to select either a representative sample of Orientalists or the most influential ones and then to attempt some assessment of all of their works or, more manageably, their most important ones. Yet, at the outset, Said makes clear he intends no such exercise. "My argument . . . depends," he says, "neither upon an exhaustive catalogue of texts dealing with the Orient nor upon a clearly delimited set of texts, authors, and ideas." On what, then? "I have depended instead upon a different methodological alternative—whose backbone in a sense is the set of historical generalizations I have so far been making."[54]

These "historical generalizations" are the central assertions of his book. In other words, his "methodological alternative" is simply to search for examples that fit his hypothesis. Thus does he brazenly announce, albeit with a voice muffled by jargon, his intent to omit Orientalists, however important, such as Goldziher, whose work contradicts his thesis and to include others, however unimportant, such as Gobineau, who confirm it. Moreover, even with some of the serious figures he treats, experts point out various cases in which he finds a handy quote from some minor piece of writing while ignoring their more influential books. For example, Irwin notes that "[Bernard] Lewis was one of the main targets of *Orientalism* and later publications by Said, though Said tended to concentrate on Lewis's later essays of popularization and failed to engage with the early major works."[55]

To top it off, as we have seen, Said expands the definition of "Orientalist" to include every Westerner who ever uttered a word (or drew an image) about the East. This would make the challenge of submitting his theses to rigorous examination virtually impossible since it makes the universe to be tested almost infinite. But this methodological fillip gives him a license to drag in a quote from Flaubert or Dante or Macauley when it suits his purposes.

Said may have had little choice other than to rig his methodology, especially because he was eager to show that the imperialist/racist attitudes he was flaying were still dominant. They "persist without significant challenge in the academic and governmental study of the modern Near Orient," he said.[56] However, three years before the publication of *Orientalism*, the British specialist Charles F. Beckingham published an essay titled "Misconceptions of Islam: Medieval and Modern." In it, says Varisco, "Beckingham recounts a number of the same overt errors of Christian polemicists that infuriated Said. . . . But, as Orientalist Beckingham observes and critic Said ignores, such gross opinions are 'explicitly held by hardly anyone today and certainly not by any reputable scholar.'"[57]

The illegitimate methods Said employed—selecting (and sometimes distorting) evidence that fit his argument and willfully omitting that which contradicted it—were themselves sufficient to invalidate his work. But, in addition, *Orientalism* was riddled with profound errors of logic.

Regarding Said's central postulate about the critical relationship between scholarship and imperialism ("knowledge of subject races . . . is what makes their management easy and profitable"), we have already seen that Said left German Orientalists out of his study. A reader new to this esoteric subject has no way to gauge the importance of this omission, but it is widely agreed that for at least a large portion of the era that is the focus of Said's attention the importance of German contributions to the field of Oriental studies was second to none.

If there are, thus, strong examples of scholarship without imperialism, there are even more of imperialism without scholarship. The Europeans who conquered North and South America dallied little with studying the "Indians" whom they found there. Russia built itself as a country and then an empire by conquering neighbors in all directions, but there is no great tradition of Russian study of Baltic, Caucasian, Central Asian, or Eastern European cultures. In the nineteenth century when the Germans led Oriental studies they possessed no relevant colonies; but in the twentieth when Germany launched two world wars, it exhibited no special exertions of academic learning about Poles, Russians, Jews, or others.

Then there is the Orient, itself. As Irwin notes wryly, "If the Persians needed to make play with the notion of an 'other' or to construct an archive of racial stereotypes . . . those activities have gone unrecorded. They just seem to have set about trying to conquer their neighbors."[58] Even more apropos is the history of Muslim conquest. Western rule in the Muslim world, enduring in most places only a few decades, was short-lived compared to Muslim rule in Spain, Greece, and various Slavic lands where it lasted for centuries. Yet, none of this was facilitated or accompanied by any notable efforts by the conquerors to study the native cultures.

Writing about the period of Western supremacy, Said notes: "It has been estimated that around 60,000 books dealing with the Near Orient were written between 1800 and 1950; there is no remotely comparable figure for Oriental books about the West."[59] His comment on the disparity reprises his mantra about the link between power and knowledge: "Orientalism is all aggression, activity, judgment, will-to-truth, and knowledge." But the number of Arab/Muslim books about Western culture was minuscule not only in the

era of Western conquest; this was also so in the era of Muslim conquest when the power relations were reversed. In that period, the
Islamic approach to the Occident could be characterized by the first
half of Said's litany, namely "aggression, activity, judgment," but not
the second half: "will-to-truth and knowledge."

Much more could be said about Islamic imperialism, for example
Ibn Warraq's observation that India, the part of the Orient ruled
longest by the West, was ruled even longer by Islam with far greater
cruelty and fewer benefits.[60] But the key point here is that Said's
thesis about the nexus of imperialism and Orientalism cannot withstand scrutiny. There has been much imperialism, including by the
West, without concomitant study of "the other," and much such
study without imperialism.

A central theme of Said's is that Orientalism produced a false or
distorted image of the Orient tailored to suit Western appetites and
prejudices. "The Orient was almost a Western invention," he says.
"European culture . . . produce[d] . . . the Orient."[61] He hastens to add
the clarification that "there were—and are—cultures and nations
whose location is in the East, and their lives, histories, and cus-
toms have a brute reality."[62] Nonetheless "Orientalism is more . . . a
sign of European-Atlantic power over the Orient than . . . a veridic*
discourse about the Orient."[63] In sum, he says, the Orientalist approaches his subject with an "absence of sympathy" and "weighted
heavily with all the orthodox attitudes, perspectives, and moods of
Orientalism. His Orient is not the Orient as it is, but the Orient as it
has been Orientalized."[64]

This provokes Warraq to ask impudently about the relationship between the distorted image of their subject produced by the
Orientalists and the contribution he says they made to Western
ascendancy:

> If Orientalists have produced a false picture of the Orient . . .
> then how could this false or pseudoknowledge have helped
> European imperialists to dominate [the region]? "Information

---

* One part of Said's rhetorical strategy of creating a miasma of prose, in
which precise meanings are difficult to pin down, is the use of uncommon
words. Veridical means truthful, and "truthful" would have made the sentence clearer to many readers. Said's choice—"veridic"—is found in neither
the unabridged *Webster's* nor the full *Oxford English Dictionary*.

and control," wrote Said, but what of "false information and control"? [65]

Thus Irwin was exactly on target when he rendered what he ac-knowledged was an extreme judgment, namely, that *Orientalism* was at bottom "a work of malignant charlatanry." [66] His autobiography shows that Said was quite capable of writing lucid prose. But *Orientalism* was intentionally dense. In addition to the uncommon (even nonexistent) words and endless sentences, subjects, predicates, and modifiers are compounded throughout (and not merely to the ex-tent of two at a time, but often three, four, or five), so it is hard to make out exactly who did what how, leaving the precise meaning of any assertion elusive and therefore not susceptible to proof or disproof.

Through this haze, what made the book electrifying was that Said had found a new way to condemn the West for its most grievous sins: racism and the subjugation of others. With great originality, Said even extended the indictment through the millennia, a depic-tion that drew a protest from Sadiq al-Azm, a Syrian philosopher of Marxist bent (and one of that country's most admired dissidents). Wrote al-Azm:

> Said . . . trac[es] the origins of Orientalism all the way back
> to Homer, Aeschylus, Euripides, and Dante. In other words,
> Orientalism is not really a thoroughly modern phenomenon,
> but is the natural product of an ancient and almost irresist-
> ible European bent of mind to misrepresent other . . . cultures
> . . . in favor of Occidental self-affirmation, domination, and
> ascendency. [67]

Al-Azm may have thought this wrong, but it was heady stuff. If we are talking about a mentality that is continuous before and af-ter Christ then we are talking less about European culture, which is in large measure defined by Christianity, than about the Euro-pean race. Thus did *Orientalism* fit the temper of a time when it was widely asserted that all white people were inherently bigoted, and encounter groups met at campuses and workplaces so that whites could discover and confront their inner racist. The white race stood condemned of . . . racism. And nowhere was the evidence laid out in greater depth and seeming sophistication than in Said's pages.

In this atmosphere, wrote *The New York Times*, "*Orientalism* established Dr. Said as a figure of enormous influence in American and European universities, a hero to many, especially younger faculty and graduate students on the left for whom that book became an intellectual credo and the founding document of what came to be called postcolonial studies."[68]

It was not only American Leftists who seized on the book. *The Guardian* observed that:

> Orientalism appeared at an opportune time, enabling upwardly mobile academics from non-western countries (many of whom came from families who had benefited from colonialism) to take advantage of the mood of political correctness it helped to engender by associating themselves with "narratives of oppression," creating successful careers out of transmitting, interpreting and debating representations of the non-western "other."[69]

Orientalism, added *The Guardian*, "is credited with helping to change the direction of several disciplines," a thought echoed by supporters and detractors alike. Stuart Schaar, a professor emeritus of Middle East history at Brooklyn College, wrote admiringly that "the academic community has been transformed and the field of literary criticism has been revolutionized as a result of [Said's] legacy."[70] Less admiringly, Varisco wrote: "Literary and postcolonial studies focused on Orientalism as a kind of touchstone, at times, a launch pad for legitimizing their own posturing. . . . Citing Said almost became a kind of initiatory *bismillah* in literary texts about colonial discourse."[71] And Irwin lamented that "the malign influence of Said's *Orientalism* . . . has been surprisingly effective in discrediting and demoralizing an entire tradition of scholarship,"[72] that tradition, of course, being Orientalism.

Without ever relinquishing his claim to personify a "glamour-garlanded ideal of 'outsiderdom,'" as one disillusioned reviewer of a series of lectures Said delivered in London put it,[73] Said and his disciples became regnant in academia, as reflected in the astonishing number of courses that assigned his books and the frequency with which they were cited. Varisco observed that "a generation of students across disciplines has grown up with limited challenges to the polemical charge by Said that scholars who study the Middle East and Islam still do so institutionally through an interpretive sieve that divides a superior West from an inferior East."[74] The new Saidian orthodoxy became so utterly dominant in the Middle East Studies Association, and so unfriendly to dissenting voices, that in 2007 Bernard Lewis and Fouad Ajami took the lead in forming an alternative professional organization, the Association for the Study of the Middle East and Africa.

Said was fond of congratulating himself for "speaking truth to power." This was an easy boast for someone who opted to live in America and made a career of denouncing the West and Israel. Had Said chosen to live out his life in his native region and to speak out to its powers, his calling would have cost more. Habib Malik, a historian at the Lebanese American University and a cousin of Said's, recalls hearing him deliver a talk at the American University of Beirut: "On one occasion he blasted Saddam Hussein and a number of other Arab dictators but stopped short of mentioning Hafez Assad for obvious reasons: the Syrian *mukhabarat* in Beirut would have picked him up right after the lecture!"[75] Said's courage, it seems, consisted in speaking truth to tolerant powers or safely distant ones.

The impact of all this on Israel lay in Said's success at redefining Arabs and Muslims as the moral equivalent of blacks. Four years after the UN General Assembly had declared Zionism to be a form of racism, Said gave this same idea a high-brow reiteration. Israel did not give Arabs the same right of immigration as Jews, he said mockingly, because they are "less developed."[76] Mary-Kay Wilmers, the Jewish editor and financier, who turned the *London Review of Books* into Britain's leading anti-Israel periodical, explained her stance by saying, "Edward Said converted me."[77] And Jacqueline Rose, who called Zionism "collective insanity," dedicated her book to Said. Its title, *The Question of Zion*, was a deliberate echo of his *The Question of Palestine*, and the parallelism continued but with a twist: Said's book was a fervent statement of the Palestinian case while Rose's was an equally fervent statement *against* the Zionist case. In other words, both books basically said the same thing. It was an unintentional reprise of the clever toastmaster's quip, "Everything that needs to be said has been said, but not everyone has yet said it."

Decades after *Orientalism* was published, Said confessed that Israel had been its covert target all along:

I don't think I would have written that book had I not been politically associated with a struggle. The struggle of Arab and

Palestinian nationalism is very important to that book. *Orientalism* is not meant to be an abstract account of some historical formation but rather a part of the liberation from such stereotypes and such domination of my own people, whether they are Arabs, Muslims or Palestinians.[78]

Said had not acknowledged this agenda within the pages of *Orientalism* or at the time of its publication, although its ideological subtext could be discerned in his ferocity toward Bernard Lewis who, observed Irwin, "was not really attacked by Said for being a bad scholar (which he is not), but for being a supporter of Zionism (which he is)."[79] It was also implicit in the identity of those Said exempted from his generalization about Westerners. In the concluding pages of *Orientalism*, he allowed that a very few "decolonializing" voices could be heard in the West, and in a footnote he offered just two American examples, Noam Chomsky and MERIP, the Middle East Research and Information Project. Chomsky of course is not a Middle East expert or someone who writes often on the Middle East, but had already carved out a place for himself as the leading Jewish voice of vituperation against Israel. MERIP was a New Left group formed to cheer Palestinian guerrillas and other Arab revolutionaries. It was so single-minded in its devotion that it found words of praise for the massacre of Israeli athletes at the 1972 Olympics.[80]

Although (or perhaps because) Said's assault on the Jewish state was thus initially camouflaged, it was devastatingly effective, as his approach came to dominate Middle East studies and with it, his stance on Arab/Israel questions. UCLA historian of the Middle East, Nikki Keddie, whose sympathetic work on revolutionary Iran had won Said's praise in his book, *Covering Islam*,[81] commented:

There has been a tendency in the Middle East field to adopt the word "Orientalism" as a generalized swear-word essentially referring to people who take the "wrong" position on the Arab-Israeli dispute or to people who are judged too "conservative." It has nothing to do with whether they are good or not good in their disciplines.[82]

His reputation made by the success of *Orientalism*, Said devoted much of the rest of his career to more direct advocacy of the Arab/Muslim/Palestinian cause, starting with the publication of *The Ques-*

tion of Palestine in 1979, by which time he was already a member of the PLO's top official body, the Palestinian National Council. The book was a full-throated polemic. The Jews were the aggressors; and the Palestinians their victims—on all counts and with little nuance. Even on the matter of terrorism, Said waxed self-righteous. "There is nothing in Palestinian history, absolutely nothing at all to rival the record of Zionist terror," he asserted.[83]

And yet, he also made a touching appeal for peace, invoking the common humanity of the two sides, that was soothing to Western ears although jarring against the rest of his text:

> Peace between neighbor states will mean common borders, regular exchange, mutual understanding. In time, who cannot suppose that the borders themselves will mean far less than the human contact taking place between people for whom differences animate more exchange rather than more hostility.[84]

He conveyed his own humanistic sensitivities without giving an inch to the other side. Said proclaimed himself "horrified" by the terrorist acts that "Palestinian men and women . . . were driven to do."[85] The passive verb is a tip-off. All blame ultimately rested with Israel, which had "literally produced, manufactured . . . the 'terrorist.'"[86]

Further, he insisted his own benign attitudes reflected the stand of the PLO. Thus, he wrote with what a *New York Times* reviewer called "stunning disingenuousness"[87] that "at least since the early seventies, the PLO had avoided and condemned terror."[88] Said published this just one year after the organization's bloodiest attack on Israeli civilians, the March 1978 "coastal road massacre" in which thirty-eight civilians, thirteen of them children, were randomly gunned down, with scores of others injured—and not by any "renegade" faction but by the PLO's mainstream group, Fatah. Said himself was already a member of the PLO's governing body when this "action" was carried out.

Said further claimed that: "On occasion after occasion the PLO stated its willingness to accept a Palestinian state in the West Bank and Gaza," citing resolutions of the Palestinian National Council in 1974 and 1977.[89] This was true, but no less disingenuous, for these resolutions did not convey, as Said went on to claim, "an implicit recognition of Israel." Rather, they envisioned a strategy in which Palestinians would form a government in the West Bank and Gaza, in the event that international diplomacy afforded them this opportunity, not as a step toward peace but with the declared intent of using this territory as a base to fight on to "liberate" the rest of Palestine— that is, Israel proper. As the PNC's 1974 resolution stated: "the PLO will struggle against any plan for the establishment of a Palestinian entity the price of which is recognition [of Israel], conciliation, secure borders and renunciation of the national rights of our people, its right to return and self-determination on its national soil."[90]

In 1988, a decade after Said's book appeared, the PLO did renounce terror and imply its willingness to acquiesce in Israel's existence, albeit equivocally. Then, in the 1993 Oslo Accords, it avowed these two pivotal concessions more clearly. When Arafat finally took this indispensable step toward peace, one might have expected Said to praise him; one might even have forgiven Said a claim of vindication, however belated, for having insisted during the PLO's episodes of greatest violence that it really wanted peace. But, on the contrary, Said now denounced Arafat, wailing that he had "sold his people into enslavement." Said branded the agreement—in which Israel and the PLO recognized each other and pledged to hammer out a two-state settlement—an "instrument of Palestinian surrender."[91] Back in Arafat's terrorist days, Said had seen him as "a man of genius . . . his people . . . loved him." Indeed, "Arafat and the Palestinian will . . . were in a sense interchangeable," he gushed.[92] But, by agreeing to the terms of Oslo, Arafat had become, in Said's eyes, "a strutting dictator."[93] Arafat and his circle were now a bunch of "losers and has-beens" who "should step aside."[94]

Said himself adopted a new position on the Israeli–Palestinian conflict. No longer did he envision a two-state solution, as he had professed to do back when the idea was safely academic, since the main Palestinian organization (on whose board he sat) was not prepared to suffer the existence of Israel in any shape or form. Now, however, he sought instead to devise a different means "where the two peoples can live together in one nation as equals."[95]

This was not a proposal to be taken seriously. Of course, Arabs and Jews do live together peacefully in the United States where both are very much minorities. But Said was talking about the Middle East where these two groups predominate. There, we have only the example of Israel, where large numbers of Arabs do live albeit not in complete equality, a fact over which Said often protested; and then there are the Arab states, where many Jews once lived but from which nearly all were expelled. In other words, Said's new position was nothing more than a precious way of opposing the only genuine possibility of peace: two states for two peoples.

This position—a prescription for endless bloodshed and a duel to the death—was phrased in terms chosen to sound idealistic. In that sense it was characteristic of Said's *oeuvre* and of the movement whose intellectual commitments he helped to define. Leftism is the stance of those who aspire to make the world a better place through political action. For roughly a century its modal idea was Marxism, which identified the proletariat as the engine of redemption, a choice that resonated with the age-old Christian belief that the meek shall inherit the earth. As the twentieth century wore on, however, Mahatma Gandhi, Martin Luther King, and Nelson Mandela displaced Joe Hill, Mother Bloor, and Walter Reuther as objects of veneration. People of color and strugglers against colonial oppression stirred the hearts of idealists more than leaders of strikes and fighters for a fair day's pay. Once, Zionism had tapped into that older Leftism, seeing itself as a workers' movement. But in the latter twentieth century—and in considerable part thanks to the impact of Edward Said—it became redefined against its will as a movement of white people competing for land with people of color. This transformation meant that from then on the Left would be aligned overwhelmingly and ardently against Israel.

eight

Israel Shows a Less Endearing Face

By 1977, the support and sympathy Israel had enjoyed in its moment of peril a decade earlier had been eroded by counter blows both physical and intellectual. Already the conflict had been redefined to pit Israel against the displaced Palestinians rather than the Arab world as a whole. Already the crude force of terrorism and oil embargoes had softened up Western resistance to the Arab/Palestinian version of the issue. Already the United Nations had become a theater featuring nonstop performances of a passion play scripted by the "non-aligned" with Israel cast as the villain. Already the moderate Left represented by the Socialist International had opened its arms to Arab radicalism, dropping its historic criterion of democratic bona fides. Already a New Left embodying the sensibilities of a rising generation had emerged in Europe and America, having been taught by thinkers like Edward Said to regard race as a more salient axis of oppression than class and to see the likes of the Palestinians as the new proletariat.

Against this background, Israelis went to the polls and elected a government from a slate they had never chosen before, one whose principles and attitudes played into the hands of the country's growing number of detractors. The winner was Likud, a coalition of right-of-center parties led by Menachem Begin who had commanded the *Etzel*, or *Irgun*, in its violent underground campaign to expel the British from Palestine and create a Jewish state. Ever since, he had led a minority party in the *Knesset*, Israel's parliament, carving out a role as the government's most articulate, unrelenting, and, to some, insufferable critic.

Suddenly at sixty-four, the gadfly of the past thirty years had to become a statesman. In many ways he made a surprisingly good job of it, but some of the positions on which he stood steadfast, some of his policy initiatives, and aspects of his underlying philosophy played into the hands of Israel's enemies.

Even more important in the long run than alienating various foreigners, Begin's actions also proved deeply divisive at home. Like a Newtonian law of motion, in politics, too, actions entail reactions, and Begin's harsh, hard-line policies fed the growth of an accommodationist movement in Israel that was to become a permanent source of grist for the busy mills of the country's critics and enemies.

The image of Israel presented by Begin was shorn of features that had made the country appealing to many outsiders. Since at least the 1930s, the Zionist movement had been dominated by Labor Zionism, a secular amalgam of Jewish nationalism and socialism. Around the world, socialism took many sometimes contradictory forms. But although it meant different things to different people, "socialism" was the most widely embraced political ideal in history. The Labor Zionists who led the struggle for Israel's creation and who then, in the form of the Mapai Party or Labor Alignment, governed for its first twenty-nine years, created what was arguably the world's most far-reaching and successful socialism.

Elsewhere, Communist parties had completely abolished private property in favor of state ownership but through methods of dictatorship that many saw as a betrayal of the idealistic spirit of socialism. Meanwhile, moderate social democratic parties had upheld democratic rights and procedures but had uniformly backed off from wholesale expropriations, making their peace with capitalist modes of production.

Israel, however, went further than any other democracy in establishing a system in which public or shared property predominated over private. Most land belonged to the state which made it available to individuals and groups not in title but through ninety-nine-year leases. The enormous labor union, Histadrut, became the country's largest employer, owning the leading transportation and construction companies as well as the prevailing health care system. Its leader, David Ben-Gurion, marshaled the country to independence and became its first prime minister. Agriculture was largely a function of *moshavim*, cooperative farms, and *kibbutzim*, the world's purest socialist collectives whose members practiced common ownership of all things (even clothing, in some) and raised their offspring collectively from the cradle, almost as in Plato's imagined Republic.

Fellow socialists near and far admired Israel's methods and accomplishments. Young people attracted by the socialist ideal often spent time as volunteers on *kibbutzim* to experience their dream in practice. Moreover, Labor Zionism, melding Jewish particularism with the universalistic credo of socialism, made the Jewish cause easier for others to support. Labor Zionists did not intend merely to create a home for the Jews; rather they aimed for a Jewish home that would also be a socialist model for mankind and a pillar in the worldwide movement for workers' emancipation and a new dawn.

Menachem Begin's Likud Party, however, descended from what was called General Zionism and its later offshoot, "Revisionism," formulated by Begin's mentor, Zeev Jabotinsky. Revisionist Zionism presented itself as the antithesis of Labor Zionism, not necessarily in preferring capitalism but in rejecting any addition to or dilution of Zionism. "We will never be able to come to terms with people who possess, in addition to Zionism, another ideal, namely Socialism," he said.[1] Jabotinsky called his stance "monism," declaring "we do not recognize the permissibility of any ideal whatsoever apart from the single ideal," namely, a Jewish state.[2]

As such, Revisionism had a narrower basis than Labor Zionism on which to appeal for the support or sympathy of non-Jews. Jabotinsky did nurture the idea that the Zionists could curry favor with the British on the grounds that Jews were more advanced than the Arabs, and thus would make sturdier allies. But London showed little inclination to buy this argument, which was no surprise to Jabotinsky's young disciple, Begin, who believed that the Jews could hope for nothing from the world except what they could wrest with their own hands.

The anarchy that seemed to prevail within and among nations beginning in 1914 confirmed the lesson he had learned in the microcosm of his Polish elementary school:

> I remember that red-bricked, big, terrible house where we
> learned the foreigner's language. . . . The children of the goyim
> in their hundreds, the Jewish children in their tens. We bought
> knowledge with a price, being beaten day after day, insulted,
> shoved, but through all this we learned to defend ourselves.[3]

This early conviction was burned into him indelibly by the Holocaust in which his father, mother, and older brother perished.

Begin harbored bitterness toward Britain over its adoption of the

1939 White Paper that contradicted the Balfour Declaration, choking off Jewish immigration into Palestine just as Hitler was launching his campaign of annihilation. Thus, under Begin's leadership
the *Irgun* launched a "revolt" against Britain that involved beating,
kidnapping, and killing British soldiers in retaliation for their like
actions against Jews. The *Irgun* (short for *Irgun Tzvai Leumi*, National Military Organization) was a 1931 split-off from the main
Jewish armed force in Palestine, *Haganah* (The Defense). Although
the split was not strictly on party lines, the *Irgun* was dominated
by the revisionist movement, and it pursued a more militant policy
than the *Haganah*, notably in retaliating against Arab civilians for
Arab attacks on Jewish civilians. The group's reputation for terrorism was indelibly reinforced by its 1946 bombing of the King David
Hotel, which housed British headquarters, but in which scores of
others died, as well, and by its responsibility for the massacre of
Arab civilians in the village of Deir Yassin during Israel's 1948 war
of independence.*

Perhaps even more problematic in terms of public relations was
the ideology of Begin's movement. It held that all of Palestine, as defined by the League of Nations, including that which lay east of the
Jordan River and was designated by the British as Transjordan and
later the Kingdom of Jordan, was rightly a part of the Jewish homeland. This larger ambition was no mere abstraction, but, in the early
days of Israeli statehood, a main plank in the platform of Begin's
Herut Party, the heir to Jabotinsky's revisionism and the predecessor to Likud.

Likud was formed through a merger of Herut with other parties
and factions, mostly more moderate, and it dropped the claim to
the east bank. But the reasoning behind it remained, resting less on
the League of Nations than on the Bible. Begin believed to his core
that "the Jewish people have an eternal historic right to the Land
of Israel," as the founding principles of his 1977 government put it.[4]
The obvious problem in this was that the Jewish bible offered a compelling basis for Israel's claims only to those who took this as Holy

---

* Deir Yassin, near Jerusalem, was a legitimate military target, but the
Irgun-led assault on the town included the killing of women and children.
The atrocity was exaggerated in some Arab propaganda, but was also
denounced by mainstream Zionists who sent a letter of apology to King
Abdullah of Jordan.

Scripture, and even among them, only to those who inferred it to be a basis for contemporary rights.

Many Israelis and other Jews found Begin's brand of nationalism repugnant, and some went beyond all bounds in expressing their distaste. David Ben Gurion, setting a lamentable precedent for Israel's latter-day enemies, likened Begin to Hitler and called his followers "Nazi-Jews." In contrast, Begin found a natural constituency among Israelis who had come from the Arab countries and their progeny. These *Sephardi* or *Mizrachi* Jews* often felt ignored or looked down upon by the country's inbred *Ashkenazi* establishment (*Ashkenazis* being Jews of Germany, Poland, Russia, and nearby lands). In addition, Begin's ideology made sense to them. As political scientist and Middle East expert Mark Tessler put it:

> Compared to other Israelis, those whose families once lived in Muslim and especially Arab countries were disproportionately likely to regard Arabs as untrustworthy, to think peace with the Arab world is impossible, and to favor retaining most or all of the territory captured in 1967.[5]

For the same reasons, Begin's assumption of the office of prime minister in 1977 was greeted with dismay in many quarters. In the United States, reported the *Los Angeles Times*, "White House and State Department officials took a publicly noncommittal stance . . . on the triumph of the right-wing Likud Party . . . but the predominant private view in the capital was that prospects for peace in the Middle East had suffered a setback."[6] Yehuda Avner, an aide who accompanied Begin on his first post-election visit to Washington, recalls being pulled aside by Arthur Goldberg, the former Supreme Court justice and US representative to the United Nations, and dressed down in these words:

> To most Americans, Begin's ideology is an enigma. To the president, the "not an inch" posture on the Land of Israel is baffling. It is equally puzzling to most American Jews. Sure, American Jews will support the prime minister in public. It's the right

* The term *Sephardi* refers to Jews who migrated to the Middle East from Iberia following their expulsion in the fifteenth century. *Mizrachi* refers to those who came to the region even earlier, perhaps as far back as the Roman era. In contemporary Israel, where these groups are hard to distinguish, the terms are often used interchangeably.

thing to do. Begin, after all, is the head of a freely elected democratic government. But in private, many Jews are troubled and
confused, myself included.[7]

If Begin's persona made some friends of Israel uneasy it also em-
boldened some long-time nonfriends. *TIME* magazine, which had
for years distinguished itself among major US news outlets by its
critical tone toward Israel, greeted Begin's arrival with the information that the man's name "rhymes with Fagin," the fictional symbol
of Jewish avarice.[8] Whether the critics were well-intentioned, like
Goldberg, or otherwise, like *TIME*, Begin took few pains to assuage
anyone's unease. As *The New York Times* reported: "Each time ques-
tioners on ABC-TV's 'Issues and Answers' program asked about the
countries occupied by Israel, Mr. Begin would interrupt to change
the word to 'liberated.'"[9] And when asked during his visit whether
his government planned to annex some of those territories, his reply did not placate: "We don't use the word 'annexation.' . . . You
don't annex your own country."[10]

Begin's combative posture drew a sharp warning from pro-Israel
columnist George Will:

> The world's sense of Israel's legitimacy rests on a particular un-
> derstanding of Zionism, an understanding that Mr. Begin can
> jeopardize with reckless talk. Zionism began as a movement of
> salvation to enable a people to save itself by becoming a na-
> tion, concentrated and sovereign. . . .
>
> Israel's existence depends on its tenuous hold on the imagi-
> nation of the West, and especially of the American people. That
> hold depends on Israel appearing familiar – part of the Western
> family. So Israel must not begin to appear bizarre.
>
> Israel cannot seem to be hearing mysterious voices and obey-
> ing strange impulses. It must express its claims to legitimacy in
> the west's shared vocabulary of liberal democratic politics. Its
> aspirations must be intelligible to the secular people who could
> not care less what God promised Abraham.
>
> Israel's right to exist securely rests, insecurely, on the fact
> that Israel is right: right as a response to centuries of injustices
> against Jews, right as an embattled enclave of worthy values in
> an inhospitable region. Thus Israel has a claim upon the con-
> science, not the calculations, of other peoples. Mr. Begin must
> walk, and talk, softly because merely being right is a weak reed
> on which to rest a nation.[11]

The sorest point between Begin and his detractors as well as Israel's worried friends like Will was Begin's opposition to relinquishing any part of the West Bank or Gaza, now being seen as the patrimony of the Palestinians. Security Council Resolution 242, the basis of all peace proposals, called for Israel to withdraw from occupied territories but implicitly not *all* occupied territory. In the view of many, including the US government, this implied a substantial Israeli withdrawal on all fronts.* But Begin held that withdrawal on *any* front would suffice to fulfill Israel's obligations. The Labor governments that had preceded his had taken no precise stance on territorial issues, but they clearly stood closer to the US position than he did.

In a pre-election newspaper column Begin had pledged to give top priority to establishing large Jewish settlements throughout the occupied lands, a sharp break with the policies of the incumbent Labor government.[12] After the 1967 war, Jewish Israelis had been all but unanimous in favoring *some* changes in the boundary lines that had made Israel feel so vulnerable that its dovish UN ambassador, Abba Eban, had labeled them, "Auschwitz borders." There were, however, many different ideas about what Israel needed to hang onto to be more secure. Plus, there were some powerful emotional attachments. Almost all Israelis wanted to keep possession of the Old City of Jerusalem, the historic and spiritual center of Judaism. Some also coveted other venues that evoked emotional attachments, such as Hebron, burial site of the biblical patriarchs and matriarchs, and Kfar Etzion, a landmark of Zionist martyrdom in the 1948 war.

Labor politicians had been all over the map on these issues, leading the successive governments of Levi Eshkol, Golda Meir, and Yitzhak Rabin to muddle through. They had sponsored or countenanced a score or so of small settlements in the West Bank, the Sinai, and the Golan Heights but had sought to keep settlements away from Arab population centers, so as to minimize frictions. And in secret talks with Jordan's King Hussein, they had presented proposals for dividing the West Bank accordingly.

This approach was challenged by *Gush Emunim*, a militant group

---

* Some American officials may have condoned an exception for the territory captured from Syria simply because the country's government was so unremittingly hostile to Israel, and for that matter to America, too. But all believed that Israel must be prepared to make withdrawals from the territories taken from Jordan and Egypt, both.

convinced of the Jews' God-given right to sovereignty over their entire biblical homeland. Days after Likud's electoral victory, Begin, and his new key ally, Ariel Sharon, a hawkish military hero who had bolted from the Labor Party, visited Kadum, a West Bank encampment that had been the test case of the militants' determination to settle everywhere in Palestine regardless of official policy. Founded in 1975, this settlement, originally called Elon Moreh, had been declared illegal by successive Labor governments because it lay near Nablus, a major Arab city. This had set off a game of cat-and-mouse in which the army forcibly evacuated the outpost on repeated occasions, only to have the settlers return. Finally a deal had been struck allowing twenty-five families to remain in makeshift quarters. Now, Begin threw his prestige, as well as the legal weight of his government, behind Kadum. Celebrating with the settlers who had illicitly augmented their numbers, Begin exulted: "The elections have brought about a turning point . . . with regard to settlements within the Land of Israel. Soon there will be no need for a temporary camp, and there will be many more Elon Morehs."[13]

Begin appointed Sharon, who had assisted the militants in defying the law, to be minister of agriculture. "He was something of a farmer in private life," notes political scientist Amos Perlmutter dryly, "but in this case . . . the only thing he planted was settlements."[14] Sharon presented the cabinet with a "settlement plan" that had been rejected by the government of Labor Prime Minister Yitzhak Rabin, and it was approved by Begin's. Sharon justified it in terms of security, the need to protect Jerusalem, and to control the Jordan River crossing and the high grounds overlooking Israel's narrow central plain. But Begin's deeper goal, shared by Sharon, was ideologically driven and none too democratic in spirit, notwithstanding Begin's ostentatious devotion to parliamentarianism. They aimed, as scholar Mark Tessler puts it, to "make it impossible for a withdrawal to be effected should Labor return to power."[15]

Labor governments had envisioned returning much or most of the West Bank to Jordan. Here and there, others thought of some sort of independence for this area, governed by non-Palestine Liberation Organization (PLO) Palestinians and without all the attributes of sovereignty. In those years, virtually no one in Israel countenanced the idea of a Palestinian state, much less one headed by the PLO. Gershom Gorenberg, a writer on the Israeli Left, faults Labor officials such as Moshe Dayan, Shimon Peres, Yitzhak Rabin, even the notoriously cautious Prime Minister Levi Eshkol for having allowed the settlement enterprise to begin.[16] But Begin and Sharon enlarged and accelerated it and gave it a new meaning.

Decades later, the Likud Party under Prime Minister Binyamin Netanyahu would agree to sit down with leaders of the PLO and to accept the idea of a Palestinian state, a position that Labor had already reached in the 1993 Oslo Accords. By this time, however, hundreds of thousands of Israelis lived in scores of settlements, complicating diplomacy and compromising Israel's standing in foreign eyes even though the claim that they constituted the principal obstacle to a settlement was highly tendentious.

But Begin was not indifferent to his image abroad and sought to counterbalance an unyielding position on Palestine with compromise elsewhere. He "burned to achieve some sort of peace," says Perlmutter.[17] In this, he found a willing partner in Egypt's President Anwar Sadat.

Both leaders were alarmed by President Carter's plan for an international peace conference cochaired by the United States and the Soviet Union at which the Arab delegates would form a single bloc. Sadat, who had only recently expelled thousands of Soviet military advisers, was chary of awarding Moscow a central role, and to Israel, the USSR was simply an enemy. And both disliked the idea of a pan-Arab delegation—Begin because he could foresee concessions to Egypt that he would not make on other fronts, and Sadat because he thought it led to paralysis. The Syrians, he said, posed "never-ending objections to everything proposed" about the make-up of the pan-Arab delegation because "in reality they had no desire to see the conference take place."[18]

So the two leaders made an end run around the American plan—oddly through the good offices of Romania's dictator Nicolae Ceausescu, a maverick Communist who had maintained good relations with Israel. Sadat visited Bucharest on Begin's heels and later recalled that Ceausescu told him, "Begin wants a solution."[19] Soon after, Sadat made the historic gesture of traveling to Jerusalem, meeting Israel's leaders, and addressing the Knesset, shattering the Arab's boycott of Israel, demonstrating dramatically his readiness to recognize the Jewish state.

Peace, however, was not easy to achieve. Gradually Begin yielded to Sadat's insistence on recovering every inch of the Sinai which meant that Israel's settlements there were dismantled. But the sticking point was the future of the West Bank and Gaza. Although Sadat's diplomacy was renounced by all the other Arab states—who even suspended Egypt from the Arab League—he nonetheless viewed himself as negotiating not only on behalf of Egypt but also the larger Arab cause, which meant the Palestinians. This circle proved almost impossible to square.

Sadat sought an independent Palestinian state. Begin was prepared to go no further than to grant the Palestinians autonomy under Israeli sovereignty. His position, says Kenneth Stein, Middle East advisor to President Jimmy Carter, "bitterly infected" US–Israeli relations until Carter left office.[20] Nonetheless, a peace treaty was hammered out, putting off final resolution of the Palestinian question until after five years of autonomy.

Sadat was reviled for settling for so minor a step toward Palestinian self-determination, since Begin insisted that he would not in the end agree to a Palestinian state. Perhaps because of Begin's obduracy or perhaps because they themselves were not ready for peace, the Palestinians refused to partake in the talks on their final status envisioned in the agreement, as did the Jordanians. Thus, the negotiations ended before they began.

Nonetheless, the implications of this stillborn deal were more profound than most first recognized. It made Begin "the first Israeli Prime Minister to give de jure recognition of the rights of the Palestinian people," notes Shilon.[21] And President Carter's advisor, Kenneth Stein, goes so far as to say that for Begin to formally acknowledge the "legitimate rights" of the Palestinians "was an ideological compromise and distance whose only remote equivalence was perhaps Sadat's brazen trip to Jerusalem."[22] Shimon Peres characterized the deal as "the Balfour Declaration of the Palestinians,"[23] an apt analogy because that declaration had not promised the Jews a state but had consecrated the legitimacy of the Zionist project.

Excoriated by his Herut comrades for having sold out, Begin denied having made any such momentous concession. But his aide, Dan Meridor, recalled years later that privately Begin conceded this was "the biggest ideological break with the past."[24] And according to an account of another conversation, Begin acknowledged he had opened a door. He reportedly said that he would "never preside over the transfer of one inch of the Land of Israel to anyone else's sovereignty," but that "others may come after me who might feel differently."[25]

Although Begin's apparently minor concession was in fact momentous, he nonetheless looked small in comparison to Sadat's largeness of vision and spirit, and not only in the jaundiced eyes of Jimmy Carter. An editorial in *The Baltimore Sun* put it, "It is Mr. Begin's style, unfortunately, to respond ungenerously to large favors. He never adequately recompensed Anwar el Sadat after the Egyptian president went to Jerusalem, risking isolation in the Arab world to give Israel the acceptance it so long had craved."[26]

If even in his finest moment Begin did not cut a sympathetic figure, all the worse was his performance in the final chapter of his career, which was far from his finest: Israel's 1982 invasion of Lebanon. The purpose of the war was to expel the PLO from Lebanon where, after having been driven from Jordan by King Hussein's forces in 1970, it had built up a "state within a state," immune to control by the weak, confessionally divided Lebanese government. The PLO had created its own standing army, and it carried out terror raids and occasional shelling into northern Israel's Galilee region. After the last Israeli retaliatory strike, the United States had mediated a cease-fire between the rival artilleries. But Israel still found it intolerable to have a military/terrorist force whose declared purpose was its destruction camped on its border, still sponsoring violent acts and capable of attacking civilian targets whenever it wished.

Israel's thrust into Lebanon initially enjoyed overwhelming domestic support, and even though it evoked knee-jerk condemnation from abroad, its moral basis was strong. But several aspects of the three-month-long campaign greatly intensified the international opprobrium directed at Israel and opened painful divisions at home.

First, the war was mired in political deception aimed at the Israeli public and cabinet; at Israel's ally, America; and even at the Israeli prime minister, himself. The deceiver-in-chief was Ariel Sharon, who had been elevated to defense minister and who planned and orchestrated the war. Initially, he told the cabinet—and Begin had told Washington and announced to the world—that the goal of "Operation Peace for Galilee" was to push PLO guns beyond a line forty kilometers from Israel so that their fire could not reach across the border. As the war unfolded, this perimeter kept being extended until it was forgotten completely whereas the operation's other declared goals were enlarged. A final stage of this process was the occupation of Beirut.

This step exemplified the fog in which Sharon had deliberately shrouded the entire war. Israel's preeminent military correspondents, Zeev Schiff and Ehud Yaari, capture the absurdity:

> Begin was as astonished as his ministers to discover that Israeli
> troops were in Beirut. As countless Israelis were driving openly
> through the streets of East Beirut, taking in the sights and
> shops, quite unaware that they weren't supposed to be there,
> Begin was continuing to deny that the IDF was in Beirut at all.
> In one particularly ironic coincidence, his statement of denial
> was quoted by the Israeli state radio in its hourly news bulletin
> only to be immediately followed by a live report from Beirut de-
> scribing the streets of the city jammed with Israeli vehicles.[27]

That he himself was at least sometimes among the victims of Sharon's duplicity scarcely exonerated Begin and not only because the buck stops with the prime minister. At each stage at which Sharon was revealed to have expanded the war beyond what had been agreed within the cabinet, not only in its Lebanese aims but also by initiating or provoking clashes with Syrian forces, Begin gave it his retroactive endorsement.

Moreover, Sharon's unstated goals, which enjoyed Begin's full sympathy even if not his prior operational assent, were more ambitious than ousting the PLO. He also aimed to remake Lebanon's political landscape by installing a new government headed by the Maronite Christian, Bashir Gemayel of the Phalange Party. In principle there was nothing wrong with wanting Lebanon's embattled Christians to be protected and to see the formation of a Lebanese government that would make peace with Israel. Sharon envisioned that its accession would be achieved through constitutional processes, albeit under Israel's patronage—a procedure that may have been no less democratic than Lebanon's politics had already become thanks to civil war and Syrian intervention. But, in practice, Lebanon's complex ethnic tapestry could not be rehung so readily. Nor did this scheme reckon with the likely response of Syrian dictator Hafez al-Assad who had Gemayel assassinated just days after he was sworn in.

Third, the war culminated in an especially vicious episode, the massacre of noncombatants in the Palestinian refugee camps of Sabra and Shatilla. Israel's bombardment and siege of West Beirut, the Muslim half of the city where Palestinians lived and the PLO was based, forced Arafat to accept evacuation from Lebanon with his forces. But Israeli intelligence learned of his plans to leave some two thousand fighters behind in civilian guise. On the heels of Gemayel's assassination, Sharon arranged for the Phalange Party to send its militia into the camps to eliminate this underground force. Predictably, the Phalangists took revenge for the murder of their leader and for other depredations of Palestinians against Christian Lebanese by killing whichever Palestinians they could get their hands on, including women and children. Israel's investigative commission later reported that "the dead counted by the Lebanese Red Cross, the International Red Cross, the Lebanese Civil Defense, the medical corps of the Lebanese army, and by relatives of the victims" amounted to 460, including 15 women and 20 children. It added that some bodies may have been carted away by the killers and others buried under rubble, leading Israel's military intelligence to estimate a death toll of seven to eight hundred.[28]

The sad truth was that Lebanon had seen worse in the course of years of internecine bloodletting. In fact, another Palestinian camp in Beirut, Tel Zaatar, had suffered a larger massacre at Christian hands in 1976, with the perpetrators in that case abetted by Syrian rather than Israeli forces while attracting little notice. In contrast, Sabra and Shatilla evoked an international storm thereby symbolizing not only the horrors of the Lebanon War, but also the incongruousness of the international response to it. This was exemplified by the esteemed *NBC Nightly News* commentator, John Chancellor, who asserted breathlessly about the damage that Israel wreaked on Beirut, "nothing like it has ever happened in this part of the world,"[29] as if unaware of, say, the Bible, the Roman Empire, or the Crusades or of such more recent events as the destruction of the Iranian city of Khorramshar in the Iran-Iraq war in 1980 or the razing of his own rebellious city of Hama by Syrian President Hafez al-Assad's forces earlier in 1982, in each of which the damage and death toll far surpassed Beirut's.

But if some of Israel's critics were guilty of selective indignation, this was beside the point to many Israelis. In their view, their country had been complicit in a shameful act, and the weight on their conscience was not lightened by knowledge of how brutally Arabs might treat one another. Discontent with the Lebanon War had been building for months, but Sabra and Shatilla was the last straw, sparking a demonstration that brought crowds into the streets variously estimated at two hundred thousand to four hundred thousand. Even the lower figure would amount to 5 percent of the entire population of Israel, making it proportionately perhaps the largest demonstration the world had ever seen.

"Shock and revulsion led the whole country to take a new, deeply sobered look at the aims of the war and the means used to achieve them," write Schiff and Ya'ari. "It seemed to have changed the face of Israel and debased its cherished rectitude."[30] The protests forced the government to appoint an independent investigative commission which was chaired by the President of the Supreme Court Israel Kahan. After a four-month inquiry, it concluded that although the Phalange forces bore "direct responsibility" for the killing, Israel bore "indirect responsibility" for sending the Phalange into the camps. Blame was apportioned to individuals, including some top military and intelligence officers and also to Sharon himself. The commission called on him to resign which he did only after failing to persuade the cabinet to reject the commission's report, although he remained in the cabinet as minister without portfolio.

During the course of the commission's work, Begin's beloved wife of forty-three years, Aliza, succumbed to illness. Under the twin blows of personal loss and a sense of disgrace surrounding the Lebanon War, Begin seems to have sunk into depression, performing his functions in a desultory way until resigning from office in the summer of 1983 even while his party remained in power. He lived nearly another decade, mostly as a recluse, neither writing memoirs nor giving interviews, and appearing in public only rarely. The war, says one of his biographers, had sapped his "spirit" and "faith," leaving him "bitter, disappointed, adrift and feeling betrayed."[31] His resignation, says another, was "an act of contrition."[32]

The work of the Kahan Commission—and its contrast with a Lebanese government inquiry that whitewashed the massacre—partially rehabilitated Israel's reputation after the body blow it had taken over Sabra and Shatilla. But the harm done by the whole Lebanon venture was never fully repaired. Public opinion polls in the United States showed that support for Israel eventually returned to its pre-Lebanon War levels, but in Europe the recovery was only partial. The combined impact of Lebanon and Begin's settlement-building campaign would become specters haunting Israel's global standing.

nine

Israel Spawns Its Own Adversary Culture

The harm to Israel's reputation caused by Begin's policies was multiplied many times over by the divisions they exacerbated within Israeli society. There they nurtured a subculture of alienation that proved to be an inexhaustible resource for Israel's enemies, much as the Vietnam War gave rise to an "adversary culture" in America that stoked an anti-Americanism that strengthened the hand of Communist forces.

Whereas America's Vietnam debates were rendered moot by the ending of the Cold War, Israel's divisions continued to fester. In 2008, screenwriter Ari Folman, who had been a nineteen-year-old soldier in the Lebanon War, brought out an animated documentary, *Waltz with Bashir*, about the nightmares and guilt that he and other soldiers suffered. It was acclaimed in Israel and the United States, where it won the Golden Globe Award for best foreign language film. Twenty-six years after the Lebanon War, apparently, it remained the formative experience of Folman's generation—or at least some members of it.

Of course, dissent in Israel did not begin with Begin's administration. In fact, it stretched back decades before the state was even born. Take, for example, the famous philosopher, Martin Buber. He was the prodigy of the Zionist movement in the early days of the twentieth century, but not for long, repudiating the political cause in favor of a more religious and mystical version. In the 1930s he found refuge from Hitler in Palestine, teaching at the Hebrew University of Jerusalem, the land's preeminent academic institution. He remained there after the war, living out his years in Israel, without ever renouncing his opposition to the idea of a Jewish state. Buber's stance was not a solitary one: throughout these years he was active in organizations of Palestinian Jews, and later Israelis, who rejected Zionism. In his book, *The Jewish State*,[1] Yoram Hazony writes that views like Buber's reigned at Hebrew University.

Once Israel came into being, anti-Zionism lost its influence in the new country. Fierce disputes continued, however, among Zionist factions. The foremost critic of the government before Begin came to office was of course Begin himself. But criticisms aimed from the domestic Right had different international ramifications from those aimed from the Left. Since Begin faulted Labor governments for being insufficiently nationalistic, his complaints were of no use to Israel's enemies. With Begin in power, however, the argument was reversed: those to his left charged that his policies made Israel too aggrandizing, and such statements were naturally seized on by Arabs and other foreign detractors of the Jewish state.

Initially, the opposition to Begin's government was parliamentary and made up primarily of Labor Zionists who couched their criticisms in terms that gave little comfort to Israel's enemies. But the Lebanon War inflamed the debate and moved more political action into the streets, where it was even punctuated by violence. In February 1983, someone—presumably a rightist—tossed a hand grenade at marchers demanding that Begin's government embrace the Kahan Commission's findings of blame for Sabra and Shatilla. The blast killed one demonstrator and wounded several others. The Left committed no comparable acts, but its rhetoric grew increasingly shrill and extreme, lending an indigenous imprimatur to the most jaundiced interpretations of the country's actions and motives. Some voices went so far as to challenge Israel's right to exist or the legitimacy of its birth. Hazony discerned in this discord a revival of the anti-Zionism of Buber and his co-thinkers.

Lebanon changed the tone of debate, but the rise of an influential movement of Israelis blaming their own country for its international predicament began earlier in Begin's tenure, during the peace negotiations with Egypt. Sadat's visit to Jerusalem, signaling an Arab willingness to accept Israel's existence, was a dream come true for Israelis. But there was a legion of devils in the details. The major sticking point was the fate of the Palestinians. To vindicate himself in the eyes of the Arab world, Sadat sought some kind of national liberation for them. Begin, on the other hand, although ready to return the Sinai to Egypt, would not relinquish territories in Israel's historic patrimony. Within months after Sadat's speech to the Knesset, it seemed that the promise of that magical moment might not be fulfilled.

At this crucial juncture, an open letter to Begin signed by 348 reserve officers, all combat veterans, some highly decorated, was released to the press in March 1978. Its core paragraph read:

> We write to you with profound anxiety. A government that prefers the establishment of the State of Israel in the borders of a Greater Israel above the establishment of peace through good neighborly relations instills in us many doubts. A government that prefers the establishment of settlements beyond the "green line" to the elimination of the historical quarrel and the establishment of normal relations in our region will awaken in us questions as to the justice of our cause. A government policy which will continue the domination over millions of Arabs may damage the democratic and Jewish character of the state and make it difficult for us to identify with the path taken by the State of Israel. We are aware of the security requirements of the State of Israel and of the difficulties facing the road to peace, but we know that true security will be achieved only when peace will come. The strength of the Israeli Defense forces lies in the identification of its citizen-soldiers with the posture of the state.[2]

As soon as it was published thousands of others added their names to this statement, and demonstrations began to be held. In the next months the group grew into a mass movement, adopting the name Peace Now.

Its positions were not outside the mainstream of Israeli thought about relations with the Arabs. Nor did it present itself as a radical force. One of its first acts was to ask for and receive an audience with the prime minister. Later that year, as Begin prepared to leave for the United States meetings at Camp David with Sadat and President Jimmy Carter, one hundred thousand Peace Now supporters saw him off, the biggest demonstration Israel had ever seen. Its slogan eschewed rancor: "Go in peace and return with peace." Later, Begin wrote to Amos Oz, the famous novelist who supported the peace movement, that the demonstrators were on his mind throughout his stay at Camp David. This may have moved him to make key concessions—relinquishing every last inch of Sinai and embracing a transitional plan for the Palestinians that might have led to an independent state—opposed by some of his advisers.[3]

Following the treaty's signing, Peace Now's activity diminished until a few weeks into the Lebanon War when it reappeared with a new urgency and bitterness. It cosponsored a series of demonstrations culminating in the enormous turnout to protest the Sabra and Shatilla massacre. Anger continued to simmer, but with the dismissal of Sharon as defense minister and the resignation of Begin, the peace movement again lapsed into quiescence.

It sprang back to life once again in the late 1980s with the outbreak of the first Palestinian *intifada*. Ill-equipped and unprepared Israeli troops were sent to suppress mobs hurling rocks and Molotov cocktails in Gaza and the West Bank. They responded with force that was sometimes lethal, and other times sublethal but brutal, to the dismay and embarrassment of many Israelis. The uprising also proved a sense of national identity had permeated Palestinian society and could no longer be dismissed as just the dream of radicals or intellectuals. In December 1988, while this unconventional conflict was going on, Yasser Arafat uttered a statement crafted by Western diplomats in which he "totally and absolutely renounce[d] all forms of terrorism" and recognized Israel's right to exist. Seizing this basis for negotiations with the PLO, the Israeli peace movement turned to the goal of ending Israeli occupation of the territories captured in 1967.

In contrast to the American protests against the Vietnam War, whose slogans invariably accused America's leaders and soldiers of vile acts, whose marchers sometimes waved Viet Cong flags, and whose spokesmen sometimes traveled to Hanoi to express solidarity with America's enemies, Israel's peace movement struck no chord of disloyalty to the nation. An unshakeable Israeli patriot, performing the required military service and prepared to die for his or her country, might still demand that the government make the concessions needed for peace with Egypt, might still oppose Sharon's deceitful war in Lebanon, and might still be eager to negotiate with the PLO a withdrawal from the West Bank and Gaza Strip.

Indeed, with the signing of the Oslo Accords in 1993 the Israeli peace movement was vindicated. With Labor back in power, Foreign Minister Shimon Peres, who had grown increasingly dovish, persuaded the more hawkish Prime Minister Yitzhak Rabin to authorize secret negotiations in Norway that resulted in an agreement on mutual recognition between Israel and the PLO and a step-by-step plan for the creation of a Palestinian state. The deal was sealed with a ceremonial handshake on the White House lawn between Arafat and a visibly repelled Yitzhak Rabin.

Rabin's thoughts were easy to guess: Arafat was the vile architect of unforgivable acts of terror, but he was also—or appeared to be—the key to Israel's dream of acceptance in the region. Rabin warmed to his role as champion of peace (if not to Arafat), and he keynoted a Peace Now rally in 1995 where he was gunned down. The bullets of the fanatic young assassin, Yigal Amir, however, did not stop the peace movement. On the contrary, they covered the Israeli right wing with shame and led to the accession of the more dovish Shimon Peres. What brought the peace movement low, however, leaving only a radical remnant, were the events of the year 2000. Yasser Arafat spurned the peace terms offered by Israel at Camp David in July and the more generous ones proposed by President Bill Clinton at Taba in December, and his rejections were punctuated by the uncorking of a new Palestinian *intifada*, this one not of rocks and Molotov cocktails but of suicide bombers in Israeli buses, cafes, and markets.

This violence struck forcefully at the weakness that had all along lay at the center of the peace movement's outlook. The reserve officers who demanded that Begin not allow his attachment to the biblical land of Israel to stand in the way of peace with Egypt made an irresistible argument. But Sadat needed Begin to make concessions to the Palestinians who spurned peace. Begin's plan for Palestinian autonomy finessed the issue until negotiations between Israel and the Palestinians commenced in the 1990s. Then it had to be faced. The peace movement's compelling argument that Israel should not put settlements and West Bank territory ahead of the chance for peace was rendered moot by Arafat's obduracy, and the bloody new *intifada* seemed to demonstrate that the Palestinians were not in fact ready for peace.

To most Israelis—including many who had adhered to the peace movement—the nightmare of suicide bombings signified that the Palestinians cherished the goal of annihilating Israel more than the hope of a state of their own. Emblematic of the shift in mood was Alexander Yakobson, a newspaper columnist and professor of ancient history at Hebrew University. Unlike most other immigrants from the USSR, Yakobson stood on the political left, serving as a member of the executive of the Meretz Party, to Labor's left, and on the board of the New Israel Fund. An activist in Peace Now, Yakobson used his column in Israel's leading Russian language news-paper to advocate relentlessly for the peace process. Now, however, he sounded a different note. Under the heading, "Peace, not now," he wrote: "The basic situation has not changed. . . . The only solution is two states for two peoples. [But] this attempt to have it with Arafat was no more than a hypothesis. It was right to test this hypothesis, [but one must now] admit that the experiment has failed."[4]

Yakobson resigned from his positions with Meretz and the New Israel Fund. Then, in the summer of 2001, on receiving an invitation from Peace Now to join a demonstration outside the Israeli Ministry of Defense under the slogan "no to an unnecessary war," he penned this reply:

> Since I can no longer regard myself as either a member or a sup- . porter of Peace Now, I would like to ask you to take me off your mailing list. . . .
>
> An unnecessary war is in fact being waged now in this coun-try, and it was started by Yasser Arafat in September 2000 after he had been offered an independent Palestinian state with a capital in East Jerusalem. . . .
>
> The slogan "No to an unnecessary war" should today be ad-dressed to Arafat. . . . By constantly creating the impression that the danger of an all-out war comes from Israel, you do not serve the cause of peace at all—all you serve is the vicious propa-ganda war waged by the P[alestinian] A[uthority] and the Arab countries against Israel.
>
> I am writing all this with a heavy heart, remembering that I have been taking part in Peace Now demonstrations for some 20 years. . . . [F]inally and irrevocably breaking with Peace Now is not an easy decision.[5]

While few former adherents of the peace movement had the will or the skill to express their disillusionment as sharply as Yakob-son, most of them dropped out. Those who remained stalwart—attending the demonstration that Yakobson spurned and more that followed—naturally tended to be the most extreme or to grow extreme because of their isolation. An exemplar of this group was Avraham Burg, son of Yosef Burg, leader of the National Religious Party who served in Begin's cabinet.

Avraham had been among those injured by the lethal hand grenade thrown into the Peace Now march protesting Sabra and

Shatilla. Twenty-eight at the time, Avraham had already moved left-ward from his father's politics while continuing to sport the knitted skullcap that marked him as an orthodox observer. Thanks to this combination of ideology and religious status, as well as his luminous patrimony and quick tongue, he rose rapidly through the ranks of the Labor Party. When Arafat's rejectionism and the new *intifada* drove Labor from office and Ehud Barak (temporarily) from politics in 2001, Burg contended to succeed him as the party's leader. Falling short, he nonetheless became speaker of the Knesset in which he served until resigning in 2004.

Burg's Labor Party was not as far left as Yakobson's Meretz, but the two men's paths crossed like ships in the night. While Yakobson deserted the Left for the Center, Burg grew increasingly extreme in his views, calling Israel "fascist" and comparing it to Nazi Germany. He eventually renounced Zionism altogether, urging Israelis to consider dismantling their state in favor of a bi-national one.[6] Perhaps as a step toward his own post-Israel existence, he acquired citizenship in France, where his wife had been born, and revealed in 2007 that he had voted in that country's presidential election.[7]

Thus, within the span of six years, Burg lurched from competing to be Israel's prime minister to forsaking his loyalty to the Jewish state. If this made him uniquely mercurial, he was far from alone among Israelis in his radical alienation from his country. Another figure who made a dramatic transition was Meron Benvenisti, the former deputy mayor of Jerusalem. In 2012 he published (in Hebrew) *The Dream of the White Sabra*, spelling out in detail the case he had been espousing in op eds for some years in favor of replacing Israel with a bi-national state.

"I am drawn to the Arabs," he explained in an interview. "I love their culture, their language, their approach to the land," in comparison to which Jewish attachment to it, was merely "an acquired love." While expressing such warmth for the Arabs, he heaped scorn on the Israelis who came from the Arab lands: "If we had not been here to take them in . . . what would they be worth? . . . We made a heroic decision to take them all in. And by that decision we effectively committed suicide."[8] Of course, these refugees were culturally similar to the Arabs among whom they had lived for centuries, but apparently the same characteristics he found appealing in an Arab were repulsive in a Jew.

By "suicide," Benvenisti appeared to mean Israel's departure from socialism. "I am very proud of my kibbutz past," he said "and of socialism. . . . I am thrilled to hear the 'Internationale' and to sing the Internationale." A similar feeling apparently motivated another Israeli dissident, the celebrated novelist, Amos Oz. Speaking against the background of the Lebanon War which he opposed, Oz delivered a much broader lamentation on his country's lost potential: "Israel could have become an exemplary state. . . . the most egalitarian and creative social democratic society in the world." Why had it failed to do so? "One of the major factors was the mass immigration of Holocaust survivors, Middle Eastern Jews and nonsocialist and even antisocialist Zionists." These types, said Oz, "wanted bourgeois coziness and stability;" they "chose 'respectability' over egalitarianism."[9]

While blaming the fading of Israeli socialism mostly on the moral failings of Israelis, Oz acknowledged that Soviet support for the Arabs and European New Leftists "who questioned Israel's very right to exist" had alienated Israelis, making it hard to remain simultaneously a leftist and a Zionist. Oz performed that feat, but most others chose one side or the other, like Yakobson, who abandoned Leftism, and Burg and Benvenisti, who abandoned Zionism.

This dilemma points to a profound vulnerability in Zionism which is perhaps the deepest source of Israeli alienation. The dominant stream of Zionism was Labor Zionism, an amalgam of nationalism and socialism, a mixture that elsewhere produced history's most horrible regimes, those of Hitler, Mao, Pol Pot, and Kim Il Sung. In Israel it produced something wholly different and indeed admirable. But in the latter portion of the twentieth century the entire world came to realize, from many different experiences, that socialism, although a beautiful idea, simply did not work. One of the most telling revelations that contributed to this realization was the voluntary transformation of Israel's kibbutzim away from socialism.*

The global realization of the fallacy of socialism left Labor Zionism incoherent, and few voices were able to fill the void by articulating a compelling vision of Zionism without the "Labor" part. Was it

---

*Although both Oz and Benvenisti blamed *Sephardim* and other later immigrants for Israel's retreat from socialism, these groups could not have been implicated in transforming the kibbutzim since few of their members ever joined kibbutzim. The turn from collective living was the doing of native-born Israelis of European lineage. Oz and Benvenisti, for all their nostalgia, had themselves each moved away from a kibbutz.

sufficient for the Jewish people to have a state of their own, or did that state have to have some higher purpose? For some, that purpose inhered in Scripture, but other devout Jews rejected Israel as the fulfillment of prophecy, and the pioneers who forged the state of Israel were mostly secularists who found higher purpose in a socialist vision that had proved illusory.

This death of the socialist dream created a spiritual vacuum in Israel. Yoram Hazony put his finger on the problem in his 2000 book, *The Jewish State: The Struggle for Israel's Soul*. A prime symptom was the voluble disenchantment of Israel's intellectual elite. "Israeli culture has become a carnival of self-loathing," complained Hazony.[10] Hazony stands somewhere on the political right, but the same point had already been made by the prominent novelist, Aharon Megged, whose background was on the left. Writing in *Ha'aretz* in 1994, he decried "a phenomenon which probably has no parallel in history: an emotional and moral identification by the majority of Israel's intelligentsia with people openly committed to our annihilation."[11]

The name usually put on this phenomenon is "post-Zionism," a label that carries no consensual definition. Some have used it to designate nothing more than the wish for a less heroic, more objective account of the nation's history than had been taught in the schools. But for others the term represented something far more radical, namely, a challenge to the very idea of Israel as a Jewish state.

This view was embodied in the 2004 "Olga Statement" (named for the place, Givat Olga, where it was hammered out) signed by more than two hundred Israeli professors, artists, and others. It described Israel as a "living hell," "a benighted colonial reality," and "the heart of darkness." "Zionism," it said, was "based . . . on [a] refusal to acknowledge the indigenous people of this country and on denial of their rights, on dispossession of their lands." The solution? "Peace and reconciliation are contingent on Israel's recognition of its responsibility for the injustices done to the indigenous people, the Palestinians, and on willingness to redress them. Recognition of the right of return follows from our principles." The statement made clear that those who signed it understood that this formula meant the end of Israel as the prerequisite for "spiritual healing" and its replacement with something else, although when it tried to explain what this might be the rhetoric grew childish. Jews and Palestinians it affirmed "are brothers and sisters," adding: "It is pointless, now, to guess the material future form of the vision of life together: two states or one?! perhaps a confederation?! or maybe a federation?! and what about cantons?!" [*sic*].

Such public statements became a staple of the post-Zionist movement, prompting Israel's leading political scientist, Shlomo Avineri, himself a man of the Left, to recall the history of Jewish opposition to Zionism. He concluded: "Those who call themselves 'post-Zionists' are simply anti-Zionists of the old sort."[12]

Petitions and circular letters became a common format in which the post-Zionist movement found expression. Two months after the Olga statement was issued, most of its signers and hundreds more put their names on a new appeal, this one in defense of Tali Fahima, an Israeli Jew who had traveled to Jenin in 2004, during the *intifada*. Jenin had a reputation as the hotbed of terrorism on the West Bank, and the home court of the main group organizing the suicide bombings, the Al Aqsa Martyrs Brigade. In Jenin, Fahima befriended Zakaria Zubeidi, the Brigade's local commander, volunteering to serve as a human shield for him and reportedly becoming his lover.[13] Her subsequent arrest by Israeli authorities sparked the petition demanding her immediate release. "The Israeli government," the signers said, "continues to operate as a police state, thinking that forcefully silencing Tali Fahima would deter and prevent other women and men from following her groundbreaking path." She was not "an activist against the security of Israel," but rather "an agent of peace and solidarity on behalf of the disillusioned and sane voices in this hell created by the Israeli policy of occupation."[14]

Nonetheless, her lawyers' plea-bargained down the charge of assisting the enemy in time of war, and she served more than two years in prison before being released in 2007. By then the *intifada* was over, Mahmoud Abbas had succeeded Yasser Arafat as president of the Palestinian Authority, and peace feelers had resumed. As one confidence-building measure, various militants were removed from Israel's most wanted list in return for surrendering their weapons and agreeing to have their movements monitored by Abbas's police who in turn communicated with Israeli security. When Zubeidi agreed to these terms, Fahima took to the press to denounce him as a "whore of the Shin Bet" and "a disgrace to the resistance."[15] Two years later, she announced that she had converted to Islam at a ceremony in Umm al-Fahm, Israel's largest Arab town, and apparently abandoned Fatah which was no longer militant enough to suit her.

She now had a new mentor, Sheikh Yusuf Albaz, one of the leaders of the more radical northern branch of the Islamist movement among Israeli Arabs. "I liked her mentality," said Albaz. "Tali Fahima is an example of resistance."[16] In short, with Fatah apparently returning to the peace process, she seems to have transferred her allegiance to the still-rejectionist Hamas.

One of the signatories of the appeal on behalf of Fahima and one of the initiators of the Olga Statement was Anat Biletzki, a philosophy professor at Tel Aviv University. She went on to become a leader of *B'Tselem*, a group that began as a human rights watchdog and evolved into one of the most influential bastions of post-Zionism.

B'Tselem, which means "in the image," an allusion to the biblical assertion that humans are made in God's image, was formed during the first *intifada* for the purpose of monitoring the mistreatment of Palestinians by the Israeli army. At first it employed a single Palestinian, Bassem Eid, to look into complaints. An investigative reporter who had written in both the Arab and the Hebrew press, Eid was expert at ferreting out the facts and evidence that would prove an abuse had occurred. He was equally good at assessing the stories of accusers for false notes or exaggerations. This aptitude enabled *B'Tselem* to build a strong reputation. "For me, Bassem Eid *is* B'Tselem," wrote *Ha'aretz* columnist Gideon Levy in 1995. "He brings them their hard information, their raw material."[17]

In the mid-1990s, a rift developed between Eid and *B'Tselem*. Under the Oslo Accords, Yasser Arafat and his colleagues had returned to the occupied territories and established the Palestinian Authority. Eid, now widely known in the territories as a kind of tribune, began to receive complaints against Arafat's security services as well as against Israelis. He wanted to investigate these cases and to have *B'Tselem* report on them, but this divided *B'Tselem*'s directors, some of whom argued that it was not appropriate for an Israeli organization to comment on violations by Palestinian authorities.

Eid prevailed, and in 1994 *B'Tselem* issued a report on the torture and killing of hundreds of Palestinians accused of being Israeli "collaborators."[18] In 1995, it produced a broader report on Palestinian-on-Palestinian abuses,[19] prompting Jabril Rajoub, Arafat's security chief for the West Bank, to denounce Eid as a "collaborator" and "Israeli police agent."[20] This was like putting a bounty on his head, and forced Eid to circumscribe his work with new precautions.

Ongoing tension within *B'Tselem* on this issue led Eid to leave the organization in 1996 to establish his own, the Palestinian Human Rights Monitoring Group. Other Palestinian rights groups focused on protesting Israeli actions, but Eid systematically investigated and documented malfeasance by Arafat's regime. For this he was dogged by accusations of "collaboration." As *B'Tselem's* 1994 report had shown, this term was an epithet rather than a description, applied to homosexuals and other nonconformists, critics of the leadership, and targets of grudges. In this case, its sole meaning was to threaten Eid so he would cease publicizing Palestinian misconduct. Astonishingly, it was explicitly echoed by Uri Avnery,* the elder statesman of the Israeli radical left, for the same purpose.

Avnery had been one of the *B'Tselem* board members who opposed Eid's wish to report Palestinian abuses. He had long been an anti-Zionist, propounding since at least 1947 "the unity of the Semitic sphere."[21] He was also a close friend of Bruno Kreisky's and had encouraged the Austrian chancellor in his courtship of Yasser Arafat. Like Rajoub, Avnery did not even pretend to have any information that Eid was an actual collaborator. He meant simply that Eid's work embarrassed Arafat and "whoever destroys [Arafat's] standing in the international arena is pulling the carpet from under the feet of the Palestinian cause."[22] Having argued within *B'Tselem's* board that mistreatment of Palestinians by Arafat's regime should not be publicized by an Israeli organization, Avnery now objected to its being publicized by Eid's indigenous Palestinian organization. Apparently he found criticism of Arafat objectionable whatever the source, and by adding an Israeli imprimatur to the charge of "collaboration" he quite wittingly made it more likely that Eid would be murdered.

To say that any government should be exempt for whatever reason from criticism for abusing its citizens is an anomalous stance for an officer of a human rights organization. This highlighted a duality in *B'Tselem's* work. While monitoring rights violations, it also served as an advocacy group which, in its own words, "acts primarily to change Israeli policy in the Occupied Territories."

This dichotomy was not unique but the tension between the roles of monitor and advocate intensified as the balance within the board tilted in the late 1990s and 2000s toward the more radical, even anti-Israeli, voices like Avnery's. Biletzki, coauthor of the anti-Zionist "Olga Statement," rose to the chairmanship of *B'Tselem* in

---

* Not be confused with Shlomo Avineri, quoted previously.

2001, holding this position until 2006. The "Free Tali Fahima" petition that she had signed, along with one of her successors as chair, the academic Oren Yiftachel, entirely prejudged the case, presuming that any prosecution by Israeli authorities amounted to "persecution." This contrasted dramatically with Bassem Eid's careful sifting of evidence on which *B'Tselem* had made its reputation.

At the height of the second *intifada*, Biletzki and Yiftachel also both signed a petition initiated by Gush Shalom, a radical group led by Avnery, that declared: "While we totally condemn acts of terror against innocent civilians, we regard Palestinian violence as being, on the whole, a legitimate revolt against colonial occupation."[23] Since Palestinian violence consisted mainly of terror against innocent civilians this was double talk. In any case, the condemnation of terror was pro forma whereas the real import of the statement was to place a stamp of approval on the bloodshed.

While thus showing the utmost indulgence of Palestinian actions, these individuals showed none toward Israel. On the contrary, Yiftachel called Israel a "jailer state." Biletzki said it "is like the Nazis," and another *B'Tselem* official, Lizi Sagie, said the country is "devot[ed] to Nazi values." Executive Director Jessica Montell averred that "in some cases the situation in the West Bank is worse than apartheid in South Africa."[24] They said these things as individuals; nothing as extreme was asserted in the publications of *B'Tselem*. Nonetheless, the organization's pronouncements were often tendentious or hyperbolic, smacking of ideological advocacy rather than authentic human rights work. For example, a report on Gaza, years after Israel's complete withdrawal, averred: "Israel has turned the Gaza strip into the largest prison on earth."[25]

Part of *B'Tselem*'s activity is devoted deliberately to damaging Israel's standing in the world. In contrast to the early days when Bassem Eid was its one-man backbone, *B'Tselem* grew to become an enormous nongovernmental organization (NGO), with scores of staff members, most funded, as *B'Tselem* reports, by European sources. In a devastating exposé in *Commentary*, Noah Pollak charged that the group became in effect a vehicle through which Europe worked to influence Israeli policy from within.[26] The story, though, grew even more complicated when *B'Tselem* lobbied Europe to refrain from improving relations with Israel. In a 2009 letter to European Union foreign ministers, *B'Tselem* (and two other Israeli groups) urged them to refuse to upgrade ties with Israel unless it met a series of conditions including cooperation with the United Nations's Goldstone Commission.[27] In other words, in addition to using *B'Tselem* to influence Israeli policy, Europeans critical of Israel may have been using *B'Tselem* to lobby their own governments to adopt stands less friendly to Israel.

Israel had refused to cooperate with the Goldstone Commission because it was openly biased. It was created by the UN Human Rights Council, whose primary activity is to denounce Israel, and the motion establishing the commission was an exercise in prejudgment like something out of *Alice in Wonderland*. Introduced by Pakistan on behalf of the Organization of Islamic Cooperation as well as Egypt and Cuba, the resolution instructed the Council's president:

> [T]o dispatch an urgent, independent international fact-finding mission . . . to investigate all violations of international human rights law and international humanitarian law by the occupying Power, Israel, against the Palestinian people . . . due to the current aggression.[28]

It did not authorize any investigation of the behavior of Israel's adversary, Hamas, although on the face of it, Hamas did almost nothing in its violent campaign against Israel other than commit war crimes: it fired thousands of rockets into civilian areas while concealing itself among Gaza's civilian population. To the surprise of no one, this commission's report condemned Israel in the most extreme terms while faulting Hamas scarcely at all.

A group called NGO Monitor pointed out that the Goldstone report's footnotes cited *B'Tselem* more than any other source. By the time Noah Pollak wrote his article in *Commentary* on *B'Tselem*, Goldstone himself had had second thoughts, praising Israel's own investigation of alleged misconduct by its soldiers and declaring, "If I had known then what I know now, the Goldstone report would have been a different document."[29] This left *B'Tselem* in an awkward position since it was so closely associated with Goldstone's original verdict. *B'Tselem*'s executive director, Jessica Montell, now belatedly acknowledged that it had been "impossible to ignore some glaring problems with the report."[30] But *B'Tselem* had said nothing of the kind at the time. And on the most important issue—the kangaroo-court character of the entire Goldstone investigation—it had given the Goldstone Commission an unqualified endorsement, indeed it had lambasted the Israeli government for objecting to the one-sidedness of the commission's composition and mandate. Here are *B'Tselem*'s words on the subject:

> Israel's response was to immediately condemn the report as erroneous, tendentious, and biased. *B'Tselem* rejected these claims, and stated in many forums that the report was the result of a serious, professional investigation, reflecting a deep and genuine commitment to ensure that justice is done.[31]

Even while distancing itself from the Goldstone Report, *B'Tselem* strove gymnastically to prevent that report's harsh critique of Israel from being discredited by the man's own reconsideration. Mantell wrote that "Goldstone's praise of Israel's investigations seems a bit premature" and "by no means absolves Israel of all the grave allegations regarding its conduct."[32]

The activists of *B'Tselem* and public intellectuals like Burg, Benvinisti, and Avnery were not the whole of post-Zionism. A complementary part of this movement appeared in Israeli academia. At its center was a circle of scholars, styling themselves the "new historians," who claimed that the received version of the country's history was false and self-serving. They put forward an alternative account in which the actions of the Jews were far less praiseworthy or even abhorrent. Their work was analogous to that of the "revisionist historians" in the United States, who, inspired by revulsion against the war in Vietnam, rejected traditional American historiography of the Cold War and blamed Washington for the conflict more than Moscow.

The label "new historian" was coined by Benny Morris, the most esteemed of the group, in a 1988 article in the magazine *Tikkun* that instanced recent books by Avi Shlaim, Ilan Pappé, Simcha Flappan, and himself. In explaining why this group differed from its predecessors, Morris mentioned their access to state files from Israel's early years that had been newly opened after a requisite thirty-year waiting period. A second factor, he said, was "the nature" of the new historians, themselves. They had "matured in a more open, doubting, and self-critical Israel than the pre-Lebanon War Israel in which the old historians grew up."[33]* Morris acted out this doubting and self-critical attitude by refusing an order to report for reserve duty

---

* Flappan was a wild card in this deck: older and not engaging in much archival research, he met neither of these criteria.

in the occupied territories that same year, incurring a few weeks in jail for it.

Explaining the difference between the new history and the old, Morris wrote:

> The essence of the old history is that Zionism was a beneficent and well-meaning progressive national movement; that Israel was born pure into an uncharitable, predatory world; that Zionist efforts at compromise and conciliation were rejected by the Arabs; and that Palestine's Arabs, and in their wake the surrounding Arab states, for reasons of innate selfishness, xenophobia and downright cussedness, refused to accede to the burgeoning Zionist presence and in 1947 to 1949 launched a war to extirpate the foreign plant.[34]

The new historians, he said, had "significantly undermine[d], if not thoroughly demolish[ed], a variety of assumptions that helped form the core of the old history."[35] Of the various points that made up this challenge, two were especially salient. One was the matter of which side wanted war and which wanted peace. Morris's allies, Shlaim, Pappé, and Flappan strove to prove that various Arab leaders had wished for peace but the obdurate Jews had spurned their advances and feelers. The other key point was the focus of Morris's own attack on the presumed virtuousness of Zionist intentions and behaviors. In *The Birth of the Palestinian Refugee Problem, 1947–1949*[36] and subsequent works,[37] Morris emphasized deliberate acts of expulsion of Palestinians and various massacres and cruelties by Jewish forces.

Such revelations, he wrote:

> [C]ame as a shock to much of the Israeli public, which was nurtured on a belief in its own moral superiority. . . . When an atrocity nonetheless came to light, it was always dismissed as a rare exception. . . . The truth is otherwise—and not surprisingly. Underlying the series of Arab-Israeli wars has been a deep hatred by each side of the other and deep existential fears, both among Israeli Jews and Palestinian Arabs.[38]

Morris said there were Israeli atrocities in every war with the Arabs, but the first was the worst:

Jewish forces . . . committed far more atrocities in 1948 than did Arab forces if only because they were in a far better position to do so. . . . Massacres apart, 1948 was characterized by a great deal of random killing by Jewish troops of Arab civilians. . . . In retrospect, it is clear that what occurred in 1948 in Palestine was a variety of ethnic cleansing of Arab areas by Jews.[39]

These quotes come from a chapter he contributed to a 1999 compendium on war crimes around the world, in which his indictment of Israel comes across as more fierce than in his own books, perhaps because of the venue or perhaps because his views had hardened.

On the whole, however, Morris was less tendentious than his fellow "new historians," as noted by Ethan Bronner of *The New York Times* in 1999, in a combined review of books by Morris and Avi Shlaim. Whereas Shlaim, said Bronner, was "a historian with a mission and a ready set of judgments" whose "political views are jarringly evident," Morris "writes with clinical dispassion," making him "more responsible and credible."[40]

In crediting Morris with "clinical dispassion," Bronner ignored Morris's own description of the new historians' approach: "How one perceives 1948 bears heavily on how one perceives the whole Zionist/ Israeli experience. If Israel . . . was born pure and innocent, then it was worthy of the grace, material assistance, and political support showered upon it by the West. . . . If, on the other hand, Israel was born tarnished, besmirched by original sin, then it was no[t]."[41]

But Bronner was certainly right in his characterization of Shlaim's "jarring" polemical inclinations. For example, in describing the fear that gripped Israel in the weeks before the Six Day War, Shlaim wrote, "the entire nation succumbed to a collective psychosis."[42] And his most noteworthy work on Arab–Israeli relations came endorsed with a shout of joy from Edward Said: "At last, an unsentimental, demythologized history of Israel's deliberately provocative relationship with the Arabs."[43]

If Morris seemed nonpolitical by comparison with Shlaim, then the same might be said of Shlaim in comparison to the third major "new historian," Ilan Pappé, who interspersed his literary endeavors with campaigns for the Knesset on the Communist ticket and explained in the introduction to one of his books that he writes "from the trenches."[44]

Although Morris was more the historian and less the polemicist than Pappé or Shlaim, still his claim to be doing little more than reporting what was to be found in newly available records did not stand up. Daniel Polisar, editor of *Azure*, citing Morris's references to "ethnic cleansing" and "original sin," argued: "These are not 'facts' that one discovers in recently opened archives [but] profound moral evaluations. . . . Someone else examining the facts Morris presents might easily describe matters differently."[45]

Morris, himself, was soon to prove Polisar's point. Like Alex Yakobson, Benny Morris was rocked by the events of 2000 and their aftermath. In early 2002, he took to the relentlessly anti-Israel pages of *The Guardian* to announce his transformation:

> My thinking about the current Middle East crisis and its protagonists has in fact radically changed during the past two years. I imagine that I feel a bit like one of those western fellow travelers rudely awakened by the trundle of Russian tanks crashing through Budapest in 1956. . . .
>
> It is the Palestinian leadership's rejection of the Barak-Clinton peace proposals of July-December 2000, the launching of the intifada, and the demand ever since that Israel accept the "right of return" that has persuaded me that the Palestinians, at least in this generation, do not intend peace: they do not want merely, an end to the occupation—that is what was offered back in July–December 2000, and they rejected the deal. They want all of Palestine and as few Jews in it as possible.[46]

He explained further in an exchange with *Ha'aretz*'s famous interviewer, Ari Shavit:

> The bombing of the buses and restaurants really shook me. They made me understand the depth of the hatred for us. They made me understand that the Palestinian, Arab and Muslim hostility toward Jewish existence here is taking us to the brink of destruction. I don't see the suicide bombings as isolated acts. They express the deep will of the Palestinian people. That is what the majority of the Palestinians want. They want what happened to the bus to happen to all of us.
>
> There is a deep problem in Islam. It's a world whose values are different. A world in which human life doesn't have the same value as it does in the West, in which freedom, democracy,

openness and creativity are alien. A world that makes those who are not part of the camp of Islam fair game.[47]

Although Morris stood by his earlier books, he did, as Polisar suggested one might, begin to draw different conclusions. Ethnic cleansing? "When the choice is between ethnic cleansing and genocide—the annihilation of your people—I prefer ethnic cleansing. . . . From the moment the [Jewish community in Palestine] was attacked by the Palestinians and afterward by the Arab states, there was no choice but to expel the Palestinian population. . . . in the course of the war."[48] Massacres? "You have to put things in proportion. . . . All told, if we take all the massacres and all the executions of 1948, we come to about 800 . . . killed. . . . When you take into account that there was a bloody civil war here and that we lost an entire 1 percent of the population, you find that we behaved very well."[49]

This reevaluation led Morris toward a sharper sense of the moral urgency of the issues in the Middle East conflict and a new appreciation for the existential dilemma Israel faced:

> We are the greater victims in the course of history and we are also the greater potential victim. Even though we are oppressing the Palestinians, we are the weaker side here. We are a small minority in a large sea of hostile Arabs who want to eliminate us. So it's possible that when their desire is realized, everyone will understand what I am saying to you now. Everyone will understand we are the true victims. But by then it will be too late.[50]

Fellow "new historian" Avi Shlaim did not share Morris's second thoughts perhaps because he did not experience the bus and restaurant bombings of the *intifada* as Morris did. After studying in the United Kingdom in the 1970s, Shlaim had settled there, become a British citizen, and made a career at British universities, his harsh writings about Israel given added cachet by his background. He married the granddaughter of former Prime Minister David Lloyd George, the man most responsible for the Balfour Declaration, which added a curious twist and a news angle to Shlaim's vociferousness on the subject. He calls that document a "colossal blunder" and an "egregious moral failure" on Britain's part. Nonetheless, Shlaim supports Israel's right to exist within its 1967 borders, even though he argues that throughout the history of the Israeli–Arab conflict, the Arabs have sought peace but Israel has rejected it.

In that sense, Shlaim is more moderate than Pappé who calls Zionism a "racist and quite evil philosophy"[51] and who advocates the replacement of Israel by a bi-national, or nonnational, state. He envisions the return of the Palestinian refugees and their descendants to live side by side with the Jews. "What turned me into a great lover of the Palestinians," he said in a 2008 interview, "is the will of many among them to share the land with us. Even people in Hamas."[52] A year earlier, complaining of Haifa University's failure to promote him to full professor and claiming that he was receiving "death threats by phone almost on a daily basis,"[53] he, too, moved to the United Kingdom.

In 2011, the *New Republic* published a lengthy review essay by Morris about three of Pappé's recently published books. Morris clearly no longer saw himself as belonging to the same historical movement as Pappé. His article was titled pointedly, "The Liar as Hero," and it meticulously detailed misrepresentations of evidence. For example, Pappé had written that a British inquiry "reported that the Jewish presence in the country was provoking the Arab population and was the cause of the riots" of 1920. Morris wrote that the report in question had mentioned Arab disquiet at Jewish immigration while saying: "it is perfectly clear that with . . . few exceptions the Jews were the sufferers, and were, moreover, the victims of a peculiarly brutal and cowardly attack, the majority of the casualties being old men, women and children."[54] In short, the balance of British blame-placing was the opposite of what Pappé led his readers to believe. Morris was not the only critic to nail Pappé for dishonesty. Also in 2011, the media-monitoring group, Committee for Accuracy in Middle East Reporting in America (CAMERA), demonstrated convincingly that an incriminating quote Shlaim attributed to Ben-Gurion in a book and an article in the *Journal of Palestine Studies* was an outright fabrication.[55]

With the defection of Morris and the departure of Pappé to join Shlaim in the United Kingdom, the era of the "new historians" had drawn to a close. But it left a deep impact in Israel and outside. Writing in 2000, Daniel Polisar listed prestigious publications that had reviewed the original revisionist works of these three historians, all published in 1988, concluding that they had been "the most widely-discussed books on Israel to appear in the English-speaking world in the past decade."[56] In 1998 when Israel's National Broadcasting Authority sponsored a twenty-one-part documentary series on the country's history in commemoration of its fiftieth anniversary, its account of the events of 1948 leaned heavily on the work of the "new historians." In 1999, a new ninth-grade history textbook was introduced that did the same so pointedly that it was withdrawn a year or two later. Nonetheless, the school curriculum was revised "to teach history from a universal (as opposed to national) perspective," according to the only scholarly account in English.[57] Shlaim could accurately boast that "the new history . . . influenced the way the subject is taught in Israeli schools."[58]

The theme and spirit of the "new historians"—to hold the standard Zionist/Israeli narrative up to critical scrutiny, and the more critical the better—not only infected other disciplines, it echoed throughout Israeli intellectual life. As the celebrated historian, Anita Shapira, put it:

> The revisionist dispute quickly spilled over from history into sociology and cultural studies, as new topics and new heresies were added to those that treated the War of Independence and the relation to the Palestinians: the pre-state Jewish community in Palestine and its conduct during the Holocaust, the absorption of Holocaust survivors and Oriental Jewish immigrants, and so on. No longer were particular Zionist or Israeli figures impugned; Zionist ideology as a whole was now the real culprit. Several of the new school's devotees labeled themselves "post-Zionist," and charged that the "lunatic" ambition of Jews to transform themselves into a people with a state of their own was senseless, and opposed to the natural inclinations of the Jews. They claimed that the Jews had never been a people until the Zionists muddled their thinking, and had no desire for nationhood. Post-Zionism turned out to be a peculiar form of anti-Zionism.[59]

Of course, this did not come about in a vacuum. It also reflected the post-1960s rise of Leftism throughout academia in American and Europe. Benny Morris argued that although the "new historians" were influential in this respect,

> Even more important, probably, was the integration of Israeli academia into the intellectually open university life of the West. By the early 2000s, departments of political science, sociology,

Hebrew literature, and cultural studies in some Israeli universities had become bulwarks of anti-Zionism, in which professing Zionists can barely achieve a toehold, let alone tenure. And the history departments and the Middle East studies departments are also far from being redoubts of Zionism.[60]

Sociology is the discipline most deeply shaped by this post-Zionist spirit. Morris notes that the school calling itself "critical sociology" had become dominant in that discipline even before the rise of the "new history." In 2010 the Institute for Zionist Strategies, an NGO with a conservative bent, conducted a study of sociology curricula at Israeli universities, categorizing assigned readings as either "Zionist" or "post-Zionist." It found that the latter exceeded the former by a ratio of three-to-one.[61] Interestingly, the study attributed this bias in part to "the rise of a generation of post-Zionist researchers who follow the teaching of the senior academic . . . Oren Yiftachel." A "political geographer," rather than a sociologist, Yiftachel was the chairman of *B'Tselem* and a signer of the Olga Statement, the advertisement supporting Tali Fahima, and numerous other anti-Zionist circular letters.

Daniel Polisar worries about the impact of the residue of the new history on Israeli society. "No nation can retain its vitality if its entire historical narrative comes to be seen in the public mind as a long series of moral failings compounded by errors of judgment," he writes.[62] However warranted this concern, there is also the impact abroad. The new historians write less in Hebrew than in English, today's global *lingua franca*, and the Internet places their observations on the screens of literally millions, to judge from a Google search. Have a condemnatory point you wish to make about Israel? You can probably buttress it with a pithy quote from an Israeli scholar—whether based on careful scholarship or not.

An even richer source of ammunition for Israel's critics, fair-minded and otherwise, is the Israeli press. In the battle for international public opinion, Israel earns credit for being a democracy. But it also suffers the vulnerabilities of a democracy, meaning that it boasts a free press that washes the nation's dirty linen in public. Stories in the Western press that put Israel in a bad light quite often flow from leads that foreign correspondents pick up in the Israeli press. This is as it should be, but the problem for Israel is that there is no comparable independent investigatory spirit to be found in the highly censored (and self-censored) Palestinian news media to balance the picture.

Israel's vulnerability in this respect is compounded by the fact that its most prestigious paper, the one that comes tucked inside the *International Herald Tribune*, the one read most by foreign journalists, is *Ha'aretz*. Like *The New York Times* or *Le Monde*, its stance is left-of-center, but more so, and *Ha'aretz* is more politically engaged—like, say, a cross between *The Times* and the leftist magazine, *The Nation*. *The New Yorker*'s David Remnick calls *Ha'aretz* approvingly, "easily the most liberal newspaper in Israel and arguably the most important liberal institution in [the] country."[63]

That *Ha'aretz* is critical of the government is an old story: Remnick recalls that "Golda Meir once said that the only government that *Ha'aretz* ever supported was the British mandate." But since the early 1990s when management of the paper was assumed by Amos Schocken it has moved further to the left.

Although it produces much serious journalism and carries a range of commentary, its distinct coloration is provided by the writings of Gideon Levy, Amira Hass, and Akiva Eldar who contribute opinion columns as well as news reports in which their opinions are also evident. Remnick portrays Levy, for instance, as someone who "enjoys a kind of leather-jacket roué glamour in Tel Aviv and on the foreign lecture circuit." Levy boasts that "Noam Chomsky once wrote to me that I was like the early Jewish prophets."[64] But whereas the prophets' hallmark was righteousness, and their goal was to summon Israel back to the true path, Levy's hallmark is self-righteousness, and the Israel he describes is beyond redemption.

He numbers himself among "the lone few keeping the flickering flame of humanity burning" in the country, who for their pains are "accused, convicted and punished."[65] Naturally, he rages against the political Right; but its members are not alone in villainy. "The political 'center' is hollow and imaginary," he writes. "The damage they do is no less serious . . . ; they are accomplices to a crime."[66] Israelis, he believes, are suffused with "racism." If they reject this characterization, that is only because "most Israelis . . . are masters of the lie, denial and repression." They "deflect their fears and woes onto the foreigner. . . . That's how it was in Europe in the 1930s, and that's how it is with us now."

Israel, in other words, is reminiscent of Nazi Germany. And if the country appears to be a democracy, it is so only against the wishes of the public. Levy believes that what Israelis really want is to live in George Orwell's *1984*:

> Let us imagine the dream-country of most Israelis—without criticism, neither from within nor from without. It speaks in one voice and is eternally united, with devotion and cohesion; all-Jewish, that goes without saying. It stands unanimously behind its government. . . . There [are] no human rights organizations or peace movements, no nonprofit associations and no critical reports that are published here, or, heaven forbid, abroad. Its press never criticizes, never exposes, never investigates, publishing nothing but praise and admiration for the government and the state.[67]

The pro-Israeli media-monitoring group CAMERA has documented numerous factual errors in Levy's reporting—for example, tripling the number of Palestinian casualties on one occasion; halving the number of Israeli victims on another; characterizing Hezbollah fighters as "civilians" on another; and so on.[68] Late in 2012, Levy embarrassed himself and his newspaper with a story that, in his telling, confirmed his dark take on Israelis. *Ha'aretz* carried a page one headline: "Survey: Most Israeli Jews Support an Apartheid Regime in Israel."[69]

According to Levy's report, 58 percent of Israeli Jews "already believe that Israel practices apartheid," even while a large majority says it is satisfied with life in Israel. Most glaringly, "69 percent objects to giving . . . Palestinians the right to vote if Israel annexes the West Bank." This was the essence of the South African system: blacks were citizens but not allowed to vote. Levy expounded on his article in an accompanying column titled, "Apartheid Without Shame or Guilt." Here he gave full throat to his "prophetic" voice. This survey, he said,

> [L]ays bare an image of Israeli society, and the picture is a very, very sick one. Now it is not just critics at home and abroad, but Israelis themselves who are openly, shamelessly, and guiltlessly defining themselves as nationalistic racists. We're racists, the Israelis are saying, we practice apartheid and we even want to live in an apartheid state.[70]

Weaknesses in the story began to be exposed within a day of its appearance, but not before Levy's version had been echoed in the

European press. For one thing, the poll had been commissioned and designed by a Leftist advocacy group. (When asked about the poll's being ideologically driven, a spokesman replied: "So let the Right do its own poll to refute the results."[71]) What was problematic about this was that the questions used the word "apartheid" in an unusual way. The pollster acknowledged that the term appeared to be insufficiently understood by respondents. But, more importantly, the critical finding that 69 percent would deny Palestinians the vote if the West Bank were annexed to Israel was reported without its concomitant finding that respondents opposed any such annexation.

This could be readily inferred from their responses about annexing Israeli settlements. The real news in the poll was that a plurality of respondents said they were against this although every Israeli government has said that at least some would be annexed to Israel in any peace deal with the Palestinians. If a plurality opposed annexing *settlements*, a small slice of the West Bank inhabited by Israelis, then an overwhelming majority, had they been asked, would have opposed annexing the entire West Bank, which is inhabited mostly by Arabs. But respondents were not asked this question. Instead, the poll posed the hypothetical question whether, *in the event of annexation of the entire West Bank*, they would favor giving Palestinians the vote. Sixty-nine percent said no. Since annexation would mean that Jews would overnight become a minority, this implied nothing more than an unwillingness to live under Arab rule. It was, in short, a meaningless exercise.

The activist group that designed the poll had received key support from the New Israel Fund (NIF), a left-leaning philanthropy that draws prestige from the large sums of money it distributes and from serving as the channel for the Ford Foundation in Israel. The NIF hastened to disown both the poll and the group that sponsored it, and its spokesman took to the popular US Internet newszine *The Daily Beast* within a day after the *Ha'aretz* story broke to say that Levy's account "seems to amount to a misrepresentation of the data. The poll actually shows that Israelis want to separate themselves from the West Bank."[72]

Although Levy's view of Israel is extremely harsh, it is matched by that of *Ha'aretz*'s leading correspondent from the Palestinian territories, Amira Hass. She has chosen to make her home among the Palestinians for the better part of two decades, three years in Gaza, the balance in Ramallah. In a profile in *The Independent*, the sharply anti-Israel correspondent, Robert Fisk, enthused: "Amira Hass is among the bravest of reporters, her daily column in Ha'aretz ablaze with indignation at the way her own country, Israel, is mistreating and killing the Palestinians. Only when you meet her, however, do you realize the intensity—the passion—of her work."[73]

The passion, as she explains in a Gaza memoir, was imbibed with her mother's milk: "My parents' memories [were] told to me since my childhood and absorbed by me until they became my own, . . . Holocaust survivors, Communists, southeastern European Jews living in Israel, . . . My parents' heroes were my heroes; the scenes engraved on their memories were stored in mine."[74] Her mother was sent to Bergen-Belsen, and Hass sees some kind of analogy in the plight of the Palestinians.[75]

Hass's use of the expression "southeastern European Jews living in Israel," rather than, say, "Romanian-born Israelis" is not accidental. Her parents, by her account, remained unchanged in their politics, and their refusal to embrace their new land was obvious enough to be grasped by Amira by age five. That was when she says she asked them "why they had come to Israel; after all, they had never been Zionists."[76] Even as the world changed, they apparently never reconsidered their ideological position—and she has remained as faithful to it as they. She told Remnick in 2011: "I was what you call a 'red-diaper baby.' My tribe is Leftists, not liberal Zionists." And, as if to underscore the constancy of her views, she added a gratuitous swipe at a leading symbol of the Israeli peace movement. "David Grossman [a celebrated Israeli novelist and peace activist] and the rest are always waking up too late. That is their hallmark—understanding too late."[77]

Perhaps Hass's contempt for Israeli peace activists, even of the Left, is explained by her belief in violence. In 2013, the morning after a Palestinian was convicted of the murder of a twenty-five-year-old Israeli and his one-year-old son by throwing a large stone through the windshield of their car, causing a fatal crash, Hass published a column asserting that "throwing stones [at Israelis] is the birthright and duty" of Palestinians. This right, although perhaps not the duty, belonged, she went on, not only to Palestinians living in the West Bank and Gaza, "but also within Israel's recognized borders." Such exercises in conscientious violence occurred too seldom, lamented Hass, because of insufficient encouragement by Palestinian officials

due to "inertia, laziness, flawed reasoning, misunderstanding and
. . . personal gains."[78]

While faulting their leaders for inadequate commitment to militancy, Hass expresses profound admiration for Palestinians. She
contrasts them invidiously to Israelis:

> The Palestinians are heroes, . . . To live this way and remain
> sane—that's heroism. . . . [T]he Israeli dictatorship over the
> Palestinians . . . is the champion of self-righteousness and arro-
> gance [and] hypocrisy . . . Instead of going crazy with rage, the
> Palestinians know that these characteristics will hurt the Is-
> raelis themselves. Anyone who has been harmed by the Israeli
> dictatorship feels alone, weak, angry and desperate. But every
> [Palestinian] family in its own way cultivates its humanity.[79]

Every family? Given the hundreds of documented cases of "honor
killings"; of murders of accused "collaborators"; of killings and torture of Fatah members by Hamas and vice versa; given, too, the notorious brutality of the Palestinian security forces; the lionization
of suicide bombers and others who take the lives of Israeli civilians;
and the mass, spontaneous demonstrations of joy over the news of
the attacks on America of September 11, 2001—given, in short, the
abundant displays of egregious inhumanity, one can only conclude
that Hass sees what she wants to see or what her ideological blind-
ers lead her to see. This is not a good qualification for a journalist.
Unsurprisingly, Hass's reports have been challenged many times on
the facts, often for taking questionable assertions from the Palestinian side at face value.[80]

Hass and Levy's colleague, Akiva Eldar, the third of *Ha'aretz*'s ex-
emplars, was accused of such bias, but rather than denying it, he
reveled in it. In an article in *The Nation* in 2008, he cited a column
by Nahum Barnea, written during the second *intifada* when two
Israelis were lynched in Ramallah. Barnea, Israel's most respected
columnist, had taken the *Ha'aretz* trio to task for failing the "lynch
test"—that is, he said they were unable to condemn Palestinian actions unambiguously, even when they lynched Israelis. Barnea had
likened their devotion to the Palestinian cause to 1920s American
Communist John Reed's deep devotion to Bolshevism, saying their
support for it was "absolute," adding, "it does not derive from feelings about human rights but instead other motives. Some are pris-

oners of love of Palestine. Some of their hatred of Zion. . . . They have a mission."[81]

Eldar recapitulated Barnea's accusation against himself and his two colleagues, and replied: "I admit to being guilty as charged. I am a journalist with a mission, and also no small amount of passion. Every Israeli with a conscience, in particular one who watches reality from up close on a daily basis, cannot write about the occupation from an objective observer's neutral point of view."[82]

One of Eldar's recurrent themes is to liken Israeli practices to South Africa's apartheid. In 2004, when Prime Minister Ariel Sharon announced plans for Israel's withdrawal from Gaza and the northern West Bank, Eldar wrote: "South Africa will be very interested in the Israeli . . . plan for the Gaza Strip and the enclave in the northern West Bank [which is] amazingly similar to the homelands, one of the last inventions of the white minority in South Africa to perpetuate its rule over the black majority."[83] In 2010, he wrote, "It is hard to find differences between white rule in South Africa and Israeli rule in the territories."[84] And in 2012: "In the territory under Israel's jurisdiction a situation of apartheid exists. A Jewish minority rules over an Arab majority."[85]

Eldar also boasts that: "John Mearsheimer and Stephen Walt cite me in their controversial book, *The Israel Lobby*, as one of the Israeli journalists whose criticism of the occupation is even sharper than their own."[86] Walt and Mearsheimer's book argued that American policy toward the Middle East was manipulated to Israel's advantage and America's disadvantage by the machinations of an immensely powerful "Lobby." The idea that America's support for Israel was the result of excessive and shrouded Jewish power was a familiar theme in the fever swamps of politics, but the imprimatur of esteemed professors at Harvard (Walt) and University of Chicago (Mearsheimer) gave it a whole new force. To top it off, Walt and Mearsheimer accused American Jews holding high office of using their positions for Israel's benefit. And what authority did they cite for this? None other than Akiva Eldar. They quoted his 2002 column charging that Richard Perle, then chairman of the Pentagon's defense planning board, and Douglas Feith, the undersecretary of defense, "are walking a fine line between their loyalty to American governments . . . and Israeli interests."[87]

Although Walt and Mersheimer's book, *The Israel Lobby*, sold enough copies to make them rich, it generally received harsh reviews in the American press, including from papers that are often critical of Israeli policy. *The New York Times Book Review*, the daily *New York Times* (and *International Herald Tribune*), *The Washington Post*, the *Los Angeles Times*, *The Wall Street Journal*, and *Foreign Affairs*, among others, gave it bad notices. Most did not shy from saying that the book exuded the aroma of anti-Semitism even if it was not overtly anti-Semitic. For example, *The Washington Post*: "Mearsheimer and Walt have provided required reading for Jew-haters worldwide . . . [They] supply intellectual legitimacy to a blatantly slanted, inherently biased worldview."[88] Or, *The New York Times Book Review*: "No one . . . ever accused them of harboring anti-Semitic sentiments . . . until [now]. But . . . 'they asked for trouble'—by the way they make their arguments, by their puzzlingly shoddy scholarship, by what they emphasize and de-emphasize, by what they leave out and by writing on this sensitive topic without doing extensive interviews with the lobbyists and the lobbied."[89]

One paper, however, that gave it a favorable review was *Ha'aretz*. In fact it did so twice. The first time came before the book appeared when Walt and Mearsheimer's theories were published in a "white paper," prompting this sharp response from Johns Hopkins University's usually circumspect Professor Eliot A. Cohen:

> If by anti-Semitism one means obsessive and irrationally hostile beliefs about Jews; if one accuses them of disloyalty, subversion or treachery, of having occult powers and of participating in secret combinations that manipulate institutions and governments; if one systematically selects everything unfair, ugly or wrong about Jews as individuals or a group and equally systematically suppresses any exculpatory information—why, yes, this paper is anti-Semitic.[90]

Ha'aretz came to the rescue of the two authors with an op ed by Daniel Levy, a leftist Israeli expatriate living in the United States, that defended the "white paper" and attacked its critics.[91] When the book came out a year later and received even more biting reviews, *Ha'aretz* went back to Levy, giving him three thousand–plus words to amplify his polemic against Walt and Mearsheimer's critics and to render this summary judgment: "This is a difficult and challenging book. It is also an important book that deserves to be keenly debated."[92]

Ha'aretz does run guest op eds from a range of opinions including those contrary to its editorial position, and it even has some regular columnists from the Right side of the spectrum. But these are not sufficient to counter its dominant thrust. *The New Yorker's* David Remnick quotes a member of the paper's staff joshing that regular contributors Moshe Arens, a former Likud defense minister, and Israel Harel, once the leader of the settlers' movement, serve as *Ha'aretz's* "shabbos goys" (gentiles hired to turn on lights on the Sabbath when observant Jews are forbidden from doing it).

Opinion columns are one thing, reportage should be another. *Ha'aretz* continues to hold a leading position as a news source even though the same passionate positions given voice by Eldar, Hass, and Levy also color its coverage of events. The page-one treatment of Levy's misrepresentation of the dubious "apartheid poll" was one example. Another example was a 2009 *Ha'aretz* exposé of alleged war crimes by Israeli soldiers during the 2008–2009 war in Gaza.

As with Levy on the "apartheid poll," a single journalist reported the story in the news pages, and simultaneously offered commentary in the opinion section. In this case the journalist was Amos Harel (not to be confused with Rightist columnist Israel Harel). "Israeli forces killed Palestinian civilians under permissive rules of engagement and intentionally destroyed their property, say soldiers who fought in the offensive," read Harel's lead.[93] The accounts came from a group of soldiers who gathered at the invitation of the head of a preinduction military academy who had recorded and then leaked their recollections. Naturally, the story echoed throughout the international news media with the help of *The New York Times* which picked it up the next day on its own front page.[94]

In his opinion piece that accompanied the news story, Harel assured readers that, "the soldiers are not lying, for the simple reason that they have no reason to."[95] And he drew a broad generalization from their accounts: "It seems that what the soldiers have to say is actually the way things happened in the field, most of the time."

The next day, along with more excerpts from the soldiers' discussion, *Ha'aretz* ran a second opinion piece by Harel, this one criticizing the army for revealing that the man who had organized, recorded, and leaked the soldiers' meeting had once served a month's military imprisonment for refusing an order to guard a religious ritual by settlers in the West Bank—and might have an ideological ax to grind. In addition, a military spokesman reported that the soldier who had recounted the most explosive incident—the deliberate shooting of a mother and two children—had been summoned by his brigade commander to whom he explained that he had heard of such an event but had not witnessed it. Harel suggested that the army was remiss in releasing this information, and he took a shot at other news outlets for reporting it. "It is disappointing—if not surprising—to see the enthusiasm with which major news outlets adopted IDF claims."[96]Apparently trying now to bolster its case, *Ha'aretz* carried another Harel story two days later, headlined "Testimonies on IDF Misconduct in Gaza Keep Rolling In," but the article cited no testimony whatsoever, only quotes from a film clip of a blustery pre-action security briefing and Harel's own assertion that "a number of officers told *Ha'aretz* . . . that the testimonies [in the original report] did not surprise them."[97] The officers were not named.

Twelve days after its first revelation, *Ha'aretz* reported that the military had completed its formal investigation and concluded that the reports of killings were all based on rumor. What had made the story sensational was the report that soldiers had confessed to egregious misconduct or said they had witnessed it, but there turned out not to have been a single case of that from this group.

Even a couple of days before the military investigation ended, *The New York Times* had run a lengthy story intended to counterbalance its initial report, recalling the accusations and revealing the questions that had arisen about the soldiers' claims. *Ha'aretz* did not run anything similar, although it did carry a moving piece by correspondent Anshel Pfeffer, making clear his own anguish when the paper's stories damage Israel's international standing. Noting that the paper had "never made a secret of its opposition to the occupation," he explained that "for the last 40 years, *Ha'aretz* has seen the promotion of this debate as its central role."[98]

The slant of *Ha'aretz* was exemplified by David Landau who edited the paper's English edition starting in 1997 and then the Hebrew from 2004 until 2008. In 2005, when the media-monitoring group CAMERA e-mailed *Ha'aretz* to request that it correct Amira Hass's references to "Jewish-only roads" in the West Bank, an assistant editor inadvertently sent back a message that had been intended for internal circulation at the paper. The misdirected e-mail read, "We have a quasi 'policy,' on orders of David [Landau], to ignore this organization and all of its complaints, including not responding to telephone messages and screening calls from [its] director."[99] Once this slip brought it out in the open, Landau justified his position by claiming that CAMERA had a "vendetta." But, even if this were so, and there is no evidence that it was, the issue was whether or not CAMERA's complaints were valid. It this case, for example, it clearly was. Hass's reference was false and defamatory. Due to terrorist attacks, some West Bank roads were restricted to cars with Israeli plates, but these were open to all Israelis including Arabs and other gentiles. There were no "Jewish-only" roads. Barring Palestinian vehicles from certain arteries may have been harsh, but it was not racist as Hass wanted readers to believe.

Landau caused a stir in 2007 when fellow journalists revealed, and Landau later confirmed, that he had told Secretary of State Condoleezza Rice at a private dinner that Israel was a "failed state" that needed to be "raped" by the United States in order to make peace with the Palestinians.[100] Landau also vented his dim assessment of Israel in a 2010 column, saying: "Israel has slid almost inadvertently a long way down the slope that leads to McCarthyism and racism."[101] Going even farther, he added, "as history, both ancient and more recent, teaches us, there is another component in the inculcation of a whole society with xenophobia. It's the big lie." By ancient history, he explained he meant Pharaoh; the reference to "recent" history was left unexplained, but the term "big lie" is associated with the Nazi regime.

The person responsible for *Ha'aretz's* adversarial stance toward Israel was not, however, Landau but rather the paper's owner, Amos Schocken. He had inherited *Ha'aretz* from his father and grandfather, and the legacy seems to have included an ambivalent relationship with the Jewish state. His grandfather, Salman, who had fled from Germany to Palestine, had been, according to David Remnick, a supporter of *Brit Shalom*, an organization of Jews favoring a bi-national state rather than a Jewish one. Salman bequeathed the paper to his son, Gershom (nee Gustav), who once wrote an essay about the need to remove the religious prohibition on intermarriage so as to encourage the emergence of a homogeneous Israeli nationality to supersede those of Jew and Arab.[102] This seems to have been regarded as a kind of signature idea, since *Ha'aretz* chose to reprint it as a memorial to him on the twentieth anniversary of Gershom's death in 1990 when the paper passed to his son, Amos, who has given it editorial direction ever since.

Occasionally, Amos Schocken contributes his own opinion pieces, such as a 2007 column that commemorated Israel's sixtieth anniversary by urging that it replace its national anthem, *Hatikvah*, because it speaks of the Jewish people's longing for Zion and thus is impossible for "an Arab citizen [to] identify with."[103] In 2011, he devoted a lengthy column to the problem of "Israeli apartheid," which he said, doubling down on his paper's defiant support for Walt and Mearsheimer, was shielded by "the power of the Jewish lobby" in the United States.[104]

Schocken's main impact, however, comes from his management, not his writing. The first editor he chose was Hanoch Marmari. Yoram Hazony had sharply criticized Marmari as a post-Zionist, but the second *intifada* evoked a patriotic response in Marmari that set him and Schocken apart. As bombs slaughtered Israelis in buses and pizzerias, Marmari shaped coverage sensitive to the national mood of outrage, prompting Schocken to complain, as he himself put it, that his editor was "taking too much account of the readers."[105] Marmari's take on their rift was similar: "Amos was displeased because I was less radical than him. I felt the paper might derail itself to the point of irrelevancy."[106] Marmari was fired and replaced by Landau, who seemed akin to Schocken in his radicalism. But even Landau in the end proved not radical enough. He explained to Remnick:

> You don't have to soft-pedal your stance on the kind of racism or xenophobia or fascistic trends that are worryingly engulfing parts of Israeli society, but you can do it without casting yourself as antagonistic. There is a need in the paper's rhetoric for a greater sophistication and empathy. The goal is to make the newspaper a place where people are being challenged but are also made to feel welcome.[107]

Landau was replaced in 2011, but this time Schocken did not look for someone even more radical. Rather he promoted one of the paper's longtime reporters, Aluf Benn, who did not have as sharp an ideological profile as his predecessors. If Schocken intended by this appointment to signal a change in the direction of *Ha'aretz*, that has not been apparent in the paper's pages. Perhaps he concluded that he could set the tone as publisher without needing an equally opinionated editor.

Schocken and Eldar and Hass and Levy and Biletzki and Yiftachel and Montell and Avnery and Shlaim and Pappé and Benvenisti and Burg and others of their ilk are not merely critics of Israeli policy.

Nor are they like the original Peace Now marchers who feared understandably that Begin's attachment to the idea of historic Israel could cause him to squander the opportunity for peace with Egypt. Rather, they constitute an Israeli version of the "adversary culture" that challenges the foundational legitimacy of the state itself. Some do so explicitly; others by implication. If Israel's actions are as malign as they say, then what right does it have to exist? The question matters because unlike any other state, Israel's existence is under perpetual challenge in word and deed. For those who wish to rally people to the cause of Israel's destruction, these alienated Israelis constitute an unmatched resource. They provide a trove of homegrown testimony that their country is guilty of every imaginable crime and sin. Want to liken Israel to South Africa under apartheid? It is a hard case to make, but here is the publisher of the country's leading newspaper affirming that it is so. Want to compare Israelis to Nazis? Who can say that this is a vile and absurd slander when the officers of Israel's leading human rights group, *B'Tselem*, say the same? America's adversary culture was no less extreme in its alienation, no less ferocious in its condemnations of its own country. But America, the mightiest country in history, is comparatively invulnerable to the words of its detractors. The same cannot be said for Israel.

ten

On the Wrong Side of the Left's New Paradigm

> *I must walk with care*
> *As I wander in the wood*
> *That I may crush no flower beneath my shoes.*[1]

This poem was written by the American anti-Israel activist Rachel Corrie when she was ten or eleven. In another she wrote with precious angst: "My dream is to stop hunger by the year 2000."[2] The thought of hungry children was not her only torment. "I worry about the whales dying, about the ozone layer depleting, about the trees being cut down."[3] This was quite a burden of care and compassion in a child scarcely into puberty. "She was as soft as a petal," wrote a eulogist in the *Los Angeles Times* on Corrie's death at age twenty-three.[4]

In bitter irony, Rachel herself turned out to be a flower that was crushed—by an armored Israeli military bulldozer whose path she was attempting to block in the town of Rafah which straddles the border between the Gaza Strip and the Sinai. Her colleagues later explained that they feared the bulldozer aimed to demolish the home of a family with whom Rachel had stayed during part of her two months in this war zone. Israel did at times knock down the homes of terrorists, a method of deterrence or collective punishment that was later abandoned. But there was no reason to believe that Rachel's host family was targeted for such retribution, and according to Israeli records the bulldozer's mission was simply to clear undergrowth and debris that could shield Palestinian fighters and the tunnels through which they smuggled arms from Egypt. It was March 2003, and the second *intifada* was raging.

This was not the first time Rachel had played "bulldozer cowgirl," as she insouciantly termed it. But this was no game. The toll of Israeli lives taken in the *intifada* was rising toward its eventual total of more than one thousand; and the toll of Palestinians was several times that. Rafah was one of the most violent spots. Since its outbreak Israeli soldiers had counted "some 6,000 hand grenades thrown at them in the area, as well as 1,400 shooting attacks, 150 explosive devices, 200 anti-tank rockets and more than 40 instances of mortar fire," as was noted in the Israeli court's verdict dismissing the lawsuit Rachel's parents filed against the state.[5] Indeed, one grenade was tossed at a bulldozer less than an hour before Rachel's death.[6]

It is possible that Rachel did not fully grasp that she was performing a military function by obstructing bulldozers trying to clear a strip of land to deny Palestinian fighters cover from which to shoot and camouflage under which to import weapons. But it is less likely that the more senior figures of the International Solidarity Movement (ISM), the group for which she was acting, were similarly innocent. Founded within months of the start of the second *intifada*, the ISM touted nonviolent protest, but it did not see this as a moral imperative, rather as a smart tactic that would complement violent action while claiming a moral high ground.

ISM leaders and publications made clear that the group blessed the shedding of blood. Under the heading "who we are" the ISM website proclaimed: "we recognize the Palestinian right to resist . . . via legitimate armed struggle."[7] This formula has been repeated in resolutions of Arab and Muslim states and resolutions of the UN General Assembly so often that everyone understands that "legitimate armed struggle" is a euphemism for suicide bombings and other attacks on Israeli civilians.*

The ISM website also carries reports and musings by the group's

---

* For this very reason, the UN has found itself unable to agree on a "comprehensive convention on international terrorism," despite the appointment of a drafting committee as far back as 1997 and the determined efforts of Secretary General Kofi Annan in 2004 and 2005 to bring these deliberations to fruit. Annan exhorted: "the right to resist occupation . . . cannot include the right to deliberately kill or maim civilians." But his position was defeated. What prevailed was the view expressed by the Pakistani delegate in 2004: "We ought not, in our desire to confront terrorism, erode the principle of the legitimacy of national resistance." ("UN Approves Anti-Terrorism Initiative," *Washington Post*, October 9, 2004, p. A26.) See p. 76.

members embedded in Palestinian communities in the West Bank and Gaza. In one, the volunteer "Ewa" reported that she was staying in the home of a "martyr family [whose] son went and opened fire on some Israeli civilians in a market somewhere." She criticized "the lad" for not thinking about "S-T-R-A-T-G-Y" while hastening to add:

> I understand it's about attacking [Israeli] civilian life the way [Palestinian] civilian life has been crushed . . . under the occupation [but] I don't get why activists can't go and do the Knesset . . . or do a sophisticated politician bump-off like the PFLP [which gunned down cabinet member Rehavam Zeevi in a Jerusalem hotel].[8]

Nor was "Ewa" the only ISM activist to muse about which Israelis it was okay to kill. The group's cofounder, Adam Shapiro, was interviewed by Lebanon's respected newspaper, *The Daily Star*, which reported: "he justifies the Palestinian armed resistance against Israel as long as it is targeting Israeli soldiers and Jewish settlers. . . . Otherwise, he is not in favor of suicide bombings."[9]

Other ISM leaders expressed sympathy for suicide bombing, albeit not approval. Paul Larudee, a prominent ISM figure, wrote on the group's site about living with the widow of a bomber to prevent Israeli forces from demolishing the home. Larudee asked himself why "Amer" had become a suicide bomber, and ventured this answer: "It may have been the strong sense of moral right and wrong, of justice and injustice, that his parents instilled in him." Larudee acknowledged that suicide bombings constitute a "war crime," but unlike Israel whose "war crimes" in Larudee's view were countless and inexcusable, Amer's act was born of desperation, the response of "a resilient people without other means of resistance."[10]

Adam Shapiro, an American of Jewish background, and the ISM's other principal founder, Huwaida Arraf, an Arab American (the two later wed), explained in detail their view of nonviolent activism in a 2002 article in *Palestine Chronicle*: "While we do not advocate adopting the methods of Gandhi or Martin Luther King, Jr., we do believe that learning from their experience and informing a Palestinian movement with this knowledge can be quite valuable and of great utility." Thus, they urged "the use of nonviolence as a strategic element of . . . a larger Intifada." Nonviolent action, they said "is no less noble than carrying out a suicide operation. And we are certain that if [people are] killed during such an action, they would be considered shaheed Allah [i.e., martyrs]." To those with doubts about the effectiveness of nonviolence, they readily conceded that no "success-ful nonviolent movement was able to achieve what it did without a concurrent violent movement." For this reason, they urged a two-pronged strategy: "the Palestinian resistance must take on a variety of characteristics—both nonviolent and violent."[11]

The ISM's words are intentionally slippery, but a number of its actions underscore its affinity with anti-Israel violence. In 2002, Shapiro had raised his profile by holing up with Yasser Arafat inside the Palestinian leader's Ramallah headquarters when Israel, blam-ing Arafat for starting or at least encouraging the violent second *intifada*, besieged it. Some seventy ISM members lay down in front of the Israeli tanks, and the ISM's spokeswoman said, "We are here today to support the Palestinian legitimate right to resist." This last was a rather cold-blooded declaration coming as it did just days after three Palestinians had ambushed a bus near the settlement town of Emmanuel with roadside bombs, then sprayed the passengers with grenades and gunfire, leaving eleven dead and thirty wounded. Not long after this episode, several dozen armed Palestinian fight-ers took refuge in Bethlehem's Church of the Nativity, where Israeli forces felt constrained from following lest they be blamed for dam-age to Jesus's birthplace. So they resorted to besieging the church, hoping the militants within would eventually yield. The ISM worked to assist the gunmen and defeat the siege. As Arraf explained to Paula Zahn on CNN: "we . . . got the food inside . . . we also put inter-national activists inside in the hopes of providing an international civilian shield, if you will."[12]

In 2003, a local leader of Islamic Jihad fleeing Israeli arrest for masterminding various terror acts sought to hide in the ISM head-quarters in Jenin where he was eventually taken into custody. On its website, the ISM denies having been complicit with the man, say-ing that all it did was to give him "a change of clothes, a hot drink and a blanket" because he arrived "soaking wet, shivering and terri-fied."[13] Also in 2003, two British Muslims stopped at an ISM apart-ment in Rafah for tea and chat before joining several ISM volunteers at a memorial meeting for Rachel Corrie. They then went on to carry out a suicide bombing at Mike's Place, a Tel Aviv bar, but the ISM says it had only that one-time contact with the two.[14] The group's website also responds to a photo circulated on the Internet showing four ISM volunteers brandishing Kalashnikovs by explaining, "At the time the photographs were taken, these individuals had not yet become ISM volunteers."[15]

In 2008, another ISM volunteer, Richard David Hupper, was sentenced to 42 months in US federal prison for violating the ban on support for groups on the US terrorism list after "he admitted to giving about $20,000 to Hamas while working in Israel with the International Solidarity Movement," according to a report in the Hanover, Pennsylvania, *Evening Sun*.[16] In the same year, ISM leader Paul Larudee traveled to Gaza where he accepted a medal from Ismail Haniyeh, the Hamas-designated prime minister of Palestine, and had himself photographed—the gold medallion hanging from a ribbon around his neck—seated with Haniyeh at a banquet.[17]

In short, the ISM shows different faces at different moments or to different audiences. Thus, cofounder Arraf boasted of providing "an international civilian shield" to the gunmen in the Church of the Nativity, but a year later, in the wake of Rachel Corrie's death, declared at an ISM press conference in Jerusalem: "ISM activists are NOT [sic] human shields."[18] At the same press conference, Arraf also declared, "We're . . . not pro-Palestinian. . . . We are pro-freedom." But the year before she justified the ISM's refusal to work with Israeli peace groups by telling an interviewer, "this movement is a Palestinian movement."[19] To American audiences ISM often invoked the legacy of Gandhi and King, but as we have seen, in their *Palestine Chronicle* article, Shapiro and Arraf went out of their way to dissociate themselves from the methods of those two men. Likewise, ISM representatives often describe themselves as "peace activists," even while condoning Palestinian violence and spurning cooperation with the Israeli peace movement, a stance Shapiro explained this way: "the focus of most Israeli peace groups is different than ours. Ultimately, the focus of ISM is peace, but in the immediate, our focus is freedom."[20]

The nature of that "ultimate" peace that ISM leaders envision will follow on Palestinian "freedom" is not spelled out, but references to a two-state solution for Israel and the Palestinians—the only plausible vision of peace between the two sides—are rare in ISM pronouncements. Shapiro sometimes noted that this was the official Palestinian position, but *The Daily Star* of Lebanon reported from its interview with him that "his utopian wish is to bring the Palestinians and Israelis to live together within a united state."[21] This of course is a euphemism for the destruction of Israel and its replacement by a Palestinian Arab state in which some Jewish remnant would be tolerated, perhaps as a few Jews are to this day in Yemen, Egypt, Lebanon, and a few other Arab states.

For her part, Arraf denounced Israel's Peace Now movement because it "is Zionist and doesn't believe in Palestinian right to return"[22]—which seems to amount to an objection to the group's desire for Israel's continued existence. Raphael Cohen, another ISM spokesman who shared the podium with Arraf at a press conference, said, according to David Bedein, a pro-Israeli activist and journalist who covered it, that the ISM favored a "one-state solution."[23] In the same vein, a gushing review of Rachel Corrie's diaries in *The Observer* of London, described her as a "young woman who believed there would be a democratic Israeli-Palestinian state in her lifetime."[24]

In sum, the group for which Rachel Corrie was working, and to which she gave her life, was not pro-peace as that term is usually understood. Nor was it a principled advocate of nonviolence. Rather, its quite deliberate purpose was to serve as an enabler of Palestinian violence. Its strategy was indeed quite ingenious. Consider Rafah, the precinct where Rachel Corrie played her deadly game of "bull-dozer cowgirl." It was a center of Palestinian shooting and bombing and also the main hive of weapon-smuggling to fuel the *intifada*. The Israeli effort to clear level ground was a natural military move. Had Hamas sent its fighters to try to stop the bulldozers they would have been blown away in short order, but Americans and Europeans practicing "nonviolence" could indeed do much more to obstruct Israeli military operations.

Rachel was perhaps not as hardened as Shapiro, Arraf, Larudee, and other senior ISM figures, but she burned an American flag at a Gaza rally against war in Iraq, and she, too, justified Palestinian violence. In a long letter to her mother just weeks before her death, she rebutted "what you said on the phone about Palestinian violence not helping the situation." Reciting a one-sided litany of Israeli depredations, she posed the rhetorical question of whether "we might try to use somewhat violent means . . . in a similar situation?" She answered herself: "I really think . . . most people would."[25] And she worked at mastering ISM-style agitprop: "when people ask about Palestinian violence, I will talk about resisting genocide."[26]

Two other west coast Americans, Anne Marie Olivier and Paul Steinberg of Portland, Oregon, had gone to live among the people of Gaza for months during the first *intifada*, then spent six years col-

lecting paraphernalia from that struggle, in effect becoming its cura-
tors. Their book, *The Road to Martyrs' Square: A Journey into the World
of the Suicide Bomber,*[27] describes a society steeped in the glory and
romance of bloodshed. They observed "martyr cards passed around
by kids in the West Bank and Gaza Strip as if baseball cards," and
"posters of [a suicide bomber's] image decorat[ing] every conceivable
surface . . .he was the talk of the town, at least until the next martyr
took his place."[28] All this they saw during the first *intifada*, when Palestinian suicide bombing and other violence was only a fraction of
what it became during Rachel Corrie's sojourn and before the Gaza
Strip had become dominated by Hamas with its official slogan: *"Jihad* is our way. Dying in the way of Allah is our highest hope." Yet to
all of this Rachel Corrie shut her eyes and zipped her lips, claiming
that "the vast majority of Palestinians right now, as far as I can tell,
are engaging in Gandhian nonviolent resistance."[29]

On some level, no doubt Rachel Corrie remained the passionate
idealist whose young heart ached for less fortunate children, but at
another level her spirit had hardened. She had become blinded in
her perceptions and grown selective in her compassion. The delicate
child who admonished herself not to step on a flower, who could not
endure the thought of whales dying or trees being felled, exhibited
cold indifference to the death of Israelis. What force was it that had
wrought such a transformation?

It was the force that Eric Hoffer described in his 1951 classic, *The
True Believer*, the embrace of creeds that breed "fanaticism, enthusiasm, fervent hope, hatred and intolerance."[30] The mentality had
been captured in John Steinbeck's 1936 novel *In Dubious Battle* when
the protagonist Mac sees his closest comrade, Jim, shot to death,
then pauses only a moment before hauling the body up onto a speakers' platform to serve as a prop in a harangue.

The ISM did something analogous when, immediately after Rachel Corrie's death, it distributed to news organizations a doctored
photo display intended to show that the Israeli bulldozer had struck
her deliberately. The display showed her standing and gesturing in
full view of the driver, then lying mortally wounded in the vehicle's
tracks. This sequence was picked up by news organizations around
the world, but later it was shown (and eventually acknowledged by
those who provided them) that the photos of her standing were
shot hours before the fatal encounter. At the terrible moment of her
death she was kneeling and far less visible. Her colleagues insisted,

nonetheless, that the driver must have run her over knowingly, but an Israeli court heard the case in full and found to the contrary.

What interested Hoffer and Steinbeck was the paradox that humane sentiments can find expression in an ideology that coarsens humane instincts. Whatever emotion Steinbeck's Mac may feel at the sudden death of his close buddy is subordinated in the blink of an eye to his thoughts of how he can used that death for the cause. Various apostates from Communism, like Arthur Koestler and Whittaker Chambers, also wrestled with the subject of idealism versus action, ends versus means. Milovan Djilas, who helped lead the Communist seizure of power in Yugoslavia before growing disillusioned and serving years in prison as a dissident, wrote of his one-time comrades: "How could they think or act otherwise when they have been named by a higher power, which they call history, to establish the Kingdom of Heaven in this sinful world?"[31]

Of course Rachel Corrie was no Communist. By the time she came along almost no one was. But she was drawn to leftist ideology, even if its contours had grown fuzzier than those of classical Marxism. When she told her father of her plan to join the ISM in Gaza, he recalled: "I was concerned. Why not work in a soup kitchen or something like that, I said to her."[32] But she didn't want merely to help people; she wanted to be part of something momentous—a movement to change the world: history itself.

As a teen, Rachel's budding affinity with leftism had drawn her to Evergreen State College, a radical enclave describing itself as "a very different place to learn."[33] Commencement speakers, usually a Native American activist or militant feminist or radical environmentalist, have in recent years included such icons of the revolutionary Left as Angela Davis (one of the last genuine Communists, the party's vice presidential nominee in 1980 and 1984), Leonard Peltier, and Mumia Abu Jamal. The latter two delivered their remarks remotely since they are serving life terms for murder: Peltier of two FBI agents and Abu Jamal of a Philadelphia police officer. Davis, having been acquitted of providing the weapons used to murder a California judge, was able to deliver hers in person.

Rachel Corrie seemed to drink in what Evergreen had to offer: the recently decanted wine of the New Left and the dregs of the old. She wrote that she "like[d] reading about the IWW,* criminal syndical-

* The Industrial Workers of the World, or "Wobblies," was an anarchist-

ism [and] Woody Guthrie."[34] And that "trying to decode escalating fascist policy changes gave me a rabbit hole to follow into history. . . . Drawing links between historic repression, racism, propaganda campaigns and xenophobia to our present situation has been very empowering to me."[35] Coming from "the United States, perhaps one of the most racist countries in the world," as she put it, she was concerned about "healing our own racism and classism and sexism and heterosexism and ageism and ableism."[36]

Rachel Corrie's litany of malign-isms reflected the metamorphosis of Leftism. Conflict between groups continued to be seen as the engine of progress, as Marx had posited, but particularly after the upheavals of the 1960s race and other demographic categories replaced class as the crucial axis. The seeds of this transition had been sown by Lenin who observed in *Imperialism, the Highest Stage of Capitalism* that the proletariat had failed to rise up because Western capitalists had bribed the workers with colonial lucre, enabling many to "enjoy more or less petty bourgeois conditions of life." Thus, the peoples of the colonial areas, whom Marx had described contemptuously as living an "undignified, stagnant and vegetative life,"[37] now became necessary figures in the drama of birthing a new age.

The importance of the struggle of non-Western peoples grew geometrically after the second World War with revolts against colonialism and protests against the terrible disadvantages faced by newly decolonized nations. Jean-Paul Sartre, once an orthodox Stalinist, gave voice to this profound rewrite of leftist canon in his preface to Frantz Fanon's *The Wretched of the Earth*. "Natives of all underdeveloped countries, unite!" he wrote.[38] The riveting movement for civil rights of blacks in America melded with the global anticolonial cause to create a larger image of "the rest against the West," or rather against the White West.

This transformation of the main paradigm of Leftism from class struggle to a conflict of nations and ethnicities was consequential for Israel. The traditional Leftist parties had been no friends to the Jewish state (except, for a time, the social democrats, whose sympathy had been largely reversed by the efforts of Socialists such as

---

oriented radical labor organization that vied with the larger, more moderate American Federation of Labor during the first two decades of the twentieth century.

Bruno Kreisky and Sweden's Olaf Palme). But in the Left's new interpretation of history, Israel became a more central target.

As with the proletariat under classical Marxism, the favored groups—blacks, browns, former colonials—were not merely objects of sympathy; they were regarded as the vessels of universal redemption. Not only were Gandhi and Mandela seen in this light, but even, to some, Ayatollah Khomeini. The famous French social theorist, Michel Foucault, wrote rapturously of the Iranian revolution in *Le Nouvel Observateur* in 1978, seeing in it an "attempt to open a spiritual dimension in politics," a "possibility we [Westerners] have forgotten since the Renaissance and the great crisis of Christianity."[39]

The uprising led by Khomeini against the US-backed shah exemplified the rebellion of "the rest," and its triumph transformed Islamism into a vital force, just as Lenin's seizure of Russia had done for Marxism. Ali Shariati, the intellectual guide of the Iranian revolution, who formulated the idea of "Red Shiism,"[40] had argued that Islam offered a redemptive political model superior to Marxism. Now he seemed vindicated as Islam or Islamism took its place at the forefront of world revolution.

Ilich "Carlos the Jackal" Ramirez Sanchez, the most infamous of international terrorists, named after Lenin by his Venezuelan Communist parents, converted to Islam. So did Roger Garaudy, once the top theoretician of the French Communist Party, who was convicted by a French court in 1998 of Holocaust-denial which is against the law in that country. The late President Hugo Chavez welcomed Iranian President Mahmoud Ahmadinejad in Venezuela where the two "hugged, held hands, and praised each other as fellow revolutionaries," while Chavez denounced Israel as "a murderous arm of the Yankee empire."[41] The daughter of Che Guevara traveled to Lebanon in 2010 to meet with leaders of the terrorist Islamist group, Hezbollah, and lay a wreath at the grave of the group's cofounder, Abbas al-Musawi, killed by Israeli forces.[42] And Judith Butler, the professor of "critical theory" whose books are among the most widely assigned in American universities, said, "understanding Hamas/Hezbollah as social movements that are progressive, that are on the left, that are part of a global left, is extremely important"[43]—even though Butler's reputation was built on her advocacy of feminism and "queer theory" for which these groups evince murderous contempt.

Edward Said added intellectual panache, if not honest scholarship, to the glorification of the international struggle against the

Western and white world, and made the Palestinian cause its emblem. This was reinforced by the use of Israel—America's "spoiled child," in the words of Turkey's Prime Minister Recep Tayyip Erdogan[44]—as a voodoo doll for America. Boycotting Israeli universities, for example, can allow European academics to experience frissons of self-righteousness at much lower cost than taking the same stance toward, say, Harvard, Yale, and Princeton.

The Left's ardent hostility to Israel seeps into global discourse, exerting influence in more moderate or mainstream circles where talk of "revolution" would seem out of place. For example, respected human rights organizations have singled out Israel for criticism disproportionate in quantity and tone to their treatment of other Middle Eastern governments whose depredations are of an entirely different magnitude. It is like criticizing Western democracies more vociferously than Communist or Fascist totalitarian regimes.

This provoked Robert L. Bernstein, the head of Random House publishers who had been the original founder of Human Rights Watch (HRW) and served as its chairman for twenty years, to take to the op ed pages of *The New York Times* in 2009 to castigate his own creation, having abandoned hope of influencing it from within. He wrote:

> [T]he Arab and Iranian regimes . . . most[ly] remain brutal, closed and autocratic, permitting little or no internal dissent. The plight of their citizens who would most benefit from the kind of attention a large and well-financed international human rights organization can provide is being ignored as Human Rights Watch's Middle East division prepares report after report on Israel.[45]

In designing the organization, Bernstein recalled, "we sought to draw a sharp line between the democratic and nondemocratic worlds," elaborating: "We always recognized that open, democratic societies have faults and commit abuses. But we say that they have the ability to correct them through vigorous public debate, an adversarial press and many other mechanisms." In contrast to the states that surround it, Israel, he wrote "is home to at least 80 human rights organizations, a vibrant free press, a democratically elected government, a judiciary that frequently rules against the government."

Bernstein would have been less perplexed at the direction HRW had taken had he borne more carefully in mind the tortuous history of the human rights issue in US politics. As the American publisher of leading Soviet dissident, Andrei Sakharov, Bernstein was embedded in the wing of the US human rights movement that focused primarily on the abuses of Communist regimes. But there was another wing which grew out of the Vietnam antiwar movement, and it targeted anti-Communist regimes with which the United States allied in the Cold War. This element formed an effective lobby called the Human Rights Working Group which secured passage in the 1970s of laws linking foreign aid to human rights. No doubt, the legislators who voted for these bills saw them as levers to extract reforms from rightist authoritarian regimes that were America's tactical partners. But the aim of the activists in the Human Rights Working Group was different. They hoped that withdrawal of Washington's backing and US aid would make those regimes more vulnerable to insurrection. As Bruce Cameron, one of the two co-chairs of the Human Rights Working Group put it: "The motive was that if you cut the link . . . then you create more space for the revolutionary Third World people to assert their right of self-determination."[46]

"Revolutionary third world people" was a euphemism for Communist movements of which Cameron's co-chair, Jacqui Chagnon, was so enamored that she went off subsequently to live as a field worker in the Lao People's Democratic Republic. Freedom House assessed the Lao regime to be one of the world's most repressive, but Chagnon returned singing its praises, even to the point of justifying the notorious "reeducation" camps. "They simply just took the heavy-duty 'baddies' and put them in remote areas, essentially, and said, 'take care of yourselves,'" she explained.[47]

In short, the US human rights movement had two components, one anti-Communist and the other anti-anti-Communist. It is tempting to refer to these as Right and Left, but like Bernstein, most of those active in Helsinki Watch, the group he founded in 1978 to monitor the East Bloc's compliance with the human rights provisions of the Helsinki Accords, would have placed themselves somewhere on the left side of the spectrum, albeit not the extreme left. It would thus be more accurate to describe the two camps as Left and Lefter. The latter, for example, dominated the work of the parallel group, America's Watch. In the 1980s it frequently lacerated the rightist dictators of Central America, but when the Communist "Sandinista" regime in Nicaragua began to commit similar abuses,

America's Watch did not merely hold its tongue, it leaped to the regime's defense.

Explaining this odd behavior, America's Watch conceded, "Ordinarily, we do not take pains to state the abuses of which a government is not guilty." However, it went on, "in the case of Nicaragua we feel called upon to do so because the Reagan administration has engaged in a concerted effort to distort the facts, charging the Nicaraguan government with abuses far in excess of what it actually commits."[48] In other words, America's Watch saw Sandinista human rights abuses as a lesser evil than Reaganism. But it was not only hatred for Reagan that motivated America's Watch; the group also displayed a soft spot for Nicaragua's Leftist dictatorship. It worked to impeach Nicaragua's indigenous human rights movement, the Permanent Commission on Human Rights, which had defended the Sandinistas when they were insurgents but had begun chronicling their abuses once they rose to power.[49]

In short, HRW has a long history of comingling genuine human rights advocacy with an ideological agenda that was not merely divorced from human rights goals but sometimes hostile to them. In Cold War days, that agenda was anti-anti-Communism. In more recent years it has been fervent anti-Israelism.

Apart from that, the disproportionateness of the treatment of Israel by HRW is inexplicable. Consider the situation in Israel and the neighboring countries, as shown in the annual assessments issued by Freedom House, the only organization that attempts to measure the state of freedom,* on a comparative basis in every country every year. In the Middle East/North Africa region, whereas a handful of countries have been "partly free" and about a dozen "not free" (with small year-to-year shifts between the latter two categories), Israel has been the only country rated "free" by Freedom House since the destruction of Lebanon's democracy in 1975. This region, thus, has been by far the least free in the world since the end of the Soviet era, less free even than sub-Saharan Africa which is the world's poor-

---

* "Freedom," as used by Freedom House, is synonymous with the state of human rights, as can be seen from the explication of methodology Freedom House provides each year along with it survey results. See for example http://www.freedomhouse.org/report/freedom-world-2013/methodology and http://www.freedomhouse.org/report/freedom-world-2013/checklist-questions.

est. In other words, the area surrounding Israel has been in a state of perpetual human rights disaster. This does not mean that Israel's own record is pristine, but it is light years better than the other countries in that part of the world. In response to a question about HRW's priorities, its Executive Director Kenneth Roth once said: "we've got to pick and choose—we've got finite resources."[50] If that is the case, then it is hard to see how HRW could justify spending much of its time and energies on Israel. It turns out, however, that it spends more on Israel than on any other country in the region.

HRW's defense is that it does not concentrate on Israel internally where freedom admittedly prevails, but rather on the Palestinian territories occupied in 1967 which present a far different picture. Freedom House offers nuanced numerical ratings that range in half-steps from a best of 1 to a worst of 7. Internally, Israel scores a very good, but not perfect, 1.5, but in the territories it rules its score has usually been 5.5 (some years even 6.0). This is a poor score, one that would land a country in the "not free" category, certainly warranting scrutiny by human rights monitors. But the sad truth is that all but a few of the countries in the region score as poorly or worse. For example, Syria has usually scored a rock-bottom 7 and Libya invariably did until the overthrow of Muammar Qaddafi in 2011, but HRW has produced more reports on Israel than on Syria and Libya combined.

In fact, the head of HRW's Middle East and North Africa division, Sarah Leah Whitson, went out of her way after a 2009 visit to write two upbeat articles praising human right progress under Qaddafi. In "Tripoli Spring," published in *Foreign Policy*, she reported:

> The brittle atmosphere of repression has started to fracture, giving way to expanded space for discussion and debate . . . I was unprepared for the change. I left more than one meeting stunned at the sudden openness of ordinary citizens, who criticized the government and challenged the status quo with new-found frankness. . . . And while [families of those slain in a 1996 prison uprising] spoke to us with great apprehension, the very presence of a public debate on abuses by the government's internal police is breathtaking for Libya. . . . The spirit of reform, however slowly, has spread to the bureaucracy as well.[51]

Whitson credited the change to Seif Qaddafi, the dictator's son, acknowledging that it might be part of an effort to position himself to succeed his father. In fact, in that period, the younger Qaddafi was indeed reaching out to some exiles and taking a few other steps that hinted at reform. However, it all amounted to too little to move the needle on Freedom House's annual ratings off a worst-possible score of 7 for Libya even though the gauge was sufficiently sensitive that it ticked up from 7 to 6.5 that year for such other repressive countries as Syria and Saudi Arabia.

Within two years, the people of Libya rose against Qaddafi, and Seif went on national television to warn that "we will fight until the last man, until the last woman, until the last bullet" to put down the rebellion.[52] Two weeks later, Whitson took to the pages of the *Los Angeles Times* to chastise the Libyan regime, recalling that in her 2009 visit "most Libyans we spoke with never had much faith that . . . the announced reforms were anything more than an endless loop of promises made and broken."[53] If so, she had hidden this relevant piece of information from the readers of her heartening *Foreign Policy* article and another in *Foreign Policy in Focus* in February 2010.[54]

Saudi Arabia, whose slight improvement on the Freedom House scale was soon reversed, was another destination of Whitson's in 2009. There, she headlined two fundraisers, appealing for donations to "combat pro-Israel pressure groups," according to a report on one in *Arab News*, the main English-language Saudi newspaper.[55] This was picked up by a pro-Israel blogger, David Bernstein, whose post, reprinted in *The Wall Street Journal*, challenged the propriety of journeying to "one of the worst countries in the world for human rights to raise money to wage lawfare against Israel, and say[ing] not a word during the trip about the status of human rights in that country."[56] In an angry response, Whitson averred that she had "spen[t] much of the time in serious discussion about Saudi violations" and that Bernstein was guilty of the false assumption that "if they live in a totalitarian country, [Saudis] must be bad people."[57] Replying in a similar vein to queries from *The Atlantic*'s Jeffrey Goldberg, HRW chief Kenneth Roth denounced the "stereotype that Saudis . . . are interested only in Israel, not their own government," and charged that criticism of his group from Israel's supporters consists of "lies," "deception" and "obfuscation."[58]

It does not appear that there were outright "lies" on either side in this dustup, but all the "deception" and "obfuscation" belonged to Whitson and Roth. While Whitson may have raised Saudi human rights abuses in her visit, her implication, and Roth's explicit assertions, that Israel was only a passing part of the fundraising affair and that Saudi Arabia was also criticized appear to be false. *Arab News* is a relatively liberal outlet and would have highlighted any discussion of Saudi transgressions. Instead, its account of the event, headlined "HRW Lauded for Work in Gaza," recounted only discussion about Israel. "HRW presented a documentary and spoke on the report they compiled on Israel violating human rights and international law during its war on Gaza earlier this year," it said. The story quoted Whitson boasting that "Human Rights Watch provided the international community with evidence of Israel using white phosphorus and launching systematic destructive attacks on civilian targets." It said that she "pointed out that the group managed to testify about Israeli abuses to the US Congress on three occasions." The story mentioned as background that "Human Rights Watch has also leveled criticism at other states in the region, including Saudi Arabia," but it did not quote or report anything from the event itself suggesting that Whitson had mentioned the Saudis' abysmal human rights record in her remarks.[59]

Whitson and Roth both labored to give the impression that this was a gathering of Saudis with a special interest in human rights, rather than primarily in criticizing Israel. But although participants may have been relatively liberal-minded by Saudi standards, this was no gathering of dissidents. The host, Emad bin Jameel Al-Hejailan, is chairman of the Al Hejailan Group, a large Saudi conglomerate which that year listed as its clients six Saudi ministries, including those of defense and interior, as well as the Saudi National Guard, Saudi Airlines, various other government agencies, and Saudi Aramco.[60] The idea that someone whose livelihood comes from the Saudi government would step on any official toes is far-fetched.

Roth also stressed to Goldberg: "we don't get any Saudi funds for work on Israel . . . the vast majority of our funding is for our work as a whole." But the *Arab News* paraphrase of Whitson's pitch said, "the group is facing a shortage of funds because of the global financial crisis and the work on Israel and Gaza, which depleted HRW's budget for the region." In other words, HRW touted its criticism of Israel to a group of wealthy Saudis, saying this had depleted its coffers and appealing to them for replenishment. If this is not tantamount to "get[ting] Saudi funds for work on Israel," it is a distinction without a difference.

In lashing back at its critics, HRW emphasizes that its touchstone is law. This allows it to sidestep the obvious moral distinction between Israel's democracy and the tyranny of its enemies, and between Israel's desire for peace and its enemies' desire to annihilate Israel. Yet HRW's reliance on law is very uneven. In conflict situations it says it addresses only *jus in bello*, that is, the conduct of the war, and not *jus ad bellum*, the question of how the war started or who started it. Thus, in World War II, the group would have criticized the Japanese for their treatment of prisoners of war, the Americans for interning Japanese citizens, the Germans for collective punishment against the resistance, and the Allies for the bombing of Dresden—all without ever saying a word about Pearl Harbor or the invasions of Manchuria, Poland, France, and the rest. What would have been the moral force of this? In what sense would this have been faithful to human rights?

Roth argues that "the question of who started any given conflict or who is most at fault almost invariably leads to lengthy historical digressions."[61] True, Hitler claimed that Polish forces had struck Germany first, and Japanese officials said America was trying to strangle their country. But sorting out the truth was not difficult for anyone of good faith. In the case of Israel's wars with Hamas or Hezbollah, there really was no ambiguity about who started them since these two groups boasted of their exploits.

It is hard to understand HRW's insistence on not addressing causality, even from a narrow legal standpoint, since the question of when it is legitimate to resort to war is the oldest and most fundamental issue in international law. Thus, when Hamas or Hezbollah initiate violence against Israel, provoking military retaliation, they have committed a fundamental breach of the law, not to mention morality.

Roth claims that "like the Red Cross" his organization practices "strict neutrality on . . . political questions." But the analogy is misleading. The work of the Red Cross is to provide tangible succor to victims, meaning it needs the acquiescence of all belligerents and must avoid offending any. For example, it cooperated with the Hitler regime during World War II. HRW, in contrast, has never delivered a blanket or bottle of water. Like other, similar groups its work is entirely political. Its power rests on the ability to "name and shame" miscreants, and thus to bring pressure to bear on them to mend their ways. But whereas Israel is in fact sensitive to opprobrium from groups like HRW, Hamas and Hezbollah are entirely shameless with respect to their treatment of Israelis or Jews—or even, for that matter, of their respective domestic rivals. Perhaps one reason why, despite its spurious claim of neutrality, HRW chastises Israel more often than its adversaries is that it knows Israelis are listening, while rebuking Hamas and Hezbollah is like whispering in the wind.

With great displays of meretricious even-handedness, HRW calls on both sides to investigate the legal violations it has identified. Israel routinely probes reports of misconduct from any reputable source, leading to many cases of military discipline and sometimes even criminal punishment. Hezbollah and Hamas, however, commit war crimes with abandon, freely targeting civilians while caring not a whit about what Western human rights groups may think.

Indeed, for Hamas and Hezbollah, war crimes are their very *raison d'etre*. As Hezbollah's "spiritual leader," Sheikh Muhammad Hussein Fadlallah put it: "there are no innocent Jews in Palestine."[62] Or as its Charter explains, Hamas:

> [L]ooks forward to fulfill the promise of Allah [when] "the Muslims fight against the Jews and the Muslims . . . kill them, and . . . the Jews [will] hide themselves behind a stone or a tree and a stone or a tree [will] say. 'Muslim or Servant of Allah there is a Jew behind me; come and kill him.'"

As part of its posture of neutrality during the 2006 war in Lebanon, HRW addressed a letter to Iranian President Mahmoud Ahmadinejad, urging his government to "use its influence to ensure that Hezbollah forces do not undertake attacks that violate international humanitarian law."[63]

This absurd exercise points to the most striking derogation from HRW's protestations of reverence for international law, namely its indifference toward genocidal threats against Israel. It has virtually ignored not only those uttered routinely by Hamas and Hezbollah, but even the still more voluble ones from Iran. Ben Birnbaum, a reporter for the *New Republic*, recounted this exchange:

> When I asked Roth in a February interview at his office about HRW's refusal to take a position on Ahmadinejad's threats against Israel, including his famous call for Israel to be "wiped off the map," Roth quibbled about the way the statement had been translated in the West—"there was a real question as to whether he actually said that"—then told me that it was not

HRW's place to render judgments on such rhetoric: "Let's assume it is a military threat. We don't take on governments' military threats just as we don't take on aggression, per se. We look at how they behave. So, we wouldn't condemn a military threat just as we wouldn't condemn an invasion—we would look at how the government wages the war." Whitson, who sat in on the interview, offered her two cents: "You know, that statement was also matched by Hillary Clinton saying that the Iranian regime should be destroyed or wiped off the map."[64]

We see here Roth and Whitson acting like a couple of fast-talking lawyers trying to throw up any defense they can muster, however far-fetched. There is of course no question, "real" or otherwise, about Ahmadinejad's threats to annihilate Israel which have been iterated often in varying phrases by him and other Iranian officials. Needless to say, Clinton's allusion to regime change in Iran bears no similarity to these threats. And Roth's comments about not taking on "military threats" are sheer sophistry.

Sidestepping the moral issues presented by Ahmadinejad, Roth and Whitson insist their touchstone is law, but there is perhaps no more fundamental piece of international human rights law than the Convention on the Prevention and Punishment of Genocide. Its definition of the crime includes "direct and public incitement to genocide." In communications reported in *The Wall Street Journal*, Roth justified ignoring Ahmadinejad's words by drawing a distinction between "advocacy" of genocide, which he said is legal, and "incitement," which is not. How to distinguish one from the other? For an exhortation to amount to "incitement," it must be followed immediately or accompanied by the literal act of genocide. The Iranian statements, Roth said "are not incitement to genocide [because] no one has acted on them."[65] But this interpretation is entirely untenable in light of the very title of the convention which speaks first of "prevention." Its framers were quite explicit in saying that this law was intended to differ from most others in that its intent was not merely to punish a crime after the fact but to stop it before it had happened. In fact, the American government did worry that the ban on "incitement" could be read too broadly and thus inhibit free expression, especially because, at the time the convention was adopted, the Soviet bloc was pressing for far more sweeping prohibitions. So the US representative moved in the "Sixth Committee," which was responsible for producing the document, to delete the clause on incitement. The US motion was defeated by a vote of twenty-seven to sixteen with five abstentions.[66] In sum, Roth's and Whitson's arguments amounted to nothing more than best-they-could-do legal bluster, leaving us to wonder why they in effect offered their services *pro bono* to the likes of Ahmadinejad.

In addition to the disproportionateness in its unrelenting moral censure of Israel as compared to its rarer and more restrained rebukes of other countries in the region, one other action by HRW reveals its profound bias against the Jewish state. This is its official endorsement of the Palestinian "right of return." Generally, the organization does not take positions on political issues, limiting itself to addressing human rights. But the "right of return," the most politicized issue of the conflict between Israelis and Palestinians, has little to do with rights and everything to do with Israel's existence. In the usage of advocates of the Arab or Palestinian cause "right of return" means that not only the thousands of surviving Arab refugees of the 1948 war but also millions of their descendants may claim residence in Israel. It is, as everyone understands, a formula for abolishing Israel as a Jewish state, and to endorse it is implicitly to oppose a peace settlement and favor the destruction of Israel. If there were a basis for this "right" in international law there would still be a compelling diplomatic and moral interest in setting it aside. But there is no substantial legal basis for it.

Arab advocates who claim there is often point to General Assembly Resolution 194, adopted by the United Nations in 1948, which says that "refugees wishing to return to their homes and live at peace with their neighbors should be permitted to do so at the earliest practicable date." But this text does not refer to any "right." It does not refer to the not-yet-born progeny of refugees. And, unlike resolutions of the world body's Security Council, those of the General Assembly are not considered to carry the force of law, and therefore, by definition, cannot form the *legal* basis for anything. In contrast, the International Covenant on Civil and Political Rights does have the status of law, and it provides a slightly more plausible basis for the claimed "right." Article 12, point 4, says: "No one shall be arbitrarily deprived of the right to enter his own country." The entire article is about the freedom of movement: point one asserts the right to move about within one's country, and point two asserts the right to exit. Point four is its companion. Clearly this was not intended in the sense it is used by the Palestinians' advocates to address contending national claims. But beyond the matter of intent, this article, too, has nothing to say about progeny. It is hard to see on what basis a child, grandchild, or great-grandchild subsequently born to someone who fled or was expelled in 1948 can claim that Israel is "his country." (Nor, for that matter, is it easy to see how Israel's unwillingness to allow its national existence to be undone in this manner can be said to be "arbitrary.")

HRW's Kenneth Roth strenuously denies any bias in the organization's treatment of Israeli/Arab issues, but the organization's staffing decisions, for which he as director is presumably responsible, make these denials ring hollow. Sarah Whitson, in charge of its Middle East work, came to that position from the Arab American Anti-Discrimination Committee, one of the leading Arab advocacy groups. When *The New Republic*'s Ben Birnbaum interviewed her, he "noticed that a poster for *Paradise Now*, a movie that attempts to humanize Palestinian suicide bombers, hangs on her door and that two photos of bereaved Gazans hang on her wall."[67] Whitson brought Norman Finkelstein, one of the most extreme of full-time Israel-bashers, to HRW to give a talk to staff. Finkelstein's writings repeat endlessly the comparison of Israelis to Nazis, sometimes even portraying the Israelis as worse.* Apparently, he did not go over well, prompting her to admit to a colleague that "his anger sometimes gets the better of him and his brilliant mind and generous spirit. I continue to have tremendous respect and admiration for him."[68]

Whitson's deputy is Joe Stork, who came to that position from

---

* For a detailed and devastating analysis of Finkelstein's career as an Israel-basher, see Paul Bogdanor, "Norman G. Finkelstein: Chomsky for Nazis" in Edward Alexander and Paul Bogdanor, eds., *The Jewish Divide Over Israel* (New Brunswick: Transaction, 2006), pp. 135–160. First Bogdaner supplies this quote from Finkelstein: "I can't imagine why Israel's apologists would be offended by a comparison with the Gestapo. I would think that, for them, it is like Lee Iacocca being told that Chrysler is using Toyota tactics." Then Bogdanor writes: "That Norman G. Finkelstein considers friends of Israel the moral equivalent of Gestapo torturers and mass murderers might be an occasion for surprise among normal people." Scarcely less amazing, then, is a parallel observation that appears in his subsequent writings about the Jewish state. Reflecting on the excuses offered by a leading Nazi tried at Nuremberg, Finkelstein declares: "the Germans could point in extenuation to the severity of penalties for speaking out against the crimes of state. What excuse do *we* have?"

MERIP, the Midde East Research and Information Project, which
he cofounded and whose publication he edited. MERIP was an out-
growth of the 1960s New Left, perhaps the first organization in
the United States to expound the view that admiration for third
world "liberation movements" ought to extend to Palestinian terror
groups. *Middle East Report*, the journal Stork edited for twenty-five
years before being hired by HRW, served as a cheering section for
these groups, going so far as to express support for the 1972 Munich
Olympics massacre. Ridiculing "the Western establishment" for
"freak[ing] out" over that event, MERIP editorialized: "we should
comprehend the achievements of the Munich action" which it listed
as "a boost in morale among Palestinians" and "halt[ing]" moves
"for a 'settlement' between Israel and the Arab regimes."[69]

In 1976, according to a column in *The Sunday Times*, Stork "attended an anti-Zionist conference in Baghdad hosted by the Iraqi
dictator, Saddam Hussein."[70] More recently, when a columnist for
the Israeli newspaper *Ma'ariv* quoted some hair-raising quotes from
the proceedings of the conference, Stork retorted: "The quotes . . .
attributed to me are more than 30 years old. Most of them I do not
recognize, and they are contrary to the views I have expounded for
decades now."[71]

No doubt Stork's views had evolved over the decades, but he kept
editing the same journal. Most political writers who come to find
opinions they once espoused repugnant feel an inner need and a
public obligation to offer some reckoning. For many who have performed this exercise, the discarded positions stopped well short of
applauding terror attacks and accepting political hospitality from
the likes of Saddam. But there is no evidence that Stork ever did
this, nor that HRW cared when it hired him away from MERIP despite his having never worked on human rights.

Another staff member, Lucy Mair, had worked for a US phil-
anthropic organization, funding Palestinian organizations, and
contributed occasional articles to the extreme anti-Israel website,
Electronic Intifada.[72] Yet another, Nadia Barhoum, was an activist
in Students for Justice in Palestine at the University of California,
Berkeley.[73] A HRW official told *The New Republic* that some staff
members come to the organization from "solidarity backgrounds"
but "when they come through the door of this organization, they put
those things behind."[74]

Anyone with experience in radical movements will find this hard to believe, understanding how passionate are the commitments that lead to such engagement. More to the point, perhaps, for HRW's Middle East staff, "solidarity backgrounds" invariably means solidarity with the Palestinian or broader Arab cause. No staff members have come from, say, the Zionist Organization of America or the Anti-Defamation League. In fact, as detailed in *The New Republic*, a few members of the HRW board or its Middle East advisory committee who dissented from the group's anti-Israel tilt were purged or resigned in frustration.[75]

As unfair as HRW is in its treatment of Israel, human rights groups based in Europe are even more one-sided. Amnesty International, for example, has collaborated overtly with the Palestine Solidarity Campaign.[76] One of its British senior staff addressed a pro-Palestinian group, saying Israel belongs on "the list of stupid dictatorial regimes . . . along with Burma, North Korea, Iran and Sudan,"[77] while the chairman of the organization's Finnish branch blogged that Israel is "a scum country."[78] In 2013 Amnesty chose Roger Waters of the rock group Pink Floyd as the presenter of its annual Ambassador of Conscience Award, notwithstanding (or perhaps because of) Waters's notoriety as a contributor to the website *Electronic Intifada* and tireless campaigner for a boycott of Israel by performers who uses an inflatable pig sporting a Star of David as a prop in his show. Amnesty makes at most only a thin pretense of neutrality. For example, when it issued a press release in 2009 denouncing US aid to Israel, it called on "all governments to impose an immediate and comprehensive suspension of arms to Israel, and to all Palestinian armed groups." The inclusion of "Palestinian armed groups" was a throwaway line since their main supplier is Iran which has never evidenced any concern about what Amnesty says.

Human rights nongovernmental organizations (NGOs) constitute but one sector where the anti-Israel slant of the Left makes itself felt in larger, more influential institutions. Organized labor is another. While American unions remain mostly friendly to Israel, those of some other Western countries take the opposite tack. For example the British Trades Union Congress (TUC), the omnibus organization of labor in Britain, declares that "the TUC, working in conjunction with the Palestine Solidarity Campaign, is calling for a targeted consumer boycott of goods from the illegal Israel settlements."[79] Targeting the settlements sounds less severe than targeting Israel as a whole, but in practice, at least in this case, there is little difference. The Palestine Solidarity Campaign, whose lead the TUC accepts, pushes an all-out boycott of Israel and boasts on its website that it has been "has been joined by the TUC in its campaign of boycott, divestment and sanctions."[80]

Mainline Protestant churches also grew hostile to Israel as they drifted politically leftward starting in the 1960s. As Mark Tooley, president of the Institute on Religion and Democracy, describes it: "In the 1940s and 1950s, liberal Mainline Protestant elites were typically ardent Zionists. The radicalism of the 1960s and 1970s shifted them to pro-Palestinian, under the guidance of Liberation Theology."[81] The World Council of Churches functions in effect as part of the Palestinian "solidarity" movement, promoting such books as *Popular Resistance in Palestine*[82] and sponsoring an annual World Week for Peace in Israel Palestine "to work for an end to the illegal occupation of Palestine, so that Palestinians and Israelis can finally live in peace. It has been more than 64 years since the partition of Palestine hardened into a permanent nightmare for Palestinians."[83] The various major denominations each debated proposals to divest from companies doing business with Israel or said to be aiding the Israeli occupation of Palestinian territories. The Presbyterian Church (USA) did in fact adopt such a policy in 2004, only to rescind it two years later, and the issue has been fought out repeatedly since in the church's General Assembly, with pro-divestment forces losing by a vote of 333 to 331 in 2012.

The Presbyterian and United Methodist churches boycott goods produced at West Bank settlements (although it is not clear how they can identify such provenance), and the Mennonites boycott Israel more broadly. In October 2012 a letter signed by high officials of eleven Christian denominations and the then General Secretary of the National Council of Churches was sent to the US Congress, urging restrictions on US aid to Israel. And in 2003 the Church of Scotland issued a report belittling the historical connection of Jews to the land of Israel.[84]

The anti-Israel influence of Leftists or those who lean in that direction also is evident in such influential venues as the news media and academia. But perhaps the most interesting reflection, and potentially the most consequential in the long run, of the Left's turn against Israel is its impact among Jews themselves. For reasons about which many have speculated, Jews have been disproportionately represented in the radical Left in all its shades, from Karl Marx to the leading Bolsheviks surrounding Lenin, to the more moderate Mensheviks whose leadership was even more uniformly Jewish, to the United States in the 1960s where "Americans of Jewish backgrounds dominated the New Left in its early years," according to the detailed study of scholars Stanley Rothman and S. Robert Lichter.[85]

Thus, as the left turned against Israel, it was inevitable that Jews would appear in growing numbers among Israel's fiercest critics. So they have, as exemplified by Adam Shapiro of the ISM. The ISM typically claims that about 20 percent of its participants in such actions as the ill-fated 2010 Gaza flotilla are Jews. Other examples include Judith Butler, the "queer theory" philosopher and radical feminist supporter of Hamas and Hezbollah, and HRW's Kenneth Roth as well as Sarah Leah Whitson's hero, Norman Finkelstein.

Roth and Finkelstein found places of honor on John Mearsheimer's roster of "righteous Jews." Mearsheimer achieved fame as coauthor of the 2007 book, *The Israel Lobby*, which created a sensation by positing that a well-financed political network of Jews and some others had successfully deployed a mix of inducements and threats to channel US policy toward unjust support for Israel at the expense of America's own interests. The authors protested that they were no anti-Semites, but Mearsheimer dropped the other shoe in a 2010 speech at Washington, DC's Palestine Center in which he divided American Jewry into "Afrikaner Jews" and "righteous Jews." "Afrikaner" is a code word from South Africa's *apartheid* days for brutal racist, and in this category Mearsheimer included the leaders of the major Jewish organizations. "Righteous Jews" was a play on the term "righteous gentiles" that Israel's Holocaust memorial, Yad Vashem, bestows on non-Jews who risked their lives to save Jews from the Nazis. By calling anti-Israel Jews "righteous Jews" Mearsheimer was smirking at the special feelings Jews have about the Holocaust, and he was analogizing Israel to Nazi Germany. No one would choose such language except for the purpose of Jew-baiting.

In case anyone missed the import of this provocation, Mearsheimer provided a jacket blurb for *The Wandering Who*,[86] a 2011 book by the bizarre Israeli-born Gilad Atzmon who categorizes himself defiantly as a "self-hating Jew." His book argues that if indeed there was a Holocaust, a claim that Atzmon says is exaggerated, then we must ask "why were the Jews hated?"—implying it was their own fault. So outré and coarse was Atzmon's outpouring that even the US Palestinian Community Network warned its members not to tarnish their cause by association with his book and called on them to "disavow [its] racism and anti-Semitism."[87] But Mearsheimer endorsed Atzmon's work as "a fascinating and provocative book [that] should be widely read by Jews and non-Jews alike."

In addition to Roth and Finkelstein, Mearsheimer's "righteous" included Noam Chomsky, Roger Cohen, Tony Judt, Tony Karon, Naomi Klein, M.J. Rosenberg, Sara Roy, and "Philip Weiss of *Mondoweiss* fame," as well as "many of the individuals associated with J Street and everyone associated with Jewish Voice for Peace." He also mentioned Judge Richard Goldstone, but this was before Goldstone had largely repudiated the UN report that bore his name.

The first on Mearsheimer's list, the linguist Noam Chomsky, long advocated the replacement of Israel with a bi-national socialist state along the lines of what he called the "successful social revolution" of Communist Yugoslavia. The bloody disintegration of that Communist tyranny along lines of nationality in the 1990s made this a less attractive model, leaving Chomsky to focus more on lacerating Israel and less on proposing alternatives. Embracing anti-Israel advocates, one and all, Chomsky even penned a preface to a book by convicted French Holocaust-denier Robert Faurisson.[88]

A still more active personification of the anti-Israel Jew was the third name on Mearsheimer's list, Princeton University's Professor Emeritus of Law Richard Falk, who serves as the UN Human Rights Council's special rapporteur on "Israel's violations . . . in the Palestinian territories." Of his lineage, Falk writes: "I am Jewish, and proud of it, but I am equally indigenous, Sufi, Hindu, Buddhist, Muslim, and Christian."[89] While most leftist Jews are nonbelievers, Falk apparently feels as estranged from the ethnic side of Judaism as the religious, writing: "the Israeli historian, Shlomo Sand . . . has shown the absence of a Jewish ethnos that might justify the claim of being a distinct people."[90]

Yet, despite his proclaimed remoteness from any aspect of his heritage, Falk does not hesitate to invoke it to add poignancy to the analogy he makes between Israel and Nazi Germany. "It is especially painful for me, as an American Jew, to feel compelled to portray the ongoing and intensifying abuse of the Palestinian people by Israel through a reliance on such an inflammatory metaphor as 'holocaust,'" he writes. "Is it an irresponsible overstatement to associate the treatment of Palestinians with this criminalized Nazi record of collective atrocity? I think not."[91]

Like other radical Leftists who sought in Islam what they could no longer find in the proletariat, Falk embraced the 1979 Iranian revolution and its apotheosis, the Ayatollah Ruhollah Khomeini. Quoting the clerical leader's promises of enlightened rule, Falk declaimed, "To suppose that Ayatollah Khomeini is dissembling seems almost beyond belief." He added, "Having created a new model of popular revolution based, for the most part, on nonviolent tactics, Iran may yet provide us with a desperately-needed model of humane governance for a third-world country."[92]

His hopes for the Iranian revolution apparently disappointed, Falk grew invested instead in the Palestinian cause. In a 2011 blog titled "A Few Notes on WHAT IS LEFT (or Toward a Manifesto for Revolutionary Emancipation)," Falk came up with a three-point agenda: "support for the Palestinian Solidarity Movement," "struggle against global capitalism," and "the challenges of climate change."[93] Sadly, the Palestinian Authority may have proved too moderate a vessel for Falk's revolutionary dreams. In 2010 he told the press that the Palestinian Authority had urged him to resign his UN post. "They say . . . that I'm a partisan of Hamas," he said, complaining that this was "essentially untrue."[94]

As it happens, Falk, like Mearsheimer, also graced Atzmon's disgraceful book with a blurb, saying he found it "absorbing and moving" and expressing hope that it will be "not only read, but reflect[ed] upon and discuss[ed] widely." This was the second occasion on which Falk had violated the Western taboo against explicit anti-Semitism. Earlier in 2011, he had posted on his blog a cartoon of a dog wearing a skullcap embossed with a Star of David, chomping on human remains while urinating on a symbol of justice.[95] This repeated recourse to Jew-baiting evoked public rebukes from British Prime Minister David Cameron and US UN ambassador, Susan Rice, as well as a campaign of criticism by the pro-Israel NGO, UN Watch. Finally, HRW, of which he was a lay leader, seems to have concluded that he was too much of a liability. In 2012, Falk revealed on his blog that he had been asked to resign from his post with the group. It was, he said, "supposedly because of my connection with the UN, which is contrary to HRW policy. Perhaps, there is more to the issue than what I have been told."[96]

He had ample reason to wonder about the rationale that HRW offered for the decision. Falk's appointment to his UN post dates to 2008, and his official position with HRW dated back at least to that

year, according to an entry on the group's website.[97] The organization could scarcely have been unmindful of Falk's UN position since
not long after his appointment, it lacerated Israel for denying Falk
entry on the grounds of his extreme bias. "Israel [has] put itself in
the company of countries like Burma and North Korea," declaimed
HRW's Joe Stork on behalf of the organization.[98]

Falk's extremism eventually proved too much even for the United
Nations where normally no critical standards apply, what with
Qaddafi's Libya once chosen to chair the human rights panel and
theocratic Iran elected to the Commission on the Status of Women.
In response to the Boston Marathon bombing of 2013, Falk wrote:
"have the courage to connect [the] dots . . . 'Those to whom evil is
done/do evil in return'?"[99] The United Nations did not go so far as to
remove Falk from his official post of scourge to Israel, but Secretary
General Ban Ki Moon issued a public rebuke through his spokesman, saying Falk's statements "can undermine the credibility and
the work of the United Nations."[100]

The distinguishing characteristic of Falk, Chomsky, Butler, and
the other "righteous Jews" is an identity as Leftists far stronger
than any they might feel as Jews. Although they are immensely influential in the world at large, the thinness of their Jewish ties has
limited their impact within the Jewish community. Their radicalism
creates a gulf because although many radicals have been Jews, most
Jews are liberals, not radicals. In the hopes of changing this, an organization was formed in 2008 that aimed, in the words of its vice
president, at "moving Jews" further to the left and especially to a
position more critical of Israel,[101] but it takes pains to speak in tones
that do not sound so radical. The group calls itself J Street, and instead of being overtly anti-Israel it says it is pro-Israel but wants to
"redefin[e] what it means to be pro-Israel."[102]

One indication that J Street's self-presentation as "pro-Israel"
might be less than on the level is that it shrouds its funding. Its
largest donor during the period for which information is publically
available was an apparently non-Jewish mystery woman, Consola-
cion Esdicul, a resident of Hong Kong—a likely cut-out to disguise
the true source of the money. Its second largest donor was George
Soros, although until leaked tax records exposed the lie, J Street's
website and officers had strongly denied receiving funding from Soros, a Jew who is known for anti-Israel views. "We got tagged as having [Soros's] support without the benefit of actually getting funded!"

said J Street's executive director, Jeremy Ben-Ami, slyly, before the truth came out.[103] Donors to J Street's political action committee included an officer of the National Iranian American Council, widely regarded as supportive of the Iranian regime, as well as "several leaders of Muslim student groups, Saudi- and Iranian-born Americans, and Palestinian- and Arab-American businessmen who also give to Arab-oriented PACs," according to an article in the *Jerusalem Post*.[104] Ben-Ami responded to this revelation by saying that Arab and Muslim donors accounted for "at most three percent" of the budget, but this failed glaringly to explain why such individuals would donate at all to a "pro-Israel" group.

Then, too, there is the nature of J Street's activities. Writing about J Street in the *Times of Israel*, Daniel Frank nailed the essential point, "It's fine for a group that is critical of Israel to be defined as being pro-Israel, but it actually has to do stuff that is pro-Israel."[105] J Street's work is all in the opposite direction. It lobbied against the Obama administration's veto of a UN Security Council resolution that one-sidedly criticized Israel, and urged a retraction of Obama's threat to use military force as a last resort to stop Iran from getting a nuclear bomb. It denounced Israel's security barrier and opposed Israel's military action in Gaza in 2008 and 2009. It "facilitated" meetings of Richard Goldstone with members of Congress when his famous eponymous report was being promoted, before Goldstone himself repudiated it. And J Street's political action committee raised funds for the reelection of members of Congress who dissent from the pro-Israel policies of the vast majority on Capitol Hill. J Street cofounder, the Israeli ex-patriot Daniel Levy, who praised Walt and Mearsheimer's book in the pages of *Ha'aretz*, has said that the Holocaust "excused" the creation of Israel which was otherwise "an act that was wrong"[106] and that "maybe, if this collective Jewish presence" in the Middle East "can only survive by the sword, then Israel really ain't a good idea."[107] Little wonder, then, that J Street's "pro-Israel" pose did not deter Mearsheimer from mentioning it among the "righteous."

In rattling off that roster, Mearsheimer aptly noted that it was "just to name a few," and he limited himself to Americans. Had he looked overseas it could have grown exponentially. In England he might have begun with a bow to the *London Review of Books* which first published his and Walt's screed against "the Lobby." That magazine is subsidized financially and given its slant by its editor, an

American-born Jew, Mary-Kay Wilmers, who has described herself as "unambiguously hostile to Israel."[108] So common is the type in that country that it was the focus of Howard Jacobson's satirical 2010 novel, *The Finkler Question*, winner of the Booker Prize, which revolved around an organization of Jews who were "proud to be ashamed" of Israel.

If some Jews, like those portrayed by Jacobson, are moved to repudiate Israel out of ethnic self-consciousness, others, exemplified by Falk, opportunistically flaunt a Jewish lineage that is otherwise meaningless to them to lend weight to their anti-Israel pronouncements. Others, like *Tikkun* magazine's Michael Lerner, who calls himself "rabbi" without having attended seminary, shamelessly cloak their invective against Israel in invocations of the Jewish prophetic tradition. For the Falks and the Lerners and their ilk, the true motive is ideology,* and Jewishness is merely brandished as a shield for their Israel-bashing while lending cover to non-Jewish Israel-bashers, helping to protect them against the taint of anti-Semitism. The big prize of all this activity, however, is the one aimed at by J Street: namely, to divide the American Jewish community on the subject of Israel. The intended result is to overhaul America's Middle East policy by making gentiles wonder why they should support Israel when the Jews, themselves, are of two minds.

---

* So transfixed did the Left, Jewish and gentile, become with its new paradigm that it lost sight of its own core values. Whatever the historical model for achieving them, the goals of Leftism are presumably those shimmering ideals first voiced in the French Revolution: *liberté, égalité, fraternité.* As measured against these humane standards, Israel ranks as one of the world's finest—and most progressive—countries. I have spelled this out in detail in a short e-book, *Liberal Oasis: The Truth About Israel,* published by Encounter Books in 2014, available on Kindle, Nook, Apple, and other electronic platforms.

eleven

Israel in the Dock

On September 28, 2000, Ariel Sharon took a thirty-four-minute walk. His footsteps made the ground tremble—politically speaking. Sharon had rehabilitated his career after the disgrace of Sabra and Shatilla and had recently won leadership of the Likud Party which was then in opposition to the Labor government of Ehud Barak. Sharon's stroll took place on the Temple Mount, the most religiously contentious spot on the face of the earth. It is Judaism's holiest site and Islam's third holiest, and it is sacred to Christians, as well.

Sharon came accompanied by one thousand Israeli police, lest Palestinians respond with violence since the locale was highly sensitive, the moment was fraught, and Sharon was a lightning rod. American officials had appealed to Barak to prohibit the foray. But Barak said he did not want to appear to be silencing the opposition since he, himself, and not the Palestinians, was the true target of Sharon's little demonstration. Its purpose was to dramatize Likud's charge that Barak had gone too far in the peace terms he had proposed to the Palestinians at the Camp David summit two months before, including an offer to relinquish sovereignty over the Temple Mount.

But what was too much in Sharon's eyes was too little for the Palestinian leader, Yasser Arafat, who rejected Barak's proposal. This refusal and Arafat's failure to put a counteroffer on the table prompted US President Bill Clinton to blame Arafat for the impasse. Clinton didn't make his feelings explicit until years later in his memoirs, but they were apparent at the summit's conclusion, when he lavished appreciation on Barak but volunteered few words of praise for Arafat. Although Arafat's obduracy irked Barak and Clinton, the Palestinian leader, too, went away angry, feeling that the Americans had betrayed their advance promise not to place blame. The mutual recrimination, conveyed to respective publics, was still heavy in the air when Sharon took his walk.

Sure enough, Palestinians rioted in Jerusalem hard on the heels of Sharon's tour. The violence was quelled after a few hours with dozens of injuries among both rioters and police, but without loss of life. Things turned worse the next day, however.

That was a Friday, the day of special prayer services for Muslims, and it also happened to be the day before the Jewish holy day of Rosh Hashanah which would begin that evening. Worshippers packed Al Aqsa Mosque atop the mount for midday prayers, where they heard the imam, Sheikh Hayan al-Idrisi, a militant opposed to peace negotiations and with a history of anti-Semitic exclamations, exhorting the gathering to "eradicate the Jews from Palestine."[1]

Thousands swarmed out of the mosque hurling rocks and bottles, and besieged a small police outpost nearby. The mob then proceeded to the ledge overlooking the Western Wall and heaved projectiles at the Jews gathered there in pre-holiday prayer. Israeli police were summoned, and they led the worshippers to safety before storming up a steep walkway to the top of the mount to disperse the rioters and relieve the besieged police post. They fired rubber bullets and some live ammunition, and four of the Muslims fell dead.

That same day, a Palestinian policeman in Qalqilya participating in a joint patrol with two Israeli colleagues, a common exercise under the cooperative arrangements instituted as part of the Israeli–Palestinian peace process, turned his gun on them, killing one and wounding the other. The second *intifada* had begun.

Whereas the first *intifada* had been waged primarily with stones, the second employed more lethal weapons. Under the terms of the peace process, a Palestinian police force had been formed and armed. Six weeks before Sharon's stroll, a Palestinian newspaper had quoted the former commissioner of that force, General Ghazi Jabali, as predicting that "the Palestinian police will lead . . . when the hour of confrontation arrives."[2] The killing in Qalqilya was but the first shot: soon the full arsenal of the Palestinian police was aimed at Israel. More lethal, still, was the wide use of suicide bombers, carrying out massacres in markets, buses, restaurants, and schools. On the other side, the Israeli army which had reacted to the first *intifada* mostly with beatings and jailings, now brought devastating fire power into play. This was not civil disturbance; it was war.

And it brought into bold relief the transformation that had taken place in Israel's standing with the world. The sympathy the country enjoyed in 1967 had been eaten away over the following twenty-five years by terror and oil and the Arab takeover of the United Nations; by Menachem Begin's solipsistic nationalism and the war in Lebanon; and by the transformation of the paradigm of Leftism from class struggle to ethnic struggle. The signing of the Oslo Accords on the White House lawn in 1993 had completed the rehabilitation of the Palestine Liberation Organization (PLO), decades after it had blasted its way onto the world stage with dramatic acts of terror. But it also served to halt the erosion of Israel's position. With the two sides agreeing to recognize each other and to hammer out a two-state solution antipathy to Israel became moot. Now, however, as that hopeful chapter went up in smoke, the international community responded with indignation directed mostly at Israel.

The bias was symbolized at the outset by Peter Jennings of *ABC Evening News*, who opened the program on that night after Sharon's walk, that is, the night of the first deaths, with the pronouncement: "Four Palestinians were killed by Israelis on [the Temple Mount] today."[3] And what of the Israeli who had been killed in Qalqilya that day? Not a hint of it from Jennings or anyone else in the broadcast. Moreover, the phrase, "Palestinians were killed by Israelis," omitted entirely the relevant detail that (in contrast to the unmentioned Israeli who had been murdered in cold blood) the four victims were part of a mob that was trying to kill Israelis. ABC's correspondent on the scene, Gillian Findlay, who shared Jennings's reputation for chilliness toward Israel, compounded his omission by reporting falsely that Israeli forces appeared on the mount to "flex . . . their muscles." This description, which made it seem that the Israelis were the instigators of the confrontation, belied the visual evidence of the violent provocation to which they were responding. So ABC edited the footage to fit its story line. Viewers of other networks saw the Palestinians showering worshippers at the Western Wall with rocks and bottles, then Israeli forces rushing up the mount to disperse them. But ABC aired only the second part of this sequence. Neither in visual images nor in words did it provide any clue to what had precipitated the Israeli charge.

This single initial episode of journalistic malfeasance was to prove a harbinger of much of the international reaction to this nasty war as it raged over the ensuing four to five years. Much of the world shut its eyes to this essential but perhaps counterintuitive fact: however much they might be outgunned and might be suffering heavier casualties, the Palestinians were the aggressors whereas Israel was acting in self-defense.

Subsequently, considerable evidence emerged suggesting that Arafat had been planning the *intifada* and had seized Sharon's walk as an excuse to pull the trigger. This, at least, was the conclusion Palestinian Israeli journalist Khaled Abu Toameh reached in an article he published two years into the war:

> A few days after the failure of the Camp David summit . . . the Palestinian Authority's monthly magazine, *Al-Shuhada* ("*The Martyrs*"), published the following letter . . . "From the negotiating delegation led by the commander and symbol, Abu Ammar (Yasser Arafat) to the brave Palestinian people, be prepared. The Battle for Jerusalem has begun." . . .
>
> The letter was published in a magazine distributed only among PA security personnel. It did not appear in any of the daily newspapers . . . Hence the message Arafat was sending to his armed men was clear: "Be prepared for an all-out confrontation with Israel, because I refuse to accept Israeli and American dictates." . . .
>
> Freih Abu Middein, the PA Justice Minister, said he could see the writing on the wall. In an interview . . . published on August 24, 2000, he warned: "Violence is near and the Palestinian people are willing to sacrifice even 5,000 casualties." The statement came after a series of meetings that Arafat had held with his cabinet ministers. . . .
>
> Imad Faluji, the PA communications minister, admitted on October 11, 2001, that the violence had been planned in July, far in advance of Sharon's "provocation." He said: "Whoever thinks that the intifada broke out because of the despised Sharon's visit to Al-Aksa Mosque, is wrong, even if this visit was the straw that broke the back of the Palestinian people. This intifada was planned in advance, ever since President Arafat's return from the Camp David negotiations."[4]

Perhaps most telling, Abu Toameh quoted from an interview given in 2001 to the pan-Arab newspaper, *Asharq al-Awsat*, by

Marwan Barghouti, the effective field marshal of the *intifada*. Said Barghouti:

> I knew that the end of September was the last period . . . be-
> fore the explosion, but when Sharon reached al-Aqsa Mosque,
> this was the most appropriate moment for the outbreak of the
> *intifada* . . . The night prior to Sharon's visit, I participated in a
> panel on a local television station and I seized the opportunity
> to call on the public to go to al-Aqsa Mosque in the morning,
> for it was not possible that Sharon would reach [the Temple
> Mount] . . . and walk away peacefully. I . . . went to al-Aqsa in
> the morning . . . We tried to create clashes without success be-
> cause of the differences of opinion that emerged with others
> in al-Aqsa compound at the time. . . . After Sharon left . . . we
> discussed the manner of response and how it was possible to
> react in all the cities and not just in Jerusalem. We contacted all
> factions. [Later that day] I prepared a leaflet in the name of the
> Higher Committee of Fatah, coordinated with the brothers [e.g.,
> Hamas], in which we called for a reaction to what happened in
> Jerusalem.[5]

In an article in 2010, Abu Toameh reported a further revelation. It had been known at the time that once the *intifada* began, Arafat's forces released from custody hundreds of terror operatives belong-ing to Hamas and Islamic Jihad whom the Palestinian Authority had incarcerated under the system of security cooperation with Is-rael that had been a cornerstone of the peace process. Now, an addi-tional bit of information came to light, as Abu Toameh wrote:

> Former Palestinian Authority Chairman Yasser Arafat in-
> structed Hamas to launch terror attacks against Israel when he
> realized that the peace talks weren't going anywhere, Mahmoud
> Zahar, one of the Hamas leaders in the Gaza Strip, revealed
> on Tuesday. "President Arafat instructed Hamas to carry out a
> number of military operations in the heart of the Zionist entity
> after he felt that his negotiations with the Israeli government
> then had failed," Zahar told students and lecturers at the Is-
> lamic University in Gaza City.[6]

In 2012, in an interview on Dubai TV, Arafat's widow, Suha, added this to the picture:

Yasser Arafat had made a decision to launch the Intifada. Immediately after the failure of the Camp David [negotiations], I met
him in Paris upon his return, in July 2001 [she meant 2000].
Camp David has failed, and he said to me: "You should remain
in Paris." I asked him why, and he said: "Because I am going to
start an *Intifada*. They want me to betray the Palestinian cause.
They want me to give up on our principles, and I will not do so.
I do not want Zahwa's friends in the future to say that Yasser
Arafat abandoned the Palestinian cause and principles. I might
be martyred, but I shall bequeath our historical heritage to
Zahwa [their daughter] and to the children of Palestine."[7]

In contrast to this evidence, during the first weeks of the *intifada*
Western news organizations quoted numerous Palestinian figures
saying that Arafat could not have stopped the violence if he tried.
Indeed this formula was volunteered so often that it seemed to reflect a deliberate public relations strategy by the Palestinian leadership that was adopted uncritically by the international media,
which rarely asked the obvious question: why hadn't he tried?

Top US negotiator Dennis Ross recounts in his memoir the fran-
tic efforts of President Bill Clinton, Secretary of State Madeleine
Albright, CIA Director George Tenet, and other American officials
to stanch the violence and rescue the peace process in which the
US administration had invested so heavily. A high point of these efforts during the third week of the *intifada* was a summit meeting at
Sharm el-Sheikh, where Egyptian President Hosni Mubarak hosted
Arafat, Barak, Clinton, and other international leaders. A plan was
agreed for a mutual stand-down from confrontation and resump-
tion of peace talks, but nothing came of it:

> Arafat got his invitation to Washington and we got our state-
> ment at the end of Sharm but once again Arafat failed in his
> performance. In the name of the Palestinian Authority a gen-
> eral statement calling for an end to violence was issued, but the
> buffer zones did not appear, the incitement did not end, and the
> violence continued. Thus, the Israelis, after making some initial
> moves, stopped their compliance.[8]

The evidence that Arafat orchestrated the *intifada* is substantial
but less than definitive. The Israeli journalists Amos Harel and Avi

Isaacharoff researched the issue and concluded, "Far more than . . . Arafat planned the violence, he hitched a ride on it." In their view "Palestinian violence erupted from below," and "the leadership of the Palestinian Authority. . . wanted to harness it to attempt to use force to bring about an Israeli withdrawal to the 1967 lines."[9]

Whether Arafat set the fire or merely fanned the flames, however, this was a war that only the Palestinian side wanted. The very name the Palestinians chose for the conflict, *intifada,* which means uprising, made this clear. And although the Palestinians suffered much more, the costs for the Israelis were huge: more casualties than in the 1967 Six Day War or the 1956 Sinai campaign. Because the toll was taken mostly by suicide bombers in civilian facilities, the fabric of Israeli daily life was badly damaged.

Despite the jarring photographs of buses and pizza parlors bombed in cities throughout Israel, the larger part of international reaction treated the Israelis as the wrongdoers and the Palestinians as the victims. A few examples starkly convey the flavor of that attitude. In England, *The Guardian* editorialized that Israel was waging a "campaign of terror across the Palestinian territories," and demanded that "the world . . . stand up to Sharon."[10] It carried an ad signed by over a thousand people including tens of members of Parliament (MPs), lords, labor leaders, celebrities, and Prime Minister Tony Blair's sister-in-law accusing Israel (and only Israel) of "atrocities" and "acts of barbaric ferocity."[11] Former President Jimmy Carter called for the United States to withhold economic and military aid from Israel although he recommended no pressure on the other side.[12] South Africa's Archbishop Desmond Tutu saw fit to offer the Jews a condescending lecture on Judaism: "Have our Jewish sisters and brothers . . . turned their backs on their profound and noble religious traditions? Have they forgotten that God cares deeply about the downtrodden?"[13] Portuguese Nobel prize winner Jose Samarago opined, "What is happening in Palestine is a crime we can . . . compare . . . to what happened at Auschwitz."[14] Greek composer Mikis Theodorakis declaimed that the Jews were "the root of all evil," then, in response to the ensuing uproar, clarified that the root of all evil was the Israeli government rather than Jews, per se.[15]

That much of this smacked of anti-Semitism did not silence echoes from leftist Jews in Israel and the Diaspora. The Israeli radical, Uri Avnery, celebrated the killing of his countrymen when he characterized the battle over the Jenin refugee camp, which claimed the lives of twenty-three Israeli soldiers as well as fifty-odd Palestinians, as "the Palestinian Stalingrad, a story of immortal heroism."[16] And British Labour Party MP Gerald Kaufman, perhaps the original inspiration for novelist Howard Jacobson's Jews who are "proud to be ashamed," delivered a tirade against the "barbarism" of the Israelis: "It is time to remind Sharon that the Star of David belongs to all Jews and not to his repulsive government. His actions are staining the Star of David with blood."[17]

Beyond the vitriol, various academics began to advocate a boycott of Israeli universities and scholars. Ironically, one of the first victims of this movement was the radical Oren Yiftachel, the one-time chairman of *B'Tselem*, who subjected his own country to relentless invective and believed that "Palestinian violence [is] a legitimate revolt against colonial occupation."[18] In 2002, Yiftachel submitted an article that he had coauthored with a Palestinian academic to the British scholarly journal, *Political Geography*. According to *The Guardian*, Yiftachel "said it was returned to him unopened with a note stating that *Political Geography* could not accept a submission from Israel."[19] When Yiftachel refused to let the matter end there, the journal demanded that the paper be revised to add "a comparison of Israel and apartheid South Africa."[20]

In 2005, the Association of University Teachers (AUT) in Great Britain adopted resolutions boycotting Haifa and Bar Ilan Universities and also called for circulation among all its affiliates of a resolution of a Palestinian academic association calling for a "comprehensive . . . boycott [of] all Israeli academic and cultural institutions." The boycott was rescinded by vote the next year, only to be reinstated by the larger University and College Union into which the AUT had at that point merged. That union's lawyers warned that the boycott might violate the antidiscrimination rules of the European Union, so it was dropped, although it continued to be pressed by various sections of the teachers' union movement in Britain and elsewhere. Some years later, the Irish teachers' union endorsed an academic boycott of Israel, as did academic groups in Australia, South Africa, and the United States. None of these unions or other bodies has a record of promoting boycotts against other countries, not even those that deny academic freedom or the right to form labor unions—which one might suppose would be paramount concerns of teacher unions.

This was exemplified by the famous physicist Stephen W. Hawking who announced in 2013 that he was withdrawing from the annual Presidential Conference in Jerusalem to "respect the boycott" of Israeli academia.[21] Hawking has apparently thought little of lending his eminence to vicious regimes in search of legitimacy. In 2006, he traveled to the People's Republic of China to keynote an international physics conference. "Dr. Hawking's talk was part of the very public kickoff" to the event, held in Beijing's Great Hall of the People, the seat of government, where, "his mere presence was a powerful symbol of what China is and would like to be," reported *The New York Times*.[22] A year later, he performed a similar service for the Islamic Republic of Iran whose state-run Press TV crowed: "World-renowned scientist Stephen Hawking is to spend 10 days in Iran, the first-ever visit by the famous physicist and mathematician."[23] But Israel was another story.

Hawking was not alone in his double standards. The University of Johannesburg severed its relationship with Ben-Gurion University in response to a campaign led by Archbishop Tutu, who declared, "Israeli universities are an intimate part of the Israeli regime."[24] Yet, neither Tutu nor the university seems to have applied that criterion to the People's Republic of China. The school maintains a cooperative relationship with Sun Yat-Sen University, and its professors collaborate with the Harbin Institute of Technology, both of which are state-run and the latter of which is deeply connected with the Military Engineering Institute of the People's Liberation Army and boasts on its website that "a number of graduates have . . . become generals of the PLA."[25]

Each of the tactics with which Israel attempted to quell the violence directed against it was denounced in turn. Closures and curfews were called "collective punishment." Targeted assassinations of terrorist organizers were called "extrajudicial killings." And throughout, because Israel's military force was so much mightier than that of the Palestinians, Israel's military strikes were called "disproportionate," as if the appropriate response to a Palestinian suicide bombing in an Israeli pizzeria was for Israel to send its own suicide bombers into Palestinian pizzerias.

The principle of "proportionality" in Just War doctrine does not refer to a balance between attack and counterattack. Rather, it holds that the degree of force employed must not far exceed what is needed to achieve a specific military objective. For example, to capture a city is one thing; to level it is quite another.

The rule of proportionality also assumes that the objective of any military operation is legitimate to begin with. Whereas Israeli actions aimed at Palestinian commanders and fighters and their weapons and bomb factories, what were the military objectives of the Palestinian side? A discotheque, a university cafeteria, a Passover seder. This raises a corollary to the principle of proportionality, the Just War rule of "distinction" which requires efforts to avoid harming noncombatants. Of course, noncombatants will always be among the victims of fighting, but warriors are obligated to minimize these casualties. Israel was often charged by its international critics with causing too much injury to civilians, but there was never a case in which this was intentional. In contrast, the targets of Palestinian attacks were mostly civilian and always intentional. Senator Daniel Patrick Moynihan once said that some regimes commit abominations in practice whereas Communist regimes do it on principle, and that "anyone who cares about human rights will know what type of abomination is the more destructive of those rights."[26] He was comparing the internal practices of democracies and dictatorships. But the analogous judgment could be made about the contrasting methods of warfare of Israelis and Palestinians. Yet, not merely were the two sides routinely equated, condemnations of unmistakable Palestinian war crimes were often oddly pro forma whereas Israel's alleged abuses were denounced with heat and passion.

The culmination of the international censure of Israel was the ruling of the International Court of Justice on the separation barrier (or "wall" or "fence"). Each of Israel's offensive tactics had drawn reproach, but the barrier was purely defensive, designed to prevent Palestinians concealing bombs from walking across the border. Perhaps for that very reason, Israel's detractors attacked it stridently. More reasonably, they argued that the barrier, which was placed so that about 10 percent of the land of the West Bank came out on the Israeli side, would amount to a *fait accompli* when the borders of a Palestinian state were ultimately determined. There were also complaints, including by some Israelis from the political center as well as the Left, that in places the barrier detoured to favor Israeli settlements where there was no security need to do so. In fact, legal action over some such cases won rulings from the Israeli Supreme Court which ordered that the barrier be rerouted to minimize disruption to the lives of Palestinians.

Presumably, the barrier would have met with less opposition had it been built exactly along the lines of 1967, but this, too, would have prejudged ultimate borders—in favor of the Palestinians rather than the Israelis. UN Security Council Resolution 242, the binding legal authority and the basis for peace making, specifies that the final borders remain to be determined through diplomacy; counter-proposals to stipulate a return to the prewar borders were rejected at the time. Thus, for Israel to build a barrier along the 1967 lines would have amounted to capitulation to the terror war being waged against it.

In 2004, the General Assembly, where the Arab and Muslim states, with the cooperation of the rest of the developing countries, have exercised an overwhelming and mechanical majority for many years, passed a resolution asking the International Court of Justice for an "advisory opinion" on the legality of the barrier.* The court's ruling, by votes of fourteen to one and thirteen to two, with only the American jurist, the eminent legal scholar Thomas Buergenthal, consistently dissenting, epitomized everything that is hopelessly corrupt and dishonest about the United Nations.

In a decision oddly in synch with the United Nations's parallel idea that terror is self-determination in disguise, the court dismissed Israel's explanation that the barrier was built in self-defense by saying that states have no right to defend themselves against terrorist groups! The ruling stated: "Article 51 of the Charter . . . recognizes the existence of an inherent right of self-defense in the case of armed attack *by one State* against another State. However, Israel does not claim that the attacks against it are imputable to a foreign State."[27] [Emphasis added.] Since the attack did not come from a state, Israel could not invoke self-defense.

This was not only intuitively preposterous, it was also a jaw-dropping misstatement of the Charter. Article 51 reads:

* This in itself contravened the UN Charter which barred the General Assembly from usurping the authority of the Security Council, but a precedent for this had been set during the Korean War when the United States, in order to circumvent a Soviet veto in the Security Council, engineered a vote of the General Assembly to claim for itself the right to exercise extraordinary powers in "emergency sessions." As described in Chapter 5, the United States long ago lost the hegemony it exercised in the early days of the United Nations, and this precedent had been seized upon. Most emergency sessions have been devoted to lacerating Israel, and in this case the referral to the court was made by the General Assembly acting in its tenth "emergency" session, which was by then in its eighth year.

Nothing in the present Charter shall impair the inherent right of individual or collective self-defense if an armed attack occurs against a Member of the United Nations.

Note that this refers to an attack *against* a member state, but says nothing about it having to be an attack *by* a state. The court was simply conjuring this out of thin air, as Buergenthal noted in his dissent.

The court acknowledged that legally binding Security Council resolutions adopted in response to the attacks on the United States of September 11, 2001, explicitly applied the "inherent right of self-defense" cited in Article 51 to terrorist attacks. But it claimed this was not relevant to the Israeli case because Palestinian attacks emanated from territory where "Israel exercises control." Aside from the fact that the *intifada,* which had by then been raging for four years, showed that Israel "control" of the Palestinian territories did not exist in practice, neither did it exist in principle in the eyes of the court: its entire opinion was premised on a presumption of Palestinian sovereignty, or, as Buergenthal put it, Palestine's "assimilat[ion] to a state." If the court had accepted Israeli sovereignty, it could not have objected to Israel's building a barrier *within* its sovereign domain. Indeed, it could not have heard the case at all since it does not deal with the internal affairs of states.

In short, the entire ruling was an egregious exercise in bad faith. The court knew where the politics of the United Nations required that it come out, and it was apparently willing to twist words and meanings without limit or logic to reach its preordained conclusion.

The International Court of Justice is an adjunct to the United Nations, and its rulings have no more power and legitimacy than most UN resolutions. Ignoring the court, Israel completed the barrier, and it proved effective in bringing an end to the *intifada.* This not only saved Israeli lives, it arguably benefitted the Palestinians, as well. In the absence of a barrier, Israel would have felt compelled to employ ever more aggressive tactics in rooting out the infrastructure of suicide bombing in the West Bank and Gaza, which would surely have taken a substantial toll in Palestinian lives and property.

The *intifada* had no formal end date; most observers put its conclusion somewhere in 2005. But, before Israel could catch its breath, it found itself at war again. On July 12, 2006, commandos of Hezbollah ambushed an Israeli patrol near the Lebanese border with the aim of capturing some soldiers. The month before, a radical faction in Gaza had succeeded in snatching one, Gilad Shalit, from Israeli soil. That perhaps inspired Hezbollah, which had made similar attempts in the past, to redouble its efforts. Captive Israeli soldiers were a valuable prize since Israel had previously demonstrated its willingness to swap prisoners in ratios of a thousand to one in order to get its fighters back.

Israel had withdrawn abruptly from Lebanon in 2000, after eighteen years of occupying a security belt across its border following its 1982 invasion. One of the many unforeseen consequences of that earlier war had been to abet the rise of Hezbollah, a new Shiite movement sponsored by Tehran. By taking credit for driving Israel out, Hezbollah was able to assume a mantle of national heroism even though it was arguably more loyal to Iran than to its own country. Feeling its oats, Hezbollah demanded that Israel also evacuate Shebaa Farms, an uninhabited strip about one mile wide and five miles long that Israel captured from Syria in 1967 as part of the Golan Heights. It had been ruled by Syria from the time Syria and Lebanon became independent following World War II, but Hezbollah now claimed that Shebaa Farms was properly a part of Lebanon. Although UN officials on the ground in 2000 had certified that Israel had withdrawn from every inch of Lebanon, this clouded the issue.

Hezbollah's spokesman, Hassan Ezzedin, later acknowledged that the new demand was a pretext to continue the struggle with Israel. *The New Yorker*'s Jeffrey Goldberg recounted his meeting with Ezzedin:

> "If they go from Shebaa, we will not stop fighting them," he told me. "Our goal is to liberate the 1948 borders of Palestine," he added, referring to the year of Israel's founding. The Jews who survive this war of liberation, Ezzeddin said, "can go back to Germany, or wherever they came from." He added, however, that the Jews who lived in Palestine before 1948 will be "allowed to live as a minority and they will be cared for by the Muslim majority."[28]

Hezbollah's patron, the government of Iran, often said that it aimed to wipe Israel from the face of the earth. And Hezbollah's own kingpin, Hassan Nasrallah, echoed this in a 1998 speech, perorating, "We shout in the face of the killers of the prophets, the children of pigs and monkeys . . . 'death to Israel.'"[29] In 2002, he went even further, making clear he was unappeased by Israel's withdrawal from Lebanon. Ridiculing what he said was the Christian Zionist plan "to return the Jews to Israel and rebuild their temple," he crowed "if they [Jews] all gather in Israel, it will save us the trouble of going after them worldwide."[30]*

The 2006 ambush left three Israeli soldiers dead and three others seriously wounded, and Hezbollah got its prize: two Israeli soldiers taken prisoner and whisked back across the border into Lebanon. When an Israeli tank gave chase, it hit a booby trap, killing its four crewmen, and another Israeli soldier who tried to retrieve them was cut down by mortar fire.

The military campaign that ensued over the next month was judged by prevailing opinion in Israel to have been deeply flawed, and a post-war investigative commission rendered harsh criticism of the prime minister, defense minister, and chief of staff. But there was little doubt among Israelis that Hezbollah had launched a war from which they could not shrink. The attack of July 12 was a wanton act of aggression, and its toll was large. Counting the two who were captured (and later executed), Israel lost ten men in those hours, proportionately equivalent to five hundred US soldiers.

Israel wreaked great destruction on Lebanon, but there was no question that its target was Hezbollah's military structure. Hezbollah, on the other hand, unleashed thousands of rockets at Israel aimed at the civilian population, forcing a quarter of a million Israelis to leave their homes. In short, Hezbollah had started the war. Its aims, according to its leader, were genocidal. And it backed those

---

* Charles Glass, the journalist and Middle East expert, has impugned the correspondent for *The Daily Star* of Lebanon who produced this quote, calling it an "apparent fabrication" and claiming that the account of the speech in another Lebanese newspaper, *As Safir*, "makes no reference to any anti-Semitic comments"(http://www.lrb.co.uk/v28/n16/charles-glass/learning-from-its-mistakes). Glass's take was echoed in various Leftist blogs, but the debate has been settled by Tony Badran, an American specialist on Hezbollah of Lebanese background, who discovered an audio recording of the speech on the Internet. (http://audio.moqawama.org/details.php?cid=1&linkid=189). "Anyone who claims this quote is a fabrication hasn't listened to the speech," he says. The newspaper account fails to provide full context and nuance, but Badran confirms that the quote is accurate and that "the speech is loaded with anti-Semitic remarks." (Tony Badran to author, e-mail, May 9, 2013.)

words by targeting the Israeli population. Nonetheless, Israel was the focus of international opprobrium.

Within the first days, UN Secretary-General Kofi Annan said, "I condemn without reservations the attack in southern Lebanon."[31] The government of Finland, speaking in the name of the European Union, of which it was president at that time, denounced Israel for "the disproportionate use of force."[32] French President Jacques Chirac called the attack "totally disproportionate."[33] Spanish Prime Minister Jose Luis Rodriguez Zapatero declared, "Israel is wrong."[34] In England, *The Guardian* editorialized that, "Israel's disproportionate response has now brought the area into chaos."[35] In *The Independent*, correspondent Robert Fisk saluted Hezbollah's "spiritual leader," Sheikh Mohammed Fadlallah, who declared he sought to "obliterate" Israel, as "among the wisest and most eloquent of clerics."[36] And *The Daily Telegraph* carried a cartoon showing "Tyre 2006" as a mirror of "Warsaw 1943" (the year the Nazis razed the Warsaw Ghetto).[37] Conservative British MP Sir Peter Tapsell put this last ugly analogy into words, calling Israel's actions "gravely reminiscent of the Nazi atrocity on the Jewish quarter of Warsaw."[38] A Danish parliamentarian sought to have visiting Israeli Foreign Minister Tzipi Livni arrested for "war crimes."[39] And US Senator Chuck Hagel, later to become secretary of defense, accused Israel of "systematic destruction" of Lebanon.[40]

Hagel also criticized the stance of the US government for signaling tacit approval of Israel's action. He was echoed by former President Jimmy Carter who seemed never to tire of second-guessing his successors, in contrast to the decorum exercised by other former presidents, just as he never tired of criticizing Israel.[41] Carter weighed in with an op ed in *The Washington Post* notable for its mendacity as well as its bias.[42] He began by chiding Israel over the fact that its soldier, Gilad Shalit, was being held hostage in Gaza. The captors, he said, "offered to exchange the soldier for the release of 95 women and 313 children who are among almost 10,000 Arabs in Israeli prisons, but . . . Israel rejected a swap." Aside from the facts that the number ten thousand was an exaggeration and the "children" were mostly sixteen- and seventeen-year-olds convicted of violence, the main point of that sentence was simply a lie. No such exchange had been offered. As *The New York Times* (and many other news sources) reported, "The groups holding [Shalit] said that before any information on him would be disclosed, Israel must release all Palestinian women in its jails and all Palestinian prisoners under the age of 18."[43] The four hundred-plus prisoners mentioned by Carter might get Israel some evidence that Shalit was still alive; the price for his freedom would be far steeper.

Turning to Lebanon, the former president said that Hezbollah sought to exchange the two Israeli soldiers it had captured for "some of the several thousand incarcerated Lebanese." In fact, at that moment, Israel and Hezbollah were arguing over how many Lebanese were held in Israeli prisons. Israel said the number was two—yes, two—whereas Hezbollah insisted it was four. Where Carter got his "several thousand" is anybody's guess. Then Carter prescribed that Israel withdraw from Shebaa Farms and "release the Lebanese prisoners." Whether the reality was two prisoners or four, the most prominent of these was Samir Kuntar, who in 1979 had infiltrated into Israel where he murdered a policeman before invading a home at random and killing a man and his four-year-old daughter by smashing her head against a rock. Kuntar was sixteen at the time, one of the "children" for whom Carter had cried crocodile tears.

"There will be no substantive and permanent peace for any peoples in this troubled region," concluded the former president, without even a pretense of evenhandedness, "as long as Israel is violating key U.N. resolutions, official American policy and the international 'road map' for peace by occupying Arab lands and oppressing the Palestinians." Was it possible that the Palestinian Authority or Hamas or Hezbollah were also doing anything to stand in the way of peace? Carter had not a word to say on this score.

Human Rights Watch, too, weighed in heavily against Israel. In the first days of fighting it issued numerous short documents addressing both sides, but with lengthier and more numerous criticisms aimed at Israel. Within three weeks of the onset, it published a fifty-page booklet, *Fatal Strikes*, directed solely at Israel, although no similar compendium was released about Hezbollah's military campaign. According to *Fatal Strikes*, "The pattern of attacks during the Israeli offensive in Lebanon suggests that the failures cannot be explained or dismissed as mere accidents; the extent of the pattern and the seriousness of the consequences indicate the commission of war crimes."[44] Moreover, "In some cases, the [evidence] suggest[s] that Israeli forces deliberately targeted civilians."

How plausible was this? According to the government of Lebanon (and the United Nations) the total number of deaths in Lebanon from this war was 1,191.[45] Among them were Hezbollah fighters: 250 by Hezbollah's count, 600 to 800 by Israel's. Either number means that civilian deaths totaled in the hundreds. According to a book-length study of the war by the Rand Corporation commissioned by the US Air Force, Israeli forces flew 18,900 sorties and released 21,600 munitions from the air.[46] If they were "targeting civilians," as Human Rights Watch would have it, then Israel's military proficiency has been extremely overrated.

In reality, the reason so many flights caused so few deaths is that Israel was not for the most part hunting people, whether fighters or civilians. It was aiming for infrastructure and weapons, particularly Hezbollah's ten to twenty thousand rockets, of which some four thousand were indeed fired across the border during the fighting. That the number of deaths was so low implies the exact opposite of Human Rights Watch's allegation—that Israel in reality was targeting with great discrimination.

The Human Rights Watch report debunked Israel's explanation for the civilian casualties, namely Hezbollah's use of civilians as human shields:

> The Israeli government claims that it targets only Hezbollah, and that fighters from the group are using civilians as human shields, thereby placing them at risk. Human Rights Watch found no cases in which Hezbollah deliberately used civilians as shields to protect them from retaliatory Israeli attack.[47]

Whatever the formulation—"to protect them from retaliatory . . . attack"—may have meant, Hezbollah's entire military apparatus was embedded in Lebanon's civilian society. We have this on no less authority than Hassan Nasrallah himself, who boasted on Al-Manar, Hezbollah's television network, just weeks before the war that his cadres "live in their houses, in their schools, in their mosques, in their churches, in their fields, in their farms, and in their factories. You can't destroy them in the same way you would destroy an army."[48] This use of civilian facilities is itself a violation of the laws of war.

That Human Rights Watch was willfully blind to this may be illustrated by the case of the village of Srifa (or Sreifa) that was discussed at length in *Fatal Strikes* and was the first instance offered by Kenneth Roth in a letter to *The New York Sun* of "the most serious

Israeli abuses." According to the report, during a site visit to that village two weeks after it was struck by Israeli bombs, "Human Rights Watch saw no evidence that there had been Hezbollah military activity around the areas targeted by the IDF during or just prior to the attack: no spent ammunition, abandoned weapons or military equipment, trenches, or dead or wounded fighters."[49] It went on to add color: describing the discovery of a decomposing female body, naming some of the deceased and quoting villagers insisting "there was no Hezbollah in the neighborhood." One even said, "Except for one person, who didn't even belong to Hezbollah, no one in that neighborhood knew how to handle weapons."[50]

But the day after the bombing of Srifa, the Associated Press had reported, "In the village of Srifa . . . airstrikes flattened 15 houses after rockets were fired from the area."[51] *The Guardian* had reported the same day, "Srifa . . . was a local beauty spot . . . but it is also in the Hizbullah heartland from which rockets have been fired into Israel."[52] And the next month, with the fighting over, *The New York Times* reporter Hassan M. Fattah wrote from the scene: "[a] Sreifa official . . . estimated that up to two-thirds of the town's homes and buildings were demolished, leaving more than 43 people buried in the rubble. A majority of them were fighters belonging to Hezbollah and the allied Amal Party, residents said."[53]

In short, the reality of Srifa was quite the opposite of what Human Rights Watch had proclaimed with such certainty and indignation. There is no reason to believe it was accurate in any of the other cases it reported. The Israeli legal scholar Avi Bell has cited other examples in which Israel was taxed by Human Rights Watch for civilian casualties when in fact there was evidence of legitimate military targets.[54] While Human Rights Watch focused its fire on Israel, the crimes committed in this war were all by Hezbollah, both in attacking Israeli civilians and in hiding its own forces among Lebanese civilians.

Two years later, in late 2008, Israel went to war once again against the irregular army of an Islamist movement—this time in Gaza. Its adversary, Hamas, was regarded as a terrorist group by the European Union and the United States, but once again Israel incurred the preponderance of blame. Israel had withdrawn from Gaza in 2005, although it was criticized for maintaining partial control over the flow of people and goods between Gaza and the outside.

The next year Hamas won legislative elections, empowering it to form a government of the Palestinian Authority in a power-sharing arrangement with Fatah whose leader, Mahmoud Abbas, had won the presidency in 2005. But in 2007, chafing at its limited authority in the parliamentary system of the Palestinian Authority, Hamas seized sole control of Gaza in a bloody coup, in which some Fatah cadre were thrown to their deaths from rooftops.

Hamas's unyielding avowal of intent to eradicate Israel, made real by a daily barrage of rocket fire over the border, prompted Israel to tighten its hold on Gaza and to launch recurrent strikes at terrorists and their facilities. Palestinian advocates began to call Gaza "the world's largest prison." In 2008, the Egyptian government brokered a cease-fire, but when it expired and Hamas declined to renew it, Israel launched Operation Cast Lead, an invasion of Gaza aimed at crippling Hamas's offensive apparatus.

European governments, human rights organizations, public figures like Jimmy Carter and Archbishop Tutu, the global Left including Israel's home-grown Leftists, all once again raised their voices to rebuke Israel. This outpouring reached its apex in the action of the UN Human Rights Commission. Normally, in response to allegations of abuses it will appoint a "special rapporteur." But in this case, at the instance of the Organization of Islamic Cooperation, it voted to conduct a full-blown examination of the Gaza War.

The resolution authorizing this "investigation" also specified what its findings should be. In it, the council declared that it "strongly condemns the ongoing Israeli military operation . . . which has resulted in massive violations of the human rights of the Palestinian people," and created an "independent international fact-finding mission . . . to investigate all violations of international human rights law and international humanitarian law by . . . Israel."[55] No investigation of Hamas was authorized.

Initially, the position of chair of the commission was offered to Ireland's former president, Mary Robinson, who, as UN High Commissioner of Human Rights, had borne responsibility for the 2001 Durban Conference, where the scapegoating of the Jewish state and of Jews caused Secretary of State Colin Powell to order a US walkout. But even Robinson, no friend of Israel's, wanted no part of this rigged proceeding, turning down the job with the explanation that the mission was "guided not by human rights but by politics." After one or two other candidates reportedly also declined that post, Richard Goldstone, a prominent South African jurist and member of the board of Human Rights Watch, accepted it.

Goldstone and the three others who made up the panel had each gone on record during the Gaza War criticizing Israel's actions. In other words, to carry out an "investigation" producing findings it had already mandated, the commission fittingly selected "investigators" who had already made up their minds. Most flamboyant among them was retired Irish military officer Desmond Travers who claimed in a subsequent interview that "Gaza has now come into the history books in the same way as Guernica, Dresden, Stalingrad"— all of them cities that had experienced utter devastation.[56] In the same interview, he claimed outrageously that Ireland had turned pro-Palestinian because "so many Irish soldiers had been killed by Israelis . . . with a significant number who were taken out deliberately and shot (in South Lebanon)"—although no reputable source in Ireland or anywhere else has ever reported a single such event and Travers offered no source or evidence for this bizarre charge.

To no one's surprise, the commission concluded that Israel should be formally investigated for "war crimes" and "crimes against humanity" for perpetrating "violence against civilians" as "a deliberate policy." The problem with this accusation (apart from the fact that it rested on unverified claims, denied by Israel, coming from Hamas or people subject to its control) was that it could not be squared with the death toll. By Israel's count the number was just over 1,100, of whom some 700 were Hamas "operatives," leaving a total of 400-odd civilian dead. According to Palestinian sources 1,400 died in Gaza, and initially Hamas said only dozens of its men had been killed, meaning civilian deaths would have totaled 1,300 or so. But even accepting the dubious Hamas numbers, if Israel had been aiming to kill Palestinian civilians, its twenty-two-day campaign, employing tanks, infantry, air power, and gun boats, would have exacted a toll a hundred times higher.

A year later, Hamas's Interior Minister of Gaza Fathi Hamad confirmed what Israel has said about the number of Hamas fighters who fell: it was around seven hundred.[57] This means that even if the higher number of total deaths—1,400—was accurate, the ratio of civilians to fighters who were killed by Israel was low by the standards of modern warfare, and extremely low in view of the population density of Gaza. This corroborates Israel's clams that, far from targeting noncombatants, it took pains to hold down civilian casualties.

Then, in April 2011, Goldstone himself repudiated the conclusions of the Goldstone Commission, taking to the pages of *The Washington Post* to declare: "We know a lot more today about what happened in the Gaza war. . . . If I had known then what I know now, the Goldstone Report would have been a different document. . . . [C]ivilians were not intentionally targeted as a matter of policy."[58] It is, however, hard to think of what Goldstone knew in 2011 that he could not have known in 2009. A more plausible explanation for his about-face is that his original conclusions were shaped by the atmosphere of the United Nations, where fierce animus toward Israel reigns, and that once he returned to the outside world he felt embarrassed that he could not defend those conclusions.

In the meantime, yet another violent episode involving Gaza had roused the always-blame-Israel crowd yet again. In May of 2010, a militant Islamist group in Turkey organized a flotilla of ships to break the Israeli naval blockade of Gaza. The group framed its voyage as a humanitarian mission, and numerous Western leftists, including Jews and apparently a few Israelis, took part. Just as with the efforts of Rachel Corrie and her colleagues to block Israeli bulldozers, this was in fact a military operation in the guise of a nonviolent action. And indeed the International Solidarity Movement, the master of this technique, was the principal Western cosponsor.

Israel's blockade was designed to interdict weapons and explosives because Gaza's rulers had resumed their low-level warfare against Israel after the 2008 war ended. Israel offered to allow the boats to land at its own docks and then transport civilian goods over land to Gaza, but the flotilla's organizers turned this down. They were not at bottom interested in providing relief but in forcing Israel to abandon the blockade so that lethal goods could enter. Israeli naval commandos intercepted the flotilla and boarded it without weapons drawn. They were set upon by militants armed with metal bars, and in defense of their lives they opened fire, killing nine.

A familiar chorus sung out. A group styling itself "the Elders," twelve retired public figures including Jimmy Carter, Desmond Tutu, Mary Robinson, Nelson Mandela, and Kofi Annan issued a declaration that Israel's action was "completely inexcusable."[59] The European Parliament passed a resolution by a vote of 470 to 56 saying it "condemns the attack against the flotilla in international waters."[60] An editorial in *The Guardian* analogized Israel's action to that of "Somali pirates" and regretted that North Atlantic Treaty Organization warships were not dispatched to attack Israel.[61] Human Rights Watch called for an Israeli investigation to determine if excessive force had been used, but in the same breath it discredited the results in advance. "Given Israel's poor track record of investigating unlawful killings by its armed forces, the international community should closely monitor any inquiry to ensure it meets basic international standards and that any wrongdoers are brought to justice," said Sarah Leah Whitson.[62] Representing the "international community," the UN Human Rights Council promptly established a "fact-finding mission" that in short order produced a sixty-six-page report along the lines of what Whitson may have been looking for. Its principal conclusion was:

> The conduct of the Israeli military and other personnel towards the flotilla passengers was not only disproportionate to the occasion but demonstrated levels of totally unnecessary and incredible violence. It betrayed an unacceptable level of brutality. Such conduct cannot be justified or condoned on security or any other grounds. It constituted a grave violation of human rights law and international humanitarian law.[63]*

Once again, with the flotilla incident, as with the wars in Gaza and Lebanon and the second *intifada,* Israel was the focus of blame, as if to exemplify the French witticism, *cet animal est très méchant, quand on l'attaque it se défend* ("that animal is so vicious that when attacked it defends itself"). The logic of Israel's critics lies in the tautology that if only there were peace these outbreaks would not happen, and in the charge that, as *TIME* magazine, which has long

---

* A year later, when the incident had receded from the headlines, a second UN report, issued by a four-member panel appointed by the secretary-general amid diplomatic efforts to restore Israeli-Turkish relations, contradicted the one-sided one issued by the UN Human Rights Council. The later panel's composition—one Turk, one Israeli, the president of Colombia, and the former prime minister of New Zealand—was unusually balanced for the United Nations, and so, too, were its conclusions. It found that "Israel's blockade was legal," although it deemed Israel's boarding "excessive and unreasonable." It also said that it "seriously questions the true nature and objectives of the flotilla organizers." (United Nations, Secretary-General, *Report of the Secretary-General's Panel of Inquiry on the 31 May 2010 Flotilla Incident*, pars. 81, 86, 117.)

viewed Israel in a jaundiced light,[64] put it in a 2010 cover story, "Israel doesn't care about peace."[65]

A grain of truth in this topsy-turvy interpretation is that the Arab world has come a considerable distance since the Arab summit following the 1967 war that declared "no peace with Israel, no recognition of Israel, no negotiations with Israel." In contrast, the Arab summit of 2002 endorsed the Arab Peace Initiative launched by the Saudis that offered Israel an end to the conflict and "normal relations" with the Arab states if it would withdraw from all territory occupied in 1967 and grant the Palestinian "right of return" in some form. Hopeful though they are, Israel cannot accept these terms as given, particularly not the "right of return," and the Arabs have refused to bargain about them. Nonetheless, apart from the Islamists whose influence is growing in the region and who are unreconciled to Israel's existence, the prevailing position of the Arabs is that they will accept Israel if it makes peace with the Palestinians. But what stands in the way of that?

A second grain may be that many Israelis have grown cynical, coming to believe with heavy hearts that whatever concessions they make, the Arabs will not make peace with them. But anyone who knows Israelis knows that peace is the fondest wish of most, and Israel has a long record of grasping for whatever prospect of peace seemed in reach, including some that proved illusory. When Anwar Sadat offered peace with Egypt he insisted that Israel return every inch of the Sinai, which it did. He insisted, too, on some deal for the Palestinians, and the nationalist Begin met him halfway by proposing temporary Palestinian autonomy and negotiations on their final status—even though the Palestinian organizations at that time still insisted they would never countenance peace with Israel. This compromise, accepted by Sadat, was roundly denounced in the Arab world, but had the Palestinians not spurned it, the state of Palestine might have been born in the 1980s.

Israel signed a peace treaty with Jordan as soon as Jordan was willing. It sought a peace treaty with Lebanon during its ill-conceived invasion of 1982. It conducted indirect negotiations with Syria, brokered by Washington in the 1990s, first under Yitzhak Rabin and then under Netanyahu and Barak, that nearly achieved a settlement between Israel and Syria.[66] Reportedly there were further attempts that came close under Ehud Olmert in 2008 and Netanyahu again in 2010.[67] In all of these talks, Israel, according to published accounts, agreed to yield back the entire Golan Heights, but the deals fell through over secondary issues.

Israel has constantly sought to establish relations of any kind with the Arabs, who, with a few exceptions, have spurned these overtures. The very rubric of all the peace processes, "land for peace" makes clear, as both parties understand, that peace is the goal of the Israeli side. This was illustrated at the Annapolis summit meeting of Middle Eastern leaders convoked by the Bush administration in 2007, where *Agence France Press* reported:

> The Saudis offered a cold shoulder to Israeli Prime Minister Ehud Olmert's call for the Arab world to normalize ties with the Jewish state even before a peace deal is clinched.
>
> "Normalization happens after there is peace," the Saudi ambassador to the United States Adel al-Juber told reporters following the conference. . . .
>
> "The Arab peace initiative is very specific as to what it requires and is very specific as to what the payoff will be the . . . you do not get the fruits of peace before you make peace, and we have made that very clear," al-Juber said.[68]

Foreign Minister Livni asked the Arab officials assembled, "Why doesn't anyone want to shake my hand?" and "Why doesn't anyone want to be seen speaking to me?"[69] She was addressing the representatives of the sixteen states that attended. Others were not willing even to be in the room.

The Arab answer to this complaint is that Israel wants peace on its own terms without accommodating the national aspirations of the Palestinians. It is true that Israelis did not originally accept Palestinian nationalism or viewed it as a mortal threat, but until the 1960s most Palestinians gave little sign of conceiving of themselves as constituting a distinct people (as opposed to part of the "Arab nation" or the Muslim *umma*), and those who led the way to national identity, Fatah and the PLO, did in fact intend it as a mortal threat to Israel.

Only with the Oslo Accords of 1993 did the possibility of a two-state solution, in which Israelis accept Palestinian peoplehood and Palestinians accept the existence of Israel, come clearly into focus. Over the next fifteen years, the peace process that flowed from Oslo reached three hopeful but ultimately disappointing climacterics. The first was at Camp David in July 2000 when Arafat turned down Barak's offer cold. Israelis were shocked by how much Barak was prepared to yield. But this only showed that the process was not yet ripe (and Barak bears blame for pushing for the summit under this circumstance), because what Barak offered, however generous it seemed to Israelis, was not sufficient for even the "peace camp" among the Palestinians.

However, at Taba in December 2000, in a last-ditch effort to rescue the process, President Clinton proposed terms that went considerably further than Barak's in meeting Palestinian demands regarding territory and Jerusalem, and he pursued some kind of breakthrough to the last days of his presidency. Barak secured the endorsement of the Israeli cabinet, but as Dennis Ross, the principal US negotiator, put it: "Alas, Arafat was not up to peacemaking. [He] had definitively demonstrated that he could not end the conflict."[70] One of Arafat's principal deputies at Camp David, Saeb Erekat, later quoted an exchange at Camp David that validates Ross's assessment. Speaking on Al-Jazeera TV, Erekat recalled that Clinton had asked Arafat:

[T]o acknowledge that the Temple of Solomon is located underneath the Haram Al-Sharif [the Temple Mount]. Yasser Arafat said to Clinton defiantly: "I will not be a traitor. Someone will come to liberate it after 10, 50, or 100 years. Jerusalem will be nothing but the capital of the Palestinian state, and there is nothing underneath or above the Haram Al-Sharif except for Allah."[71]

Thus did Arafat both deny any historic Jewish connection to Jerusalem and the land of Israel and affirm his conviction that in time it would all be liberated to become exclusively an Arab land and an Arab capital. That is why he would not make peace.

The third near miss in the peace process came in 2008 after Arafat had passed from the scene; it culminated a long process of secret diplomacy between Prime Minister Olmert and President Abbas. Olmert later estimated that the two had met thirty-five times over a two-year period. This ended in September 2008 with Olmert producing a map showing a territorial division in which Israel would keep 6.5 percent of the land of the West Bank but would cede in exchange a similar amount of Israeli land to a new Palestinian state, including a tunnel connecting the West Bank to Gaza. He asked Abbas to sign his acceptance on the spot. Olmert's account of what ensued was reported in *The New York Times*:

"I saw that he was agonizing. In the end he said to me, 'Give me a few days. I don't know my way around maps. I propose that tomorrow we meet with two map experts, one from your side and one from our side. If they tell me that everything is all right, we can sign.' The next day they called and said that Abu Mazen [Abbas] had forgotten that they needed to be in Amman that day, and they asked to postpone the meeting by a week.

"I haven't met with Abu Mazen since then. The map stayed with me."[72]

This version has not been denied by the Palestinians. The *Times* correspondent, Ethan Bronner, noted that, "in a separate interview, Mr. Abbas confirmed most of Mr. Olmert's account."[73] In a subsequent story, Associated Press correspondent Matti Friedman reported:

Palestinian negotiator Saeb Erekat confirmed the details of Olmert's offer . . . He said the Palestinians made a counter-offer, depositing their own map with the U.S. president three months later. He would not give details.[74]

Despite Erekat's claim, evidence of this alleged counteroffer is nowhere to be found.

Varying accounts have been given of Abbas's motives. Some say that it was because Olmert's domestic standing had been undermined by corruption charges. President Bush put it in his memoirs: "Abbas didn't want to make an agreement with a prime minster on his way out of office."[75] Other versions trace the collapse of negotiations to Israel's invasion of Gaza in December 2008. But former Secretary of State Condoleezza Rice in her memoirs recounts what was clearly the final act of these two years of diplomacy, and it occurred eight days before the Gaza War began.

I talked to the President [who was about to leave office after completing his second term] and asked whether he would be willing to receive Olmert and Abbas one last time. . . . We had one last chance. The two leaders came separately in November and December to say good-bye. The President took Abbas into the Oval Office alone and appealed to him to reconsider. The Palestinian stood firm, and the idea died.[76]

It is true that the Likud government of Prime Minister Binyamin Netanyahu that followed Olmert's was not very forthcoming in the terms of peace it was prepared to offer. Nonetheless, the Israeli public has shown that it wants its leaders to seize any convincing prospect of peace—and there is no reason to believe that this has changed. In those circumstances, Netanyahu would have either to be a peacemaker or get out of the way. The essential obstacle, however, has always been on the other side.

The achievement of peace between Israel and the Palestinians would bring such profound blessings to both peoples and perhaps their neighbors that the fact that it also would go far in restoring Israel's standing in the world would be merely a fringe benefit. The sad truth remains that if the Arabs had longed for this Promised Land with anything like the intensity of the Israelis, the Palestinians would have had a state of their own long since.

conclusion

Israel Imperiled

The children's verse "sticks and stones will break my bones but words will never harm me" is as false for countries as it is for children—but in a more material way. The opprobrium heaped on Israel whenever it finds itself in a confrontation with enemies who still, sixty-odd years after its founding, do not accept its existence, restricts its freedom of action, even though, more than perhaps any other state, its survival depends on its ability to defend itself militarily. No other country faces a near neighbor with the declared aim to "wipe it from the map" or well-armed forces on two of its borders sworn to its destruction and doing what they can to make this happen. The degree to which Israel has won acceptance by some of its neighbors and the hope that it may someday be accepted by them all are predicated on having given hard proof that it is indestructible.

Nonetheless, a hostile international atmosphere forces Israel to weigh each measure of self-defense against the political costs which can sometimes be astronomical. In 1973, on the eve of the Yom Kippur War, as Israeli leaders belatedly recognized that Egyptian and Syrian attacks were imminent, they were cautioned by the United States not to strike the first blow lest it compromise American support. Prime Minister Golda Meir, in secret testimony to an investigative commission on the war that was declassified in 2013, testified: "Had we gone to a preemptive strike, I have full confidence that the 'air lift' [of American arms that eventually turned the tide of battle] would not have come."[1] In part as a result of waiting until Egypt and Syria had attacked, Israel lost upward of 2,500 soldiers in that war, more than double, in proportion to population, the number America lost in the entirety of the war in Vietnam. Yet, Meir told the commission that she believed she had made the right choice. "I knew then, and I know now, too, that it's possible, maybe we could even say certain, that boys who are no longer would still be alive," she acknowledged. "But I don't know how many other boys would have fallen due to a lack of equipment."[2]

In the decades since, the political constraints on Israel have only increased. By narrowing Israel's maneuvering room in the face of the ceaseless threats of destruction, the global obloquy heaped on the Jewish state might indeed break its bones. This censure flows from two contradictory sources. The first is the material leverage that the Arabs exert thanks to their numbers and resources which, although insufficient to vanquish Israel on the battlefield, translate into political and economic power that intimidates the rest of the world. The second is the intellectual power of the contemporary Leftist paradigm in which the central drama of our time is the conflict of the "West against the rest"—and the conflict between Israelis and Palestinians has somehow become its apotheosis. This consigns Israel to the side of darkness and villainy, even in the face of the reality that, measured by the Left's nominal values—freedom, democracy, tolerance of racial, religious, and sexual diversity, equality of status for women, generosity to the needy—Israel is among the world's best countries and its enemies rank among the worst.

Israeli has withstood isolation and anathema thanks to its own strength of spirit and societal cohesion and also thanks to the United States which has consistently dissented from the global chorus of condemnation. Throughout the Arab world as well as among anti-Semites in the West, America's strong support for Israel is attributed to the mysterious power of "the Lobby," in other words, the Jews. But this explanation ignores how American democracy works. The American people have continued to identify with Israel, however much it is vilified. A Gallup Poll in March 2013 found that 64 percent of Americans supported Israel whereas 12 percent supported the Palestinians.[3] Other polls in 2013 were similar. (*The Washington Post*/ABC poll put the ratio at 55 percent for Israel to 9 percent for the Palestinians; Pew had it at 49 percent to 12 percent, and NBC/ *The Wall Street Journal*, 45 percent to 13 percent.[4]) Of course these numbers fluctuate, but they always show a whopping preponderance for Israel, on average by about four-to-one. Whenever public opinion is overwhelming on an issue, government policy will mirror it— lobby or no lobby. Can Stephen Walt and John Mearsheimer or any of the conspiracy theorists name a single exception to this rule? Or would they have us believe that a "Lobby" has not only manipulated office-holders but brainwashed the whole population?

Although the American people's sympathy for Israel has been durable, however, it is not guaranteed to last forever. The ideological Left, the bastion of contemporary anti-Israel sentiment, has always been weaker in America than elsewhere, but its influence is not inconsequential. For one thing, its voice is heard on college campuses from faculty who make the works of Israel-bashers like Edward Said, Noam Chomsky, and Judith Butler among the most widely assigned texts, as well as from student activists of the Muslim Student Associations, the Students for Justice in Palestine, and a miscellany of Leftist groups like those that attracted Rachel Corrie. To be sure, there are also Jewish groups that defend Israel, but today these are often defensive, even apologetic, in their advocacy and sometimes downright frightened of the rhetorically and occasionally physically violent behavior of their adversaries. Thus, they often seem to display less conviction than the anti-Israel voices which are, in Yeats's phrase, full of passionate intensity.

Few American students will earn their baccalaureate without getting an earful of the case against Israel in the classroom or on the commons or both. Even those who are not won over are bound to be affected. The anti-Israel movement knows it will score no sudden coup, but it is committed to the long war. As its patron saint Yasser Arafat put it: "I may be martyred, but I shall bequeath our historical heritage . . . to the children of Palestine."[5]

In addition, although the ideological Left may be small in numbers, it is able to exert influence with a much wider public by advancing its position through groups that present themselves as liberal rather than radical: human rights organizations, labor unions, churches, and even Jewish groups like J Street.

The osmotic process by which some of the views of the Left seep, albeit in diluted form, into the mainstream was evident at the 2012 Democratic Convention in a fight over the party's platform plank on the Middle East. The draft that was brought to the floor failed to describe Jerusalem as the capital of Israel as previous Democratic platforms had done. This was no oversight. Jerusalem is undeniably Israel's capital, but the drafters believed that saying so could be taken as prejudging the final status of the city which is one of the most contentious issues between Israel and the Palestinians.

However, refusing to say so amounted to a slap at Israel. There is no doubt that the platform was still pro-Israel. But this and a few other formulations on sensitive subjects such as refugees edged away from the staunch pro-Israel positions the Democrats had customarily taken and in this sense was a sign of the times.

When attention was drawn to the changes a ruckus ensued with both political parties spinning furiously. Republican candidate Mitt Romney said, with obvious exaggeration, that the Democrats' new language amounted to a "radical distancing" from Israel, whereas President Obama's team, which had engineered the changes, claimed they were merely semantic. The falsity of this spin, however, was brought home when Obama's camp, feeling the political heat, moved to amend the plank on the convention floor to restore the more robust pro-Israel language of previous platforms. On a voice vote, their motion failed—once and then again. On the third try the chairman ruled it to have passed although his dubious interpretation of the relative volume of the "ayes" and "nays" had delegates standing on their chairs, shouting protests.

Far from being only about verbiage, the argument was substantive to the point of evoking passions. Clearly, either a majority of the delegates or a large minority were less firmly pro-Israel than the stance Obama's campaign team thought it politic to run on. Surveys have repeatedly shown that convention delegates of both parties are more extreme than rank and file voters—Republicans more conservative and Democrats more liberal. In this case it was apparent that being more liberal meant, if not wishing to "radically distance" America from Israel, then at least to distance their party from its strongly pro-Israel stands of the past.

Such shifts can matter greatly even if they amount to less than a complete reversal of position. The anti-Israel camp does not need to win America fully to its side. Merely to neutralize it would radically alter the balance of power and put Israel in great jeopardy. The degree of Israel's dependence on America was underscored in an interview that Eitan Haber, who had been Prime Minister Yitzhak Rabin's closest aide, gave to the *Times of Israel* in September 2013. Scoffing at the freedom politicians feel to say whatever they like when in opposition, Haber said that only when one of them becomes prime minister does he or she begin to understand the "extent the state of Israel is dependent on America [f]or absolutely everything—in the realms of diplomacy, security, even economically."[6]

Were that support withdrawn, Israel's enemies would be tempted to renew their efforts to destroy it once and for all. Such are the dynamics of the "Arab street" that even governments that would prefer peace would feel pressure to support militant actions if Israel appeared vulnerable.

Should Israel's enemies succeed, the result would be a second Holocaust. This would be a tragedy of unspeakable proportions for the Jews, but not only for them. The world would have lost one of its most creative countries, and the devastation of the Jewish people would cause incalculable harm to the spiritual life of the West and perhaps beyond.

Of course, this scenario is unlikely—at least for the time being. With its formidable army and presumed nuclear weapons, Israel is not very destructible, at least not by conventional warfare. But this does not preclude new rounds of guerrilla fighting and terrorist strikes employing ever more lethal weapons. Even if Israel succeeds in defeating such assaults, the prospects for peace would recede before new torrents of blood and tears from Jews and Arabs alike.

And in the end it might not succeed. As the Vietnamese Communists showed, setting a model on which the Palestine Liberation Organization patterned itself, a conflict need not be determined by the sticks and stones of military arsenals. These can be trumped by words that transform political realities and, thus, the balance of power. For all its might, Israel remains a David, struggling against the odds to secure its small foothold in a violent and hostile region. The relentless campaign to recast it instead as a malevolent Goliath places it in grave peril.

Notes

Chapter 1

1 Conor Cruise O'Brien, *The Siege: The Saga of Israel and Zionism* (New York: Simon and Schuster, 1986), 152.

2 Paul Johnson, *A History of the Jews* (New York: Harper and Row, 1987), 427–8.

3 Ibid.

4 Walter Laqueur, *A History of Zionism* (New York: MJF Books, 1972), 189.

5 Ibid., 202.

6 Ibid., 189.

7 Ibid., 452.

8 Robert J. Donovan and the Staff of the *Los Angeles Times*, *Six Days in June: Israel's Fight for Survival* (New York: New American Library, 1967), 18.

9 Kenneth O. Morgan, *Labour in Power 1945 to 1951* (Oxford: Oxford University Press, 1984), 208.

10 Quoted in Allis Radosh and Ronald Radosh, *A Safe Haven: Harry S. Truman and the Founding of Israel* (New York: Harper, 2009), 113.

11 Ibid., 101.

12 Ibid., 47.

13 Ibid., 94.

14 Quoted in Ibid., 34.

15 Ibid., 129, 148.

16 Ibid., 95.

17 Donovan et al., *Six Days*, 18.

18 Klaus-Michael Mallmann and Martin Cuppers, *Nazi Palestine* (New York: Enigma, 2010), trans. Krista Smith, Kindle edition loc. 636–45.

19 Mallmann and Cuppers, *Nazi Palestine*, Kindle loc. 693–96.

20 Cruise O'Brien, *Siege*, 251.

21 Jeffrey Herf, *Nazi Propaganda for the Arab World* (New Haven: Yale University, 2009), Kindle edition loc. 1102–7.

22 Herf, *Nazi Propaganda*, Kindle loc. 2803–7.

23 Clifton Daniel, "Zionists Ask U.N. to Pass New Plan; Arabs Inflamed," *New York Times*, Sept. 2, 1947, 1.

24 Thomas J. Hamilton, "Arabs Call Palestine Report Source of Third World War," *New York Times*, Sept. 9, 1947, 2.

25 Associated Press, "Arab Rejection of '47 Partition Plan Was Error, Palestinian Leader Says," *New York Times*, Oct. 28, 2011.

26 Israeli Ministry of Foreign Affairs, *Israel's Foreign Relations: Selected Documents 1947–1974*, Meron Medzini, ed., 1976, 704.

27 Hassanain Haykal, "An Armed Clash with Israel is Inevitable-Why?" reprinted in Walter Laqueur, ed., *The Israel-Arab Reader*, 3rd ed., (New York: Bantam, 1976), 178.

28 "Nasser's Speech to the Arab Trade Unionists, May 26, 1967," in Laqueur, *Israel-Arab Reader*, 176–77.

29 Howard M. Sachar, *A History of Israel: From the Rise of Zionism to Our Time* (New York: Alfred A. Knopf, 1982), 625.

30 Ibid.

31 Cruise O'Brien, *The Siege*, 409.

32 Thomas S. Brady, "Arabs Voice Confidence," *New York Times*, May 21, 1967, 3.

33 Donovan et al., *Six Days*, 45.

34 M. S. Handler, "Donations Pour In For Israel Fund," *New York Times*, June 9, 1967, 11.

35 "10 From U.S. to Do Jobs Of Mobilized Israelis," *New York Times*, May 26, 1967; "38 U.S. Jews Off To Israel To Help: Will Fill Reservists Places—Big UJA Drive Due," *New York Times*, May 31, 1967.

36 Maurice Carroll, "Supporters of Israel March Here as the Police Turn Away Arab Group," *New York Times*, May 29 1967, 4; Irving Spiegel, "Jews in Capital Turn Aid Rally Into a Victory Demonstration," *New York Times*, June 9, 1967.

37 Louis Harris, "The Harris Survey: U.S. Public Shows Sympathy for Israel in Mideast Crisis," *Los Angeles Times*, June 11, 1967, E7.

38 "The Gallup Poll: U.S. Support for Israel Remains High," *Washington Post*, Mar. 19, 1970, F5.

39 "To Uphold Our Own Honor: Leading Americans Speak Out against Arab Threat to Destroy Israel," *Washington Post*, June 7, 1967.

40 "Professors Call Upon United States To Safeguard Israel's Integrity," display ad, *New York Times*, June 8, 1967.

41 Irving Spiegel, "8 Church Leaders Ask Aid to Israel," *New York Times*, May 28, 1967.

42 Spiegel, "Jews in Capital."

43 "Pause for Peace at Sinai," *New York Times*, May 25, 1967; James Reston, "Washington: Eisenhower and Johnson on Nasser," *New York Times*, May 28, 1967; Russell Baker, "Observer: the Arab Master Plan," *New York Times*, June 8, 1967.

44 "On Facing the Reality of Israel," *TIME*, June 23, 1967.

45 "The People: A Million a Minute," *TIME*, June 16, 1967.

46 "The Search for Peace . . ." *New York Times*, June 6, 1967.

47 E. W. Kenworthy, "Neutral Position of U. S. Confuses Capitol Hill," *New York Times*, June 7, 1967.

48 Peter L. Hahn, "The Influence of Organized Labor on U.S. Policy Toward Israel, 1945–1967," in *Empire and Revolution: The United States and the*

Third World Since 1945, eds. Peter L. Hahn and Mary Ann Heiss (Columbus: Ohio State University Press, 2000), 167–68.

49 "A Near-Riot Erupts At Rally For Israel," *New York Times,* June 6, 1967.

50 J. Y. Smith, "Congressional Worry for Israel Rising," *Washington Post,* June 5, 1967, A1.

51 Stuart Auerbach, "Senator McCarthy, Clergymen Express Support for Israel at Local Rally," *Washington Post,* May 31, 1967.

52 "McGovern Backs Goals of Israel," *New York Times,* June 23, 1967, 2.

53 Cited in Roy Licklider, *Political Power and the Arab Oil Weapon: The Experience of Five Industrial Nations* (Berkeley, Los Angeles, London: University of California Press, 1988), 82.

54 Howard M. Sacher, *Israel and Europe* (New York: Knopf, 1998), 174.

55 "10,000 at Rally in Support of Israel," *Guardian,* May 29, 1967, 12; Donovan et al., *Six Days,* 135.

56 Karl E. Meyer, "The British Role: Elements of Irony," *Washington Post,* June 11, 1967, C6.

57 Flora Lewis, "De Gaulle's Support Over Israel Sinks within Party," *LA Times,* July 7, 1967, A5.

58 "Polls Show French are Pro-Israel," *Guardian,* July 17, 1967, 8.

59 Henry Tanner, "Most Frenchmen Oppose a Policy of Neutrality," *New York Times,* June 6, 1967.

60 Donovan et al., *Six Days,* 134.

61 Tanner, "Most Frenchmen."

62 Norman Crossland, "Anti-Israel Campaign by Ulbricht," *Guardian,* June 12, 1967, 9.

63 Natan Sharansky, *Fear No Evil,* trans. Stefani Hoffman (New York: Random House, 1988), xiv.

64 Maurice Couve de Murville, *Une Politique Étrangère 1958–1969* (Paris: Plon, 1971), 474. Original: *un homage rendu à des qualities exceptionelles.*

65 Raymond Aron, *DeGaulle, Israel and the Jews,* trans. John Sturrock (New York: Frederick A. Prager, 1969), 24–25. Quip on *"lèse-Gaullism,"* 29.

66 Charles De Gaulle, *Mémoirs D'Espoir: Le Renouveau* (Paris: Plon, 1970), 277. (Author's translation.)

67 Aron, *DeGaulle, Israel,* 32.

Chapter 2

1 "Survey: Majority of Palestinians Believe Israel Not Partner for Peace," *WAFA,* May 4, 2011.

2 Alain Roussillon, "Republican Egypt Interpreted: Revolution and Beyond," in *The Cambridge History of Egypt, vol. 2, Modern Egypt from 1517 to the end of the twentieth century,* ed. M. W. Daly (Cambridge: Cambridge University Press, 1998), 344.

3 Ann Mosely Lesch, "The Palestine Arab Nationalist Movement Under the Mandate," in *The Politics of Palestinian Nationalism,* eds. William B. Quandt, Fuad Jabber, and Ann Mosely Lesch (Berkeley and Los Angeles: University of California, 1973), 14.

4 Ibid, 16.

5 Quant et al., "Introduction," *Palestinian Nationalism*, 1–2.

6 Alain Gresh, *The PLO: The Struggle Within: Towards an Independent Palestinian State*, trans. A. M. Berrett (London: Zed, 1985), 20–21.

7 Cited in Ibid., 21.

8 Hussam Mohamed, "The Changing Meaning of Statehood in PLO Ideology and Practice," *Palestine-Israel Journal* 6, no. 2 (1999).

9 Michael R. Fischbach, "Shuqayri, As'ad," in *Encyclopedia of the Palestinians*, ed. Philip Mattar (New York: Facts on File, 2005), 366.

10 Background on Shuqairy from Ibid., 365.

11 Conor Cruise O'Brien, *The Siege: The Saga of Israel and Zionism* (New York: Simon and Schuster, 1986), 476.

12 Thomas Kiernan, *Arafat: The Man and the Myth* (New York: Norton, 1976), 234.

13 Abdallah Frangi, *The PLO and Palestine* (London: Zed, 1983), 100.

14 Gresh, *The PLO*, 22.

15 Helena Cobban quotes Khaled al-Hassan, one of the members of the original inner circle, saying that from 1959 they had little more than the magazine and a post office box, and that it was not until 1962 that al-Fatah gelled. *The Palestinian Liberation Organization: People Power and Politics* (Cambridge: Cambridge University, 1984), 24.

16 Alan Hart, *Arafat: A Political Biography* (Bloomington: Indiana University, 1984), 30.

17 Kiernan, *Arafat,* has it on the mother's side (p. 27); Janet Wallach and John Wallach, *Arafat in the Eyes of the Beholder* (New York: Lyle Stuart, 1990) has it on the father's (p. 27); Barry Rubin and Judith Colp Rubin, *Yasir Arafat: A Political Biography* (Oxford: Oxford University, 2003), just say "a distant relative" (p. 12); whereas Andrew Gowers and Tony Walker, *Arafat: The Biography* (London: Virgin, 1994) insist "Arafat was not related . . . to Haj Amin al-Husseini" (p. 12).

18 Biographers Gowers and Walker cite a family member who attributes the connection to an uncle of Arafat's, Sheikh Hassan Abu Saoud, "who was very close to Haj Amin" (Gowers and Walker, *Arafat*, 15). Janet and John Wallach, whose book is based on many hours of interviews with Arafat, go so far as to say that Abu Saoud and Husseini, himself, "played major roles in directing Arafat's life," but they do not make clear how (Wallach and Wallach, *Arafat*, 28). Helena Cobban attributes some of the internal dynamics of Palestinian politics in the 1960s to "continuing contacts between Haj Amin and his distant younger cousin, Yasser Arafat" (Helena Cobban, *The Palestinian Liberation Organization: People, Power and Politics* [Cambridge: Cambridge University, 1984], 29, 31).

19 Abu Iyad with Eric Rouleau, *My Home, My Land: A Narrative of the Palestinian Struggle* (New York: Times Books, 1981), 33.

20 Gowers and Walker, *Arafat*, 17–18.

21 Ibid., 27.

22 Ibid., 58.

23 Quoted in Rubin and Rubin, *Yasir Arafat*, 19.

24 Hart, *Arafat*, 34.

25 Article 12. This translation probably appears first in Yehoshafat Harkabi, *The Palestinian Covenant and its Meaning* (London: Valentine, Mitchell, 1979) and may be found on the web at http://www.mideastweb.org/plocha.htm. A different translation may be found at the website of the permanent mission of Palestine to the UN http://www.un.int/wcm/content/site/palestine/pid/12363. There is no difference in meanings between the two, but the latter is rendered in stilted English.

26 Moshe Shemesh, *The Palestinian Entity 1959–1974: Arab Politics and the PLO*, 2nd (revised) ed. (London: Frank Cass, 1996), 90.

27 Ibid., 92.

28 Cobban, *The Palestinian Liberation Organization*,31–32.

29 "Mohammed Yazid on Algeria and the Arab-Israeli Conflict," *Journal of Palestine Studies* 1, no. 2 (Winter 1972): 12; and *Le Monde*, February 27, 1969, cited in Raphael Danziger, "Algeria and the Palestinians," in *The Palestinians and the Middle East Conflict*, ed. Gabriel Ben-Dor (Ramat Gan: Turtledove, 1978), 365, 364.

30 Gowers and Walkers, *Arafat*, 48.

31 Y. Harkabi, "Al Fatah's Doctrine," in *The Israel-Arab Reader*, 3rd ed., ed. Walter Laqueur (New York: Bantam, 1976), 395.

32 Abu Iyad, *My Home*, 66–67.

33 Ibid, 71.

34 Ibid, 67.

35 "Al Fatah: The Seven Points, passed by the Central Committee of Al Fatah, January, 1969," in Laqueur, *Israel-Arab Reader*, 373.

36 "An Interview with 'Abu Ammar' (Yasser Arafat)" (first published in *Free Palestine*, August 1969), in Laqueur, *Israel-Arab Reader*, 373.

37 "Abbas in Vietnam: 'We Are Comrades in Struggle and Fighting,'" "Abbas in Washington: 'We Will Not Relinquish the Path [of Peace],'" The Middle East Media Research Institute (MEMRI), Special Dispatch no. 3032, June 14, 2010.

38 Galia Golan, *The Soviet Union and the Palestine Liberation Organization: An Uneasy Alliance* (New York: Praeger, 1980), 9.

39 Quoted in Ibid., 11.

40 David Pryce-Jones, *The Closed Circle: An Interpretation of the Arabs* (Chicago: Ivan R. Dee, 2009), 300.

41 Abu Iyad, *My Home*, 139.

42 Gowers and Walker, *Arafat*, 86.

43 Ibid.

44 Translated in Yehoshafat Harkabi, *The Palestinian Covenant and its Meaning* (London: Valentine, Mitchell, 1979), 48.

45 Gresh, *The PLO*, 49.

46 Bernard Lewis, "The Palestinians and the PLO," *Commentary*, January 1975, 39fn (online fn 10).

47 Cited in Gresh, *The PLO*, 43.

48 BBC, July 30, 1969, cited in Jillian Becker, *The PLO: The Rise and Fall of the Palestine Liberation Organization* (New York: St. Martin's, 1984), 64.

49 Reprinted in Rudolf Kraemer-Badoni, "Zionism and the New Left," in *The Left Against Zion: Communism, Israel and the Middle East*, ed. Robert S. Wistrich (London: Valentine, Mitchell, 1979), 234.

50 Reprinted in Laqueur, *Israel-Arab Reader*, 373.

51 "The Guerrilla Threat in the Middle East," *TIME*, December 13, 1968.

Chapter 3

1 "Arabs Hold Israelis on Seized Jet," *Chicago Tribune*, July 24, 1968.

2 "Jet and Israelis Freed by Algeria," *New York Times*, Sept. 1, 1968.

3 "Israel Says That Arab Jets, Too, Can Be Attacked," *New York Times*, Dec. 27, 1968.

4 Interview with Mordechai Rachamim by telephone at his home, June 16, 2011.

5 James Feron, "Swiss Grant Arab's Killer Bail; Israel Welcomes Him as Hero," *New York Times*, Mar. 21, 1969.

6 Leila Khaled as told to George Hajjar, *My People Shall Live: Autobiography of a Revolutionary* (London: Hodder and Stoughton, 1973), 78.

7 Declassified U.S. diplomatic cables published in Amir Oren, "Anatomy of a Prisoner Exchange," *Haaretz*, Oct. 20, 2008. http://www.haaretz .com/anatomy-of-a-prisoner-exchange-1.255770.

8 "U.S.-Syria Deal Claimed," *Baltimore Sun*, Sept. 10, 1969, A2.

9 "Arabs Warn Travelers," *Baltimore Sun*, Sept. 10, 1969, A1; "Young Arabs Switch 'War' to Europe," *Guardian*, Sept. 9, 1969.

10 "Terrorist Blast at El Al Terminal in Athens Hurts 15," *New York Times*, Nov. 28, 1969.

11 "Arab Travelers Curbed in Greece," *New York Times*, Dec. 2, 1969.

12 "Athens Agrees to Free 7 After Arabs Seize Airliner," *New York Times*, July 23, 1970.

13 Abu Iyad with Eric Rouleau, *My Home, My Land: A Narrative of the Palestinian Struggle* (New York: Times Books, 1981), 221.

14 Andrew Gowers and Tony Walker, *Arafat: The Biography* (London: Virgin, 1994), 54.

15 John K. Cooley, "Arabs Impatient for Next Hijack Try," *Christian Science Monitor*, May 12, 1972.

16 "Arabs Hijack German Airliner and Gain Release of 3 Seized in Munich Killings," *New York Times*, Oct. 30, 1972.

17 Quoted in Aaron J. Klein, *Striking Back: The 1972 Munich Olympics Massacre and Israel's Deadly Response* (New York: Random House, 2007), Kindle edition loc. 1640–60.

18 Abu Iyad and Rouleau, *My Home*, 112.

19 Klein, *Striking Back*, Kindle edition loc. 1640–60.

20 David A. Korn, *Assassination in Khartoum* (Bloomington and Indianapolis: University of Indiana Press, 1993), 168.

21 Ibid., 179.

22 Ibid., 188.

23 Klein, *Striking Back*, loc. 2346–48.

24 Kay Schiller and Chris Young, *The 1972 Munich Olympics and the Making of Modern Germany* (Berkeley: University of California, 2010), Kindle edition loc. 5127–32.

25 Korn, *Assassination in Khartoum*, 217–18.

26 Abu Iyad and Rouleau, *My Home*, 220.

27 Ibid., 146.

28 Korn, *Assassination in Khartoum*, 207.

29 Quoted in Christopher Dobson, *Black September: Its Short, Violent History* (New York: MacMillan, 1974), 49–50

30 Helena Cobban, *The Palestinian Liberation Organisation: People, Power and Politics* (Cambridge, UK: Cambridge University, 1984), 54.

31 "Abu Daoud: No Regrets for Munich Olympics," *New York Times*, Feb. 23, 2006.

32 Klein, *Striking Back*, loc. 168–85.

33 Henry Kissinger, *Years of Upheaval* (Boston: Little, Brown, 1982), 628.

34 Gowers and Walker, *Arafat*, 142.

35 Kissinger, *Upheaval*, 629.

36 Howard M. Sachar, *Israel and Europe: An Appraisal in History* (New York: Knopf, 1998), 230–31.

37 Klein, *Striking Back*, loc. 2348–51.

38 Abu Iyad and Rouleau, *My Home, My Land*, 98.

39 "Terrorism Thwarted," editorial, *New York Times*, July 20, 1973.

40 Abu Iyad and Rouleau, *My Home*, 112.

Chapter 4

1 John Noble Wilford, "The Long-Term Energy Crisis," *New York Times*, Apr. 19, 1973.

2 Edward Cowan, "President Offers Policy to Avert and Energy Crisis," *New York Times*, Apr. 19, 1973.

3 Yehuda Avner, *The Prime Ministers: An Intimate Narrative of Israeli Leadership* (London: Toby Press, 2010), Kindle edition loc. 4851–55.

4 Daniel Yergin, *The Prize: The Epic Quest for Oil, Money and Power* (New York: Free Press, 2009; original edition, 1991), 586–7.

5 "Telcon, The President/Sec. Kissinger, 9:04 a.m., 10/14/73" (transcript of Nixon-Kissinger telephone conversation), *Digital National Security Archive*, Collection: Kissinger Telephone Conversations, item number KA11236.

6 Chris J. Krisinger, "Operation Nickel Grass: Airlift in Support of National Policy," *Airpower Journal* (Spring 1989).

7 Henry Kissinger, *Years of Upheaval* (Boston: Little, Brown, 1982), 520.

8 Edward Cowan, "A Saudi Threat on Oil Reported," *New York Times*, Oct. 16, 1973, 1.

9 The Insight Team of the London *Sunday Times*, *The Yom Kippur War* (Garden City: Doubleday, 1974), 359.

10 Ibid, 361.

11 "Saudis Cut Oil Output 10% To Put Pressure on U.S.," *New York Times*, Oct. 19, 1973, 1.

12 "How Do You Get Promoted By the Arabs?," *Economist*, Dec. 8, 1973, 29.

13 John M. Goshko, "Common Market Issues Mideast Statement to Mollify Arabs," *Washington Post*, Nov. 7, 1973.

14 Ibid.

15 "The Oil Splashes onto Pompidou's Fireside Summit," *Economist*, Nov. 10, 1973, 79.

16 "Europe's Unity on Oil Hits Troubled Water," *Guardian*, Nov. 7, 1973.

17 Richard Norton-Taylor in Ibid. (This part of the article was by-lined Norton-Taylor; the part cited in fn 16 carried no by-line.)

18 Yergin, *The Prize*, 605–6.

19 "The Souring of the Dutch," *TIME*, Dec. 3, 1973.

20 "Why Every Country Will Run Short of Oil," *Economist*, Nov. 10, 1973, 41.

21 Roy Licklider, "The Power of Oil: The Arab Oil Weapon and the Netherlands, the United Kingdom, Canada, Japan, and the United States," *International Studies Quarterly* 32, no. 2 (June 1988): 211.

22 "Declaration of the Arab Summit Conference at Algiers—28 November 1973," Israel Ministry of Foreign Affairs website. http://www .mfa.gov.il/MFA/Foreign+Relations/Israels+Foreign+Relations +since+1947/1947–1974/19+Declaration+of+the+Arab+Summit+ Conference+at+Al.htm?DisplayMode=print.

23 Saleh A. al-Mani, *The Euro-Arab Dialogue: A Study in Associative Diplomacy* (London: Frances Pinter, 1983), 71, quoted in Bat Ye'or, *Eurabia: The Euro-Arab Axis,* (Madison, NJ: Fairleigh Dickinson Univ. Press, 2005), 52.

24 Kissinger, *Upheaval*, 860.

25 Yergin, *The Prize*, 609.

26 Kissinger, *Upheaval*, 898.

27 Henry Kissinger, *Years of Renewal* (New York: Simon & Schuster, 2000), 668–9.

28 Kissinger, *Upheaval*, 900.

29 Ibid., 884.

30 "Arab Oil Has Gone Up 470% in a Year, *New York Times*, December 30, 1973.

31 Kissinger, *Upheaval*, 897.

32 Ibid., 908.

33 Ibid., 865.

34 Ibid., 897.

35 Flora Lewis, "Giscard Asserts World is in Grip of Fiscal Crisis," *New York Times*, Oct. 25, 1974.

36 Kissinger, *Upheaval*, 904.
37 Lewis, "Giscard Asserts."
38 Paul Hofmann, French Aide Sees Caution at U.N. on Oil Showdown, *New York Times*, Sept. 25, 1974.
39 Licklider, "The Power of Oil," 214.
40 Yergin, *The Prize*, 610.
41 "Move is Surprise," *New York Times*, Dec. 26, 1973, 1.
42 Michael Curtis, "Africa, Israel and the Middle East," *Middle East Review* (Summer 1985): 6.
43 Ibid., 8.
44 Yergin, *The Prize*, 613.
45 Ibid., 615–6.
46 Ibid., 613.

Chapter 5

1 "The World: China: A Stinging Victory," *TIME*, Nov. 8, 1971.
2 Bernard Gwertzman, "Soviet Accuses Zionism of Subverting Red Lands," *New York Times*, Feb. 19, 1971.
3 Daniel Patrick Moynihan, with Suzanne Weaver, *A Dangerous Place* (Boston: Little, Brown, 1975), 177.
4 Harris Okun Schoenberg, *A Mandate for Terror: The United Nations and the PLO* (New York: Shapolsky, 1989), 50.
5 Abu Iyad with Eric Rouleau, *My Home, My Land: A Narrative of the Palestinian Struggle* (New York: Times Books, 1981), 146.
6 Robert J. Donovan and the Staff of the *Los Angeles Times*, *Six Days in June: Israel's Fight for Survival* (New York: New American Library, 1967), 45.
7 Moynihan, *Dangerous Place*, 93.
8 Ibid., 94.
9 "Excerpts From Kissinger's Milwaukee Speech on the U.N.," *New York Times*, July 15, 1975.
10 Ibid.
11 Moynihan, *Dangerous Place*, 172.
12 Quoted in Ibid., 183–4.
13 Moynihan, *Dangerous Place*, 171.
14 Ibid., 185.
15 Ibid., 181.
16 UN General Assembly, Resolution 37/123, "The Situation in the Middle East," Dec. 16 1982, http://www.un.org/documents/ga/res/37/a37r123.htm.
17 Moynihan, *Dangerous Place*, 91.
18 American Jewish International Relations Institute, *Doing Business at the UN: The Arab League "Reaches Out" to the Pacific Islands States* (Chevy Chase: AJIRI, 2010; report no. 32), 1.
19 Rosemary Righter, *Utopia Lost: The United Nations and World Order* (New York: Twentieth Century Fund Press, 1995), 240.

20 See, for example, UN General Assembly, Resolution 2548 (XXIV), "Implementation of the Declaration on the Granting of Independence to Colonial Countries and Peoples," Dec. 11, 1969, http://daccess-dds-ny.un.org/doc/RESOLUTION/GEN/NR0/256/82/IMG/NR025682.pdf?OpenElement.

21 UN General Assembly, Resolution 2708 (XXV), "Implementation of the Declaration on the Granting of Independence to Colonial Countries and Peoples," Dec. 14, 1970, http://daccess-dds-ny.un.org/doc/RESOLUTION/GEN/NR0/349/73/IMG/NR034973.pdf?OpenElement.

22 Schoenberg, *Mandate for Terror*, p. 30.

23 UN General Assembly, Resolution 3236 (XXIX), "Question of Palestine," Nov. 22, 1974, http://www.un.org/en/ga/search/view_doc.asp?symbol=A/RES/3236(XXIX)&Lang=E&Area=RESOLUTION.

24 UN General Assembly, Resolution 37/43, "Importance of the Universal Realization of the Right of Peoples to Self-Determination and of the Speedy Granting of Independence to Colonial Countries and Peoples for the Effective Guarantee and Observance of Human Rights" Dec. 3, 1982, http://www.un.org/en/ga/search/view_doc.asp?symbol=A/RES/37/43&Lang=E&Area=RESOLUTION.

25 Colum Lynch, "Islamic Group Blocks Terror Treaty: Nations Demand U.N. Pact Exemption for Anti-Israeli Militants," *Washington Post*, Nov. 10, 2001.

26 Colum Lynch, "U.N. Approves Anti-Terrorism Initiative: In 15–0 Vote, Security Council Urges Nations to Prosecute Offenders and Supporters," *Washington Post*, Oct. 9, 2004, A26.

27 United Nations, Economic and Social Council, "Question of the Violation of Human Rights in the Occupied Arab Territories, Including Palestine," Resolution 2002/8, Apr. 15, 2002, http://unispal.un.org/UNISPAL.NSF/0/DF9CAA26E9BEB10485256BAB00666603.

28 Tom Lantos, "The Durban Debacle: An Insiders View of the UN World Conference on Racism at Durban," *Fletcher Forum of World Affairs* 26, no. 1 (Winter/Spring 2002): 16.

29 United Nations General Assembly, Report of the Secretary General, A/59/2005, *In Larger Freedom, Towards Developent, Security and Human Rights for All*, March 21, 2005, 45 (par. 182).

30 Richard Falk, "Time's Angel, or a Birthday Letter to Myself," *Citizen Pilgrimage*, Nov. 13, 2011, http://richardfalk.wordpress.com/category/reflections/.

31 Richard Falk, "A few Notes on WHAT IS LEFT (or Toward a Manifesto of Revolutionary Emancipation)." (sic) http://richardfalk.wordpress.com/?s=what+is+left&submit=Search.

32 American Jewish International Relations Institute, *The Focus on Israel: One Month at the UN* (Washington, DC: AJIRI, 2009; report no. 25), 1.

33 United Nations, Security Council, *Report of the Committee on the Exercise of the Inalienable Rights of the Palestinian People*, S/12090, 29 May 1976, pars. 20, 14.

34 Ibid., pars 18, 60.

35 United Nations, Division of Palestinian Rights, *Origins and Evolution of the Palestine Problem 1917–1988,* part I: 1917–1947 (1978) http://unispal .un.org/unispal.nsf/0/AEAC80E740C782E4852561150071FDB0.

36 International Festival of Audiovisual Programs, FIPA 2009 Competitive Selection, Creative Documentaries, *La Terre Parle Arab,* http://www .fipa.tm.fr/en/programs/2009/la-terre-parle-arabe-18718.htm.

37 United Nations, Division of Palestinian Rights, *United Nations International Conference of Civil Society in Support of Middle East Peace, UNESCO Headquarters, Paris, 12 and 13 July 2005,* 23, January 2006, 13.

38 United Nations, High Commissioner for Refugees, "History of UNHCR." http://www.unhcr.org/pages/49c3646cbc.html.

39 Ibid.

40 United Nations, Relief and Works Agency for Palestine Refugees in the Near East, "Who We Are," http://www.unrwa.org/who-we-are, and http://www.unrwa.org/who-we-are/organizational-structure.

41 United Nations, High Commissioner for Refugees, "The State of the World's Refugees 2000: Fifty Years of Humanitarian Action." http:// www.unhcr.org/3ebf9ba80.html.

42 UN General Assembly, Resolution 428(V), "Statute of the Office of the United Nations High Commissioner for Refugess," Dec. 14, 1950, http:// daccess-dds-ny.un.org/doc/RESOLUTION/GEN/NR0/060/26/IMG/ NR006026.pdf?OpenElement.

43 UN General Assembly, Resolution 194(III), "Palestine—Progress Report of the United Nations Mediator," Dec. 11, 1948, http://unispal. un.org/UNISPAL.NSF/0/C758572B78D1CD0085256BCF0077E51A.

44 James G. Lindsay, *Fixing UNRWA: Repairing the UN's Troubled System of Aid to Palestinian Refugees* (Washington, DC: Washington Institute for Near East Policy, 2009; Policy Focus no. 91), 16.

45 United Nations, Relief and Works Agency for Palestine Refugees in the Near East, "Palestine Refugees," http://www.unrwa.org/ palestine-refugees.

Chapter 6

1 Matthew Paul Berg in collaboration with Jill Lewis and Oliver Rathkolb, eds., *The Struggle for a Democratic Austria: Bruno Kreisky on Peace and Social Justice,* trans. Helen Atkins and Matthew Paul Berg (New York: Berghahn Books, 2000), 452–53.

2 Ibid, 435.

3 H. Pierre Secher, *Bruno Kreisky, Chancellor of Austria: A Political Biography* (Pittsburgh: Dorrance Publishing, 1993), 53.

4 Berg et al., *The Struggle,* 120.

5 Otto Bauer, *The Question of Nationalities and Social Democracy,* edited by Ephraim J. Nimni, trans. Joseph O'Donnell (Minneapolis: Univ. of Minnesota Press, 2000; original German pub. 1924), 293.

6 Ibid, 305.

7 Secher, *Bruno Kreisky*, 44.

8 Ibid., 51–52.

9 Ibid., 44.

10 Andrei S. Markovits and Anson Rabinbach, "The Dark Side of Austrian Social Democracy," *Dissent* (Summer 2000).

11 Secher, *Bruno Kreisky*, 180f.

12 Ron Grossman, "Wiesenthal's retirement Ends Historic Crusade," *Chicago Tribune*, Apr. 29, 2003.

13 Berg et al., *The Struggle*, 22.

14 Ibid., 122.

15 Evan Burr Bukey, *Hitler's Austria: Popular Sentiment in the Nazi Era, 1938–1945* (Chapel Hill: University of North Carolina, 2000), 43.

16 See Günter Bischof, Anton Pelinka, Ferdinand Karlhofer, eds., *The Vranitzky era in Austria*, Contemporary Austrian Studies, vol. 7 (New Brunswick: Transaction, 1999).

17 Gunter Bischof, "Introduction," in *The Kreisky Era in Austria*, eds. Gunter Bischof and Anton Pelinka, Contemporary Austrian Studies, vol. 2 (New Brunswick: Transaction, 1994), 4.

18 Secher, *Bruno Kreisky*, 74.

19 "Kreisky Calls Wiesenthal Nazi Collaborator," *Kurier* (Vienna), Nov. 11, 1975, trans. in Foreign Broadcast Information Service, *Daily Report*, Western Europe, FBIS-WEU-75-220, Nov. 13, 1975.

20 Secher, *Bruno Kreisky*, 191.

21 Ibid., 80, 121.

22 "Kreisky: The Jews – A Wretched People?" *Der Speigel*, Nov. 17, 1975.

23 Erich Aichinger, "Chancellor Kreisky Reiterates Attacks on Simon Wiesenthal," *Vienna Domestic Serivce* (radio), Nov. 18, 1975, trans. in Foreign Broadcast Information Service, *Daily Report*, Western Europe, FBIS-WEU-75-224, Nov. 19, 1975.

24 Markovits and Rabinbach, "The Dark Side."

25 Aichinger, "Chancellor Kreisky Reiterates Attacks."

26 Juan de Onis, "Palestinians Warn Austria to Stay Firm," *New York Times*, Oct. 2, 1973.

27 Juan de Onis, "Kreisky Becomes Hero in Arab World," *New York Times*, Oct. 4, 1973.

28 Bernard Gwertzman, "Nixon Appeals to Kreisky to Review Action on Jews," *New York Times*, Oct. 4, 1973.

29 Terrence Smith, "Austrian Rejects Mrs. Meir's Pleas on Transit Routes," *New York Times*, Oct. 3, 1973. On the chilly tone, see Yehuda Avner, *The Prime Ministers* (New Milford: Toby Press, 2010), 222.

30 Paul Hoffmann, "Austria's Leader Asks U.S. to Share Refugee 'Burden,'" *New York Times*, Oct. 1, 1973.

31 Paul Hoffmann, "Austria Hints Concession," *New York Times*, Oct. 2, 1973.

32 Henry Kissinger, *Years of Upheaval* (Boston: Little, Brown, 1982), 707–710.

33 Golda Meir, *My Life* (New York: G.P. Putnam's, 1975), 446–47.

34 Berg et al., *The Struggle*, 444–45.

35 "Report of the Socialist International Fact Finding Mission to the Middle East," Introduction by Bruno Kreisky (London: Socialist International, 1977; Circular No. B14/77).

36 Carl Gershman, "The Socialists and the PLO," *Commentary* 68, no. 4 (October 1979): 36.

37 Ibid. 41–2.

38 Aichinger, "Chancellor Kreisky Reiterates Attacks."

39 Berg et al., *The Struggle*, 432.

40 Ibid., 434.

41 Ibid., 470.

42 Barbie Zelizer-Meyouhas, "Kreisky Denounced for His Attacks on Begin, Israel, the Jewish Nation," *Jewish Telegraphic Agency*, Sept. 5, 1978.

43 Berg et al., *The Struggle*, 438.

44 Secher, *Bruno Kreisky*, 160.

45 Berg et al., *The Struggle*, 482.

46 Ibid., 468.

47 Ibid., 435.

48 Ibid., 438.

Chapter 7

1 Conor McCarthy, *The Cambridge Introduction to Edward Said* (Cambridge: Cambridge University Press, 2010).

2 Maya Jaggi, "Between the Lines," *Guardian*, Dec. 1, 2001.

3 Edward W. Said, *Out of Place* (New York: Knopf, 1999), back jacket blurb.

4 Edward W. Said, *Orientalism* (New York: Vintage, 1979), 301.

5 Said, *Orientalism*, 204

6 For example, he says of the relationship between Orientalism and imperialism: "all these earlier matters are reproduced more or less in American Orientalism." Said, *Orientalism*, 18.

7 J. H. Plumb, "Looking East in Error," *New York Times*, Book Review, Feb. 18, 1979, 3.

8 Edward W. Said, *The Question of Palestine* (New York, Vintage, 1992), xxxviii, 172.

9 Said, *The Question of Palestine*, 175.

10 Ibid., 165–66.

11 "Books of the Times," *New York Times*, Jan. 4, 1980.

12 Jaggi, "Between the Lines."

13 "Edward Said, Dead at 67," *Counterpunch*, Sept. 25, 2003, cited in Daniel Martin Varisco, *Reading Orientalism: Said and the Unsaid* (Seattle: University of Washington, 2007), 38.

14 Said, *Out of Place*, 197. All other biographical information in this paragraph is also drawn from this source.

15 Said, *The Question of Palestine*, xliv.

16 Julian Berger, "Friends Rally to Repulse Attack on Edward Said," *Guardian*, Aug. 22, 1999.

17 Justus Reid Weiner, "'My Beautiful Old House' and Other Fabrications by Edward Said," *Commentary* 108, no. 2 (September 1999): 23–31.

18 Edward Said, "Defamation, Zionist-Style," *Al-Ahram Weekly* 444 (August 26–September 1, 1999).

19 "Letters from Readers: Edward Said's Fabrications," *Commentary*, 109, no. 1(January 2000): 5.

20 Said, *Out of Place*, 20.

21 Ibid., 24.

22 Ibid., 26.

23 Said, "Defamation."

24 Said, *Out of Place*, 107.

25 Edward W. Said, *The Pen and the Sword: Conversations with David Barsamian* (Monroe, Maine: Common Courage Press, 1994), 50.

26 Edward Said, "Between Worlds: Edward Said Makes Sense of his Life," *London Review of Books* 20, no. 7 (May 7, 1998): 3–7.

27 Stephen Howe, "An Outsider's Inside Story," *The Independent*, Sept. 25, 1999, http://www.independent.co.uk/arts-entertainment/books-an-outsiders-inside-story-1121614.html.

28 Janny Scott, "Israeli Says Palestinian Thinker Has Falsified His Early Life," *New York Times*, Aug. 26, 1999.

29 Said, *Orientalism*, 36.

30 Ibid., 2.

31 Ibid., 2.

32 Ibid., 3.

33 Ibid., 3.

34 Ibid., 300–301.

35 Daniel Martin Varisco, *Reading Orientalism: Said and the Unsaid* (Seattle: University of Washington, 2007), 272.

36 Varisco, *Reading Orientalism*, 110.

37 John Rodenbeck, "Edward Said and Edward Lane," in *Travellers in Egypt*, eds. Paul Starkey and Janet Starkey (London: I.B. Tauris, 1998), 237, cited in Varisco, *Reading Orientalism*, 35.

38 Varisco, *Reading Orientalism*, 51.

39 Robert Irwin, *Dangerous Knowledge: Orientalism and its Discontents* (Woodstock and New York: Overlook, 2006), 204.

40 Ibid., 296.

41 Said, *Orientalism*, 11.

42 Ibid., 43.

43 Ibid., 3.

44 Said, *Out of Place*, 168–9.

45 Edward Said, *Orientalism* (New York: Vintage, 1994), 345. (This was a reissue of the 1979 original with a new Afterword.)

46 Irwin, *Dangerous Knowledge*, 173.

47 Varisco, *Reading Orientalism*, 111.

48 Ibn Warraq, *Defending the West: A Critique of Edward Said's* Orientalism (New York: Promotheus, 2007), 46.

49 Said, *Orientalism*, 209.

50 Quoted in Irwin, *Dangerous Knowledge*, 196.

51 Said, *Orientalism*, 209.

52 Raphael Patai, *Ignaz Goldziher and His Oriental Diary: A Translation and Psychological Portrait* (Detroit: Wayne State University Press, 1987), 20.

53 Said, *Orientalism*, 19.

54 Ibid., 4.

55 Irwin, *Dangerous Knowledge*,262.

56 Said, *Orientalism*, 301.

57 Varisco, *Reading Orientalism*, 78. The Beckingham essay is from *Journal of the Royal Society of Arts* 124 (September 1976): 606–611.

58 Irwin, *Dangerous Knowledge*, 11.

59 Said, *Orientalism*, 204.

60 Warraq, *Defending the West*, 230.

61 Said, *Orientalism*, 1, 3.

62 Ibid., 5.

63 Ibid., 6.

64 Ibid., 104.

65 Warraq, *Defending the West*, 44.

66 Irwin, *Dangerous Knowledge*, 4.

67 Sadiq Jalal al-'Azm, "Orientalism and Orientalism in Reverse," in *Forbidden Agendas: Intolerance and defiance in the Middle East, Khamsin: An Anthology*, ed. Jon Rothschild (London: Al Saqi, 1984), 351.

68 Richard Bernstein, "Edward W. Said, Literary Critic and Advocate for Palestinian Independence, Dies at 67," *New York Times*, Sept. 26, 2003.

69 Malise Ruthven, "Edward Said: Controversial Literary Critic and Bold Advocate of the Palestinian Cause in America," *Guardian*, Sept. 26, 2003.

70 Stuart Schaar, "Orientalism's Persistence in Mass Culture and Foreign Policy," Middle East Institute, Sept. 2009.

71 Varisco, *Reading Orientalism*, 9.

72 Irwin, *Dangerous Knowledge*, 276.

73 Stefan Collini, *Absent Minds: Intellectuals in Britain* (Oxford: Oxford University Press, 2006), 432.

74 Varisco, *Reading Orientalism*, 290–1.

75 Habib Malik to Joshua Muravchik, e-mail, Sept. 19, 2012.

76 Said, *Orientalism*, 306.

77 Nicholas Wroe, "Review: A Life In Writing: Mary-Kay Wilmers: I like difficult women. Not just because I'm a bit difficult myself. I like their complication," Review pages, *Guardian*, Oct. 24, 2009, 12.

78 Gauri Viswanathan, ed., *Power, Politics, and Culture: Interviews with Edward W. Said* (New York: Pantheon, 2001), 374.

79 Said, *Orientalism*, 262–3.

80 See p. 192.

81 Edward Said, *Covering Islam: How the Media and the Experts Determine How We See the Rest of the World,* (New York: Vintage Books, 1997), 158. I am grateful to Martin Kramer's *Ivory Towers on Sand* (see note 82) for alerting me to this.

82 Interview with Nikki Keddie in Nancy Elizabeth Gallagher, ed., *Approaches to the History of the Middle East,* (London: Ithaca Press, 1994),144–145 quoted in Martin Kramer, *Ivory Towers on Sand: The Failure of Middle Eastern Studies in America* (Washington: Washington Institute for Near East Policy, 2001), 37.

83 Said, *Question of Palestine,* 172.

84 Ibid., 175–6.

85 Ibid., xxxviii.

86 Ibid., 137.

87 Nicholas Bethell, "The View From the West Bank," *New York Times,* Jan. 20, 1980.

88 Said, *Question of Palestine,* 172.

89 Ibid., 224.

90 Alain Gresh, *The PLO: The Struggle Within,* trans. A. M. Berrett (London: Zed, 1985), 168–9.

91 Diana Jean Schemo, "West Bank Massacre; America's Scholarly Palestinian Raises Volume Against Arafat," *New York Times,* March 4, 1994.

92 Ibid.

93 Viswanathan, *Power, Politics, and Culture,* 433.

94 Schemo, "West Bank Massacre;" David K. Shipler, "From a Wellspring of Bitterness," *New York Times,* June 26, 1994.

95 Viswanathan, *Power, Politics, and Culture,* 433.

Chapter 8

1 J. B. Schechtman, *The Vladimir Jabotinsky Story,* vol. 2, *Fighter and Prophet: The Last Years* (New York: T. Yoseloff, 1961), 233, quoted in Walter Laqueur, *A History of Zionism* (New York: MJF Books, 1972), 367.

2 Zeev Jabotinsky, *A Jewish State: The Solution to the Jewish Question* (in Hebrew) (Tel Aviv, 1937), 89, quoted in Gideon Shimoni, *The Zionist Ideology* (Hanover, NH: Brandeis University Press, 1995), 243.

3 Quoted in Amos Perlmutter, *The Life and Times of Menachem Begin* (Garden City: Doubleday, 1987), 34.

4 Avi Shilon, *Menachem Begin: A Life,* trans. Danielle Zilberberg and Yoram Sharett (New Haven: Yale, 2012), 269.

5 Mark Tessler, *A History of the Israeli-Palestinian Conflict,* 2nd ed. (Bloomington: Indiana University Press, 2009), 503.

6 Rudy Abramson, "Peace Prospects Set Back, U.S. Officials Say Privately," *Los Angeles Times,* May 19, 1977.

7 Yehuda Avner, *The Prime Ministers* (New Milford: The Toby Press, 2010), Kindle edition loc. 8628.

8 "'Kind . . . Honest . . . Dangerous,'" *TIME* 109, no. 22 (May 30, 1977): 29.

9 "Begin Bars a Return to '67 Borders," *New York Times*, May 23, 1977.

10 William E. Farrell, "Israelis Upset by Begin's Support of Settlements on the West Bank," *New York Times*, May 21, 1977.

11 George F. Will, "Being Right is a Weak Reed on Which to Rest a Nation," *Baltimore Sun*, June 5, 1977.

12 Perlmutter, *Life and Times*, 310.

13 Shilon, *Menachem Begin*, 268.

14 Perlmutter, *Life and Times*, 326.

15 Tessler, *History of the Israeli-Palestinian Conflict*, 505.

16 Gershom Gorenberg, *The Accidental Empire: Israel and the Birth of the Settlements, 1967–1977* (New York: Times Books, 2006).

17 Perlmutter, *Life and Times*, 327.

18 Anwar El-Sadat, *Those I Have Known* (New York: Continuum, 1984), 100.

19 Anwar El-Sadat, *In Search of Identity* (New York: Harper Colophon, 1979), 306.

20 Kenneth W. Stein, *Heroic Diplomacy: Sadat, Kissinger, Carter, Begin, and the Quest for Arab-Israeli Peace* (New York: Routledge, 1999), 201.

21 Shilon, *Menachem Begin*, 298.

22 Stein, *Heroic Diplomacy*, 25.

23 Perlmutter, *Life and Times*, 355.

24 Shilon, *Menachem Begin*, 298.

25 Avner, *The Prime Ministers*, loc. 9777.

26 "Core of the Mideast Problem," *Baltimore Sun*, March 21, 1978.

27 Ze'ev Schiff and Ehud Ya'ari, *Israel's Lebanon War*, ed. and trans. Ina Friedman (New York: Simon and Schuster, 1984), 193.

28 "Report of the Inquiry into the Events at the Refugee Camps in Beirut" (The Kahan Commission), February 8, 1983. Available at http://www .jewishvirtualliberary.org/jsource/History/kahan.html.

29 *NBC Nightly News*, Aug. 2, 1982.

30 Schiff and Ya'ari, *Israel's Lebanon War*, 280.

31 Perlmutter, *Life and Times*, 18.

32 Shilon, *Menachem Begin*, 425.

Chapter 9

1 Yoram Hazony, *The Jewish State: The Struggle for Israel's Soul* (New York: Basic Books, 2000).

2 Various English translations may be found. This is from Mordechai Bar-On, *In Pursuit of Peace: A History of the Israeli Peace Movement* (Washington, DC: U. S. Institute of Peace, 1996), 96.

3 Bar-On, *In Pursuit of Peace*, 112.

4 Interview with Alexander Yakobson, Jerusalem, June 26, 2012. The English paraphrase is Yakobson's own.

5 Letter from Alexander Yakobson to Peace Now, July 31, 2001, copy in author's files.

6 Maurice Ostroff, "The Apple That Fell Far From the Tree," *Jeru-*

salem Post, June 11, 2007; Yossi Gurvitz, "The Strange Voyage of Avraham Burg, +972 *Magazine*, Nov. 6, 2010. http://972mag.com/the-strange-voyage-of-avraham-burg/4463/.

7 "Leaving the Zionist Ghetto," by Ari Shavit, interview with Avraham Burg, *Ha'aretz*, June 10, 2007 (Hebrew).

8 "Jerusalem-Born Thinker Meron Benvenisti Has a Message for Israelis: Stop Whining," by Ari Shavit, interview with Meron Benvenisti, *Ha'aretz*, Oct. 11, 2012.

9 Amos Oz, "Has Israel Altered its Visions?" *New York Times Magazine*, July 11, 1982.

10 Hazony, *The Jewish State*, 339.

11 Quoted in Benajmin Balin, "A Novelist Defends Zion's Idealists," *Forward.com*, September 23, 2005. http://forward.com/articles/2832/a-novelist-defends-ziones-idealists/.

12 Shlomo Avineri, "Post-Zionism Doesn't Exist," *Ha'aretz*, July 6, 2007.

13 Jack Khoury, "Left-Wing Activist Tali Fahima Converts to Islam," *Ha'aretz*, June 8, 2010.

14 "Free Tali Fahima," *Electronic Intifada*, Sept. 24, 2004. http://electronicintifada.net/content/free-tali-fahima/5244.

15 "Tali Fahima: Zakaria Zubeidi is Israeli Security Service's Whore," *Ha'aretz*, July 24, 2008.

16 Sharon Roffe-Ofir, "Leftist Tali Fahima Converts to Islam," *Ynetnews.com*, Aug. 6, 2010. http://www.ynetnews.com/articles/0,7340,L-3902175,00.html.

17 Larry Derfner, "Both Sides Now," *Jerusalem Post*, Nov. 3, 1995.

18 B'Tselem, *Collaborators in the Occupied Territories: Human Rights Violations and Abuses*, Jerusalem, January 1994.

19 B'Tselem, *Neither Law nor Justice: Extrajudicial Punishment, Abduction, Unlawful Arrest, and Torture on Palestinian Residents of the West Bank by the Palestinian Preventive Security Service*, Jerusalem, August 1995.

20 "Israeli-Occupied West Bank and Gaza Strip," *Human Rights Watch World Report* 1996. www.hrw.org/reports/1996/WR96/MIDEAST-06.htm.

21 Bar-On, *In Pursuit of Peace*, 15.

22 Uri Avnery, "The New Collaborators," *Ma'ariv*, Sept. 16, 1998.

23 "Israeli Citizens Appeal: International Intervention in the Israeli-Palestinian Conflict," Palestine: Information with Provenance (PIWP database), Apr. 27, 2001. http://cosmos.ucc.ie/cs1064/jabowen/IPSC/php/art.php?aid=592.

24 These three quotes appear in Noah Pollak, "*B'Tselem* Witch Trials," *Commentary* 131, no. 5 (May 2011). None has been challenged.

25 B'Tselem, *The Gaza Strip—One Big Prison* (Jerusalem, no date given), pamphlet. Pollak dates this publication to 2007, but it is available on B'Tselem's website in 2013 and contains no date.

26 Pollak, "*B'Tselem.*"

27 B'Tselem, Israeli Human Rights Organizations to EU: Use Association Council Meeting to Stop Settlements and Open Gaza, June 15, 2009.

28 United Nations, General Assembly, Human Rights Council, Ninth Special Session, "The grave violations of human rights in the Occupied Palestinian Territory, particularly due to the recent Israeli military attacks against the occupied Gaza Strip," A/HRC/S-9/L.1, Jan. 12, 2009, 5.

29 Richard Goldstone, "Reconsidering the goldstone Report on Israel and War Crimes," *Washington Post*, Apr. 1, 2011.

30 Jessica Montell, "Beyond Goldstone: A Truer Discussion about Israel, Hamas, and the Gaza Conflict," *Washington Post*, Apr. 5, 2011.

31 *B'Tselem, 19 Oct. '09: Israel Must Investigate Army's Conduct in Operation Cast Lead*, Oct. 19, 2009.

32 Montell, "Beyond Goldstone."

33 Benny Morris, "The New Historiography: Israel Confronts Its Past," *Tikkun* 3, no. 6 (Nov./Dec. 1988), 21.

34 Ibid., 20.

35 Ibid., 21.

36 Bennie Morris, *The Birth of the Palestinian Refugee Problem, 1947–1949* (Cambridge: Cambridge University Press, 1988).

37 Especially, *Righteous Victims: A History of the Zionist-Arab Conflict* (New York: Knopf, 2001).

38 Benny Morris, "Arab-Israeli War," in *Crimes of War*, eds. Roy Guttman and David Rieff (New York: W. W. Norton, 1999), 30.

39 Ibid., 31–32.

40 Ethan Bronner, "Israel: The Revised Edition," *New York Times*, Nov. 14, 1999.

41 Morris, "The New Historiography," 21.

42 Avi Shlaim, *The Iron Wall: Israel and the Arab World* (New York: W. W. Norton, 2001), 238.

43 Ibid., blurb, no page number.

44 Ilan Pappé, *A History of Modern Palestine*, 2nd ed. (Cambridge: Cambridge University Press, 2006), xxi.

45 Daniel Polisar, for the Editors, "Making History," *Azure* 9 (Spring 5760/2000): 18.

46 Benny Morris, "Peace? No Chance," *Guardian*, Febr. 20, 2002.

47 Ari Shavit, "Surivival of the Fittest? An Interview with Benny Morris," *Ha'aretz*, Jan. 5, 2004.

48 Ibid.

49 Ibid.

50 Ibid.

51 Ilan Pappe, *Out of the Frame* (New York: Pluto Books, 2010), x.

52 Ayelet Negev, "Ilan Pappe: I'm Not a Traitor," *Yedioth Ahronoth*, Mar. 15, 2008. http://www.ynetnews.com/articles/0,7340,L-3516193,00.html.

53 Ibid.

54 Benny Morris, "The Liar as Hero," *New Republic*, Mar. 17, 2011.

55 Gilead Ini and Dexter Van Zile, "*Journal of Palestine Studies* Compounds its Ben-Gurion Error," Committee for Accuracy in Middle East Reporting in America, Apr. 9, 2012.

56 Polisar, "Making History," 16.

57 Michal Ben-Josef Hirsch, "From Taboo to the Negotiable: The Israeli New Historians and the Changing Representation of the Palestinian Refugee Problem," *Perspectives on Politics* 5, no. 2 (June 2007): 247.

58 Avi Shlaim, "When Historians Matter," *Prospect*, June 29, 2008.

59 Anita Shapira, "The Past is Not a Foreign Country," *New Republic*, Nov. 29, 1999.

60 Morris, "Liar as Hero."

61 *Post-Zionism in the Academy*, abstract, Institute for Zionist Studies. http://www.izs.org.il/eng/?catid=395.

62 Polisar, "Making History," 16.

63 David Remnick, "The Dissenters," *New Yorker*, Feb. 28, 2011.

64 Johann Hari, "Is Gideon Levy the Most Hated Man in Israel or Just the Most Heroic?" *Independent*, Sept. 24, 2010.

65 Gideon Levy, "When did it Become Illegal to be a Leftist in Israel?" *Ha'aretz*, Jan. 6, 2011.

66 Gideon Levy, "Racism has Reared its Head, and the Public is Apathetic," *Ha'aretz*, Dec. 23, 2010.

67 Gideon Levy, "Israelis' Ideal State: A Country without Criticism," *Ha'aretz*, May 23, 2010.

68 Yishai Goldflam, "In Today's 'Apology,' Gideon Levy Just Doesn't Get It," Committee for Accuracy in Middle East Reporting in America, Oct. 29, 2012.

69 Gideon Levy, "Survey: Most Israeli Jews Support an Apartheid Regime in Israel," *Ha'aretz*, Oct. 23, 2012. (In the wake of the scandal over this misleading report, the headline was changed on the paper's website.)

70 Ibid.

71 The person quoted is Amiram Goldblum. The quote is given by former *Ha'aretz* editor Hanoch Marmari in the Israeli journalism review, *Seventh Eye*, which appears only in Hebrew. Marmari's article was translated and published by CAMERA: "Former *Ha'aretz* Editor Marmari Speaks Out on 'Apartheid' Poll Scandal," Committee for Accuracy in Middle East Reporting in America, Nov. 4, 2012.

72 Noam Shelef, "That Poll's Apartheid Problem," *Daily Beast*, Oct. 23, 2012.

73 Robert Fisk, "Amira Hass: Life Under Israeli Occupation—By an Israeli," *Independent*, Aug. 26, 2001.

74 Amira Hass, *Drinking the Sea at Gaza: Days and Nights in a Land Under Siege*, trans. By Elana Wesley and Maxine Kaufman-Lacusta (New York: Henry Holt, 2000), 5–6.

75 Ibid., 7.

76 Ibid., 7.

77 Remnick, "The Dissenters."

78 Amira Hass, "The Inner Syntax of Palestinian Stone-Throwing," *Ha'aretz*, Apr. 3, 2013.

79 Amira Hass, "Palestinians are Heroes, Braving Israeli Dictatorship," *Ha'aretz*, Dec. 21, 2011.

80 See Yishai Goldflam, "*Ha'aretz*: Amira Hass' Ideological Agenda Trumps Journalistic Integrity," Committee for Accuracy in Middle East Reporting in America, July 28, 2010.

81 Nahum Barnea, "Leftist Israeli reporters failed the Lynch Test," *The Seventh Eye*, Nov. 2000 (Hebrew), translated in Independent Media Review Analysis, Nov. 5, 2000. http://www.imra.org.il/story.php3?id= 5036.

82 Akiva Eldar, "On Not Passing Israel's Lynch Test," *Nation*, May 26, 2008.

83 Akiva Eldar, "Analysis: Creating a Bantustan in Gaza," *Ha'aretz*, Apr. 16, 2004.

84 Akiva Eldar, "Are Israel and Apartheid South Africa really Different?" *Ha'aretz*, Jan. 4, 2010.

85 Akiva Eldar, "The Jewish Majority is History," *Ha'aretz*, Oct. 16, 2012.

86 Eldar, "Israel's Lynch Test."

87 Akiva Eldar, "Perles of Wisdom for the Feithful," *Ha'aretz*, Oct. 1, 2002.

88 Samuel G. Freedman, "Conspiracy Theory," *Washington Post*, Oct. 7, 2007.

89 Leslie H. Gelb, "Dual Loyalties," *New York Times*, Sept. 23, 2007.

90 Eliot A. Cohen, "Yes, It's Anti-Semitic," *Washington Post*, Apr. 5, 2006. Cohen was referring to the "white paper" that the authors originally posted on a Harvard University website which they then lengthened into the book.

91 Daniel Levy, "So Pro-Israel That it Hurts," *Ha'aretz*, Mar. 24, 2006.

92 Daniel Levy, "Daniel Levy," Oct. 3, 2007. (Author's note: This may be a glitch on the *Ha'aretz* website, but it lists the title of the book review just as I have given it here, to wit, the name of the reviewer.)

93 Amos Harel, "IDF Killed Civilians in Gaza Under Loose Rules of Engagement," *Ha'aretz*, Mar. 19, 2009.

94 Ethan Bronner, "Soldiers' Accounts of Gaza Killings Raise Furor in Israel," *New York Times*, Mar. 20, 2009.

95 Amos Harel, "Analysis: can Israel Dismiss its Own Troops' Stories from Gaza," *Ha'aretz*, Mar. 19, 2009.

96 Amos Harel, "Analysis: Probe into Gaza Op Allegations Comes Too Late," *Ha'aretz*, Mar. 20, 2009.

97 *Ha'aretz*, Mar. 22, 2009.

98 Anshel Pfeffer, "How IDF Testimonies Led to the '*Ha'aretz* Blood Libel,'" *Ha'aretz*, Mar. 27, 2009.

99 Tamar Sternthal, "Updated: *Ha'aretz* Indifferent to Journalistic Norms," Committee for Accuracy in Middle East Reporting in America, Nov. 30, 2005.

100 Gary Rosenblatt, "*Ha'aretz* Editor Urged Rice to 'Rape' Israel," *New York Jewish Week*, Dec. 28, 2007.

101 David Landau, "Israel is Sliding Toward McCarthyism and Racism," *Ha'aretz*, Mar. 29, 2010.

102 Gershom Schocken, "The Curse of Ezra," *Ha'aretz*, Dec. 22, 2010.

103 Amos Schocken, "Toward the Next 60 Years," *Ha'aretz*, Apr. 19, 2007.

104 Amos Schocken, "The Necessary Elimination of Israeli Democracy," *Ha'aretz*, Nov. 25, 2011.
105 Remnick, "The Dissenters."
106 Ibid.
107 Ibid.

Chapter 10

1 *Let Me Stand Alone: The Journals of Rachel Corrie*, ed. by the Corrie family (New York: Norton, 2008), 4.
2 Ibid., 8.
3 Ibid., 14.
4 Tomas Alex Tizon and Lynn Marshall, "Activist Had Soft Spot for Underdogs," *Los Angeles Times*, Mar. 18, 2003.
5 Matti Friedman, "Court Dismisses Damages Claim in Rachel Corrie Case," *Times of Israel*, Aug. 28, 2012.
6 Joshua Hammer, "The Death of Rachel Corrie," *Mother Jones*, Sept./Oct. 2003.
7 The International Solidarity Movement, "Who We Are." http://www.palsolidarity.org/about_us.htm. The ISM has removed this from its site, but I found it at web.archive.org/web/20020805193207/http://www.palsolidarity.org/about_us.htm.
8 "2-Jenin Day 8 (from Ewa)." It is clear from the surrounding information that the writer is ISM activist, Ewa Jasiewicz. This, like other incendiary items, has been removed from the website, but I found it at: web.archive.org/web/20030814044336/http://www.palsolidarity.org/reports/olive_harvest/Nov4.htm.
9 Ghassan Joha, "Adam Shapiro Calls for Palestinian Civil Resistance: 'No Peace Can be Achieved with Occupation,'" *Daily Star* (Jordan), July 11, 2003.
10 Paul Larudee, Journal entry, Sept. 2002, web.archive.org/web/20060618231417/http://www.palsolidarity.org/main/2006/06/13/reposted-sleeping-in-the-bed-of-a-suicide-bomber/.
11 Huwaida Arraf and Adam Shapiro, "Why Nonviolent Resistance is Important for the Palestinian Intifada: A Response to Ramzy Baroud," *Palestine Chronicle*, Jan. 29, 2002. Reprinted at http://netwmd.com/anti-ism/ISM%20by%20any%20means.htm.
12 "American Morning with Paula Zahn: Interview with Adam Shapiro, Huwaida Arraf, Activists," *CNN.com*, aired May 10, 2002. transcripts.cnn.com/TRANSCRIPTS/0205/10/ltm.08.html.
13 International Solidarity Movement, "Frequently Asked Questions." http://palsolidarity.org/about/faq/.
14 Ibid.
15 Ibid.
16 Nichole Dobo, "York County Native Gets 31/2 Years for Helping Hamas," *Evening Sun*, Sept. 2, 2008.
17 Lisa, Amin Gulezian, "Gaza Activist Returns Home, Claims He Was Beaten," KGO-TV San Francisco, June 5, 2010. http://abclocal.go.com/

kgo/story?section=news/local/east_bay&id=7480941. The photo was shown on this 2010 news broadcast which can be seen on the website, but it was taken earlier. It may also be seen at Martha O'Connor, "Smoking Gun: The Free Gaza Movement and Hamas," *American Thinker*, June 13, 2010 which dates it to 2008, and in an untitled report on the ISM issued by the Meir Amit Intelligence and Terrorism Information Center http://www.terrorism-info.org.il/en/article/17984, 26, which dates it to 2009.

18 "ISM: Report from May 5th Press Conference in Jerusalem," *The Electronic Intifada*, May10, 2003. Electronicintifada.net/content/sim-report-may-5th-press-conference-jerusalem/1196.

19 "Compassionate Listening Project – in Israel and Palestine," July 10, 2002. International Solidarity Movement. http://palsolidarity.org/2002/07/compassionate-listening-project-%E2%80%93-in-israel-and-palestine/.

20 Ibid.

21 Joha, "Adam Shapiro."

22 "Compassionate Listening Project."

23 David Bedein, "Support Unit for Terror," *Jerusalem Post*, June 26, 2003.

24 Louise France, "She Was a Girl From Small-Town American With Dreams of Being a Poet Or A Dancer. So How at Just 23, Did Rachel Corrie Become a Palestinian Martyr?" *Observer*, Mar. 1, 2008.

25 *Let Me Stand Alone*, 271–3.

26 Ibid, 275.

27 Anne Marie Olivier and Paul Steinberg, *The Road to Martyrs' Square: A Journey into the World of the Suicide Bomber* (Oxford: Oxford University Press, 2005).

28 Ibid., 57, 76.

29 *Let Me Stand Alone*, 273.

30 Eric Hoffer, *The True Believer* (New York: HarperCollins, 2002; originally Harper & Row, 1951) xi.

31 Milovan Djilas, *The Unperfect Society*, trans. Dorian Cooke (New York: Harcourt, Brace and World, 1969), 131.

32 France, "Girl from Small Town America."

33 The Evergreen State College, "Academics." www.evergreen.edu/academics.htm.

34 *Let Me Stand Alone*, 194.

35 Ibid., 197.

36 Ibid., 233, 282.

37 Karl Marx, *On Imperialism in India*.

38 Jean-Paul Sartre, "Preface," Frantz Fanon, *The Wretched of the Earth*, transl. by Constance Farrington (New York: Grove Press, 1968), 10.

39 Janet Afary and Kevin B. Anderson, *Foucault and the Iranian Revolution: Gender and the Seductions of Islamism* (translated from *Le Nouvel Observateur*, Oct. 16–22, 1978) (Chicago: University of Chicago Press, 2005), 206–8.

40 Ali Shariati, *Red Shiism*, trans. Habib Shirazi (Tehran: Shariati Foundation, 1979).

41 Frank Jack Daniel, "Venezuela's Chavez Calls Israel 'Murderous U.S. Arm,'" Reuters, Nov. 25, 2009.

42 "Daughter of Che Guevara Meets Hizbullah Leaders in Lebanon: 'If We Do Not Conduct Resistance, We Will Disappear from the Face of the Earth,'" Middle East Media Research Institute, special dispatch no. 3317, October 25, 2010.

43 "Judith Butler on Hamas Hezbollah and the Israel Lobby (2006)," *Radical Archives*, Mar. 28, 2010, http://radicalarchives.org/2010/03/28/jbutler-on-hamas-hezbollah-israel-lobby/. Quotes of these remarks by Ms. Butler have appeared in numerous newspapers and websites, but the foregoing is the one I have found that gives a full transcript. Under criticism for her comments, Ms. Butler published a patently mendacious account of what she had said (Judith Butler, "Judith Butler responds to attack: 'I affirm a Judaism that is not associated with state violence'," *Mondoweiss*, August 27, 2012. Like many others, I viewed Ms. Butler's comments, myself, on YouTube at https://www.youtube.com/watch?feature=player_embedded&v=zFp_6Joe92Q#%21. However, perhaps because that video shows Ms. Butler's subsequent account of what she had said to be misleading, it is now labeled "private" on YouTube and no longer available for viewing.

44 Daniel Dombey and Tobias Buck, "Erdogan Labels Israel a 'Spoilt Child,'" *Financial Times*, Sept. 6, 2011.

45 Robert L. Bernstein, "Rights Watchdog, Lost in the Middle East," *New York Times*, Oct. 19, 2009.

46 Joshua Muravchik, *The Uncertain Crusade: Jimmy Carter and the Dilemmas of Human Rights Policy* (Lanham, MD: Hamilton Press, 1986), 170. I was quoting from an interview I held with Cameron at his home in Washington, DC, Jan. 21, 1984.

47 Muravchik, *Uncertain Crusade*, 168, quoting from an interview in her home in Washington, DC, Dec. 16, 1983.

48 Americas Watch Committee, *Human Rights in Nicaragua 1986*, February 1987, 6.

49 Ibid., passim; Americas Watch Committee, *The Killings in Northern Nicaragua*, November 1989, 17; Americas Watch Committee, *Human Rights in Nicaragua: Reagan, Rhetoric, and Reality*, 1985 (appearing as an Appendix in International Court of Justice, *Case Concerning Military and Paramilitary Activities in and Against Nicaragua* [*Nicaragua v. United States of America*]), *Volume IV*, 1986, 411–413.

50 Allison Hoffman, "Does Human Rights Watch Have an Israel Problem?" *Tablet*, Aug. 26, 2009.

51 Sarah Leah Whitson, "Tripoli Spring," *Foreign Policy*, May 27, 2009.

52 David D. Kirkpatrick and Mona El-Naggar, "Qaddafi's Son Warns of Civil War as Libya Protests Widen," *New York Times*, Feb. 20, 2011.

53 Sarah Leah Whitson, "Libya: To Oust a Tyrant," *Los Angeles Times*, Feb. 24, 2011.

54 Sarah Leah Whitson, "Postcard from . . . Tripoli," *Foreign Policy in Focus*, Feb. 11, 2010.

55 Nasser Salti, "HRW Lauded for Work in Gaza," *Arab News*, May 26, 2009.

56 David Bernstein, "Human Rights Watch Goes to Saudi Arabia," *Wall Street Journal*, July 15, 2009.

57 Jeffrey Goldberg, "Fundraising Corruption at Human Rights Watch," *Atlantic*, July 15, 2009.

58 Ibid.

59 Salti, "HRW Lauded."

60 Al-Hejailan Consultants, "Clients." http://www.alhejailan-consultants .com/clients.asp#.

61 Kenneth Roth, "Getting it Straight," *New York Sun*, letters to the editor, July 31, 2006.

62 Tom Gross, "How Hizbullah's Own al-Manar TV Website Remembered Fadlallah," Mideast Media Analysis, July 9, 2010.

63 Human Rights Watch, "Letter to President Ahmadinejad on Israel–Lebanon Conflict," July 26, 2006. http://www.hrw.org/news/2006/ 07/25/letter-president-ahmadinejad-israel-lebanon-conflict.

64 Ben Birnbaum, "Minority Report," *New Republic*, Apr. 27, 2010.

65 David Feith, "Dancing Around Genocide," *Wall Street Journal*, Dec. 4, 2012.

66 United Nations, General Assembly, *Genocide: Draft Convention and Report of the Economic and Social Council*, Report of the Sixth Committee, J. Spiropoulos, rapporteur, Third session, A/760, Dec. 3, 1948.

67 Birnbaum, "Minority Report."

68 Ibid.

69 "Who Are the Real Terrorists?" MERIP *Reports* 12 (Sept.–Oct. 1972), 13.

70 Jonathan Foreman, "Nazi Scandal Engulfs Human Rights Watch," *Sunday Times*, Mar, 28, 2010.

71 Examiner.com, "Credibility of Human Rights Watch on Israel crashes." http://www.examiner.com/article/credibility-of-human-rights-watch-on-israel-crashes.

72 Lucy Mair, "Life in Palestine," *Electronic Intifada*. http:// electronicintifada.net/content/life-palestine/4400.

73 Sarah Mandel and Gerald M. Steinberg, *Experts or Ideologues: A Systematic Analysis of Human Rgihts Watch's Focus on Israel*, NGO Monitor, Jerusalem, September 2009. Also see: http://www.c-spanvideo.org/ program/MeSt.

74 Birnbaum, "Minority Report."

75 Ibid.

76 See, for example: "Meeting: PSC and Amnesty," Cambridge Palestine Forum, Apr. 9, 2013. http://www.campalsoc.org/?p=1850. And "Palestine Solidarity Committee and Middle East Monitor invite you to: 'Complicity in Oppression: Do the Media Aid Israel?,'" May 23, 2011 at Amnesty International UK, posted on Facebook at https://www.facebook.com/events/108848145867498/.

77 "Amnesty International (UK): Key Issues & Next Steps (Middle East)," Labour Friends of Palestine and the Middle East, updated Oct. 4, 2012. http://www.lfpme.org/articles-p181.

78 Benjamin Weinthal, "Amnesty Int'l Finland: Israel Scum State," *Jerusalem Post*, Aug. 24, 2010. http://www.jpost.com/International/Article.aspx?id=185846.

79 Trade Union Congress, "Israel/Palestine." http://www.tuc.org.uk/international/index.cfm?mins=196&minors=184&majorsubjectID=7.

80 "Palestine-Israel: The Basic Facts," Palestine Solidarity Campaign, May 2011. http://www.palestinecampaign.org/wp-content/uploads/2012/12/basic-facts-sheet-jan-2012.pdf.

81 Mark Tooley, "The Religious Left and Israel," *American Spectator*, July 9, 2010.

82 Palestine Israel Ecumenical Forum, "Resources." http://archived.oikoumene.org/en/programmes/public-witness-addressing-power-affirming-peace/churches-in-the-middle-east/pief/resources.html.

83 World Council of Churches, "World Week for Peace in Palestine Israel." http://www.oikoumene.org/en/press-centre/events/world-week-for-peace-in-palestine-israel.

84 Anshel Pfeffer, "Church of Scotland: Jews Do Not Have a Right to the Land of Israel," *Ha'aretz*, May3, 2013.

85 Stanley Rothman and S. Robert Lichter, *Roots of Radicalism: Jews Christians and the New Left* (New York: Oxford University Press, 1982), x. On the Jewish presence in the Bolshevik and other Communist parties see Jerry Z. Muller, "Communism, Anti-Semitism and the Jews," *Commentary* 86, no. 2 (August 1988): 28–39. On the Jewish presence among Mensheviks see Richard Pipes, *The Russian Revolution* (New York: Vintage Books, 1990), 365.

86 Gilad Atzmon, *The Wandering Who* (London: John Hunt, 2011).

87 "Palestinian writers, activists disavow racism, anti-Semitism of Gilad Atzmon," *Electronic Intifada*, March 13, 2012. http://electronicintifada.net/blogs/ali-abunimah/palestinian-writers-activists-disavow-racism-anti-semitism-gilad-atzmon.

88 Robert Faurisson, *Mémoire en Défense* (Paris: La Vieille Taupe, 1980).

89 Richard Falk, "On Jewish Identity," *Intifada: Voice of Palestine*, Jan. 20, 2011, http://www.intifada-palestine.com/2011/01/richard-falk-on-jewish-identity/.

90 Ibid.

91 Richard Falk, "Slouching Toward a Palestinian Holocaust," *Countercurrents.org*, July 7, 2007. http://www.countercurrents.org/falk070707.htm.

92 Richard Falk, "Trusting Khomeini," *New York Times*, Feb. 16, 1979.

93 Richard Falk, "A Few Notes on WHAT IS LEFT (or Toward a Manifesto for Revolutionary Emancipation)," June 19, 2011. http://richardfalk.wordpress.com/2011/06/19/a-few-notes-on-what-is-left-or-toward-a-manifesto-for-revolutionary-emancipation/.

94 Jared Malsin, "UN Expert Richard Falk: PA Told Me to Quit," *Ma'an News Agency*, June 22, 2010. http://www.maannews.net/eng/ViewDetails.aspx?ID=267176.

95 UN Watch, "Before he hit delete: Richard Falk's anti-Semitic cartoon." http://blog.unwatch.org/index.php/2011/07/06/before-he-deleted-it-richard-falks-anti-semitic-cartoon/.

96 Richard Falk, "54 Responses to 'Responding to the Unspeakable Killings at Newton, Connecticut.'" http://richardfalk.wordpress.com/2012/12/15/responding-to-the-unspeakable-killings-at-newtown-connecticut/#comment-10897.

97 Human Rights Watch, "Keyword Search: Falk." http://www.hrw.org/search/apachesolr_search/Falk.

98 "Israel: Reverse Expulsion of Human Rights Rapporteur," Dec. 17, 2008. http://www.hrw.org/news/2008/12/17/israel-reverse-expulsion-human-rights-rapporteur.

99 Richard Falk, "A Commentary on the Marathon Murders," April 19, 2013. http://richardfalk.wordpress.com/2013/04/19/a-commentary-on-the-marathon-murders/.

100 "U.N. Chief Scolds Envoy for Implying U.S. Policy Sparked Boston Attack," Reuters, Apr. 24, 2013.

101 Elder of Ziyon, "Purpose of J Street is not to reflect US Jewish opinion, but to change it," May 14, 2012. http://elderofziyon.blogspot.com/2012/05/purpose-of-j-street-is-not-to-reflect.html.

102 "About J Street," *jstreet.org*.

103 Ron Kampeas, "Ben-Ami's blunder: Why did J Street chief fudge on Soros' role?" *Washington Jewish Week*, Sept. 29, 2010.

104 Hilary Leila Krieger, "Muslims, Arabs Among J Street Donors," *Jerusalem Post*, Aug. 14, 2009.

105 Daniel Frank, "Stop Calling J Street Pro-Israel," *Times of Israel*, Apr. 30, 2013.

106 Omri Ceren, "J Street Co-Founder Daniel Levy: Israel's Creation 'An Act That Was Wrong'," *Mere Rhetoric*, Oct. 5, 2010. http://www.mererhetoric.com/2010/10/05/j-street-co-founder-daniel-levy-israel%E2%80%99s-creation-an-act-that-was-wrong/.

107 Lori Lowenthal Marcus, "J Street: 'Maybe Israel really ain't a good idea'," *American Thinker*, Mar. 15, 2011. http://www.americanthinker.com/2011/03/j_street_maybe_israel_really_a.html.

108 Anne McElvoy, "Mary-Kay Wilmers: Queen of Plots," *Times* (London), Oct. 18, 2009.

Chapter 11

1 Lee Hockstader, "Street Army Spearheads Arab Riots," *Washington Post*, Oct. 4, 2000.

2 *Al-Hayat al-Jadida*, Aug. 24, 2000, quoted in Khaled Abu Toameh, "How the War Began," *Jerusalem Post*, Sept. 20, 2002.

3 ABC Evening News, Sept. 29, 2000.

4 Khaled Abu Toameh, "How the War Began," *Jerusalem Post*, Sept. 20, 2002.

5 Ibid.

6 Khaled Abu Toameh, "Arafat ordered Hamas attacks against Israel in 2000," *Jerusalem Post*, Sept. 29, 2010.

7 "Suha Arafat, Widow of Yasser Arafat: The 2000 Intifada Was Premeditated, Planned by Arafat," Middle East Media Research Institute, clip 3689, Dec. 16, 2012. http://www.memritv.org/clip_transcript/en/3689 .htm.

8 Dennis Ross, *The Missing Peace: The Inside Story of the Fight for Middle East Peace* (New York: Farrar, Straus, 2004), 741.

9 Amos Harel and Avi Isaacharoff, "Years of Rage," *Ha'aretz*, Oct. 1, 2010.

10 "Time to Get Serious, *Guardian*, Apr. 9, 2002.

11 "End the Israeli Occupation Now! For a Palestinian State" (adverstisement), *Guardian*, Apr. 19, 2002.

12 Jimmy Carter, "America Can Persuade Israel to Make a Just Peace," *New York Times*, Apr. 21, 2002.

13 Desmond Tutu, "Apartheid in the Holy Land," *Guardian*, Apr. 29, 2002.

14 Jose Samarago, "An Incurable Malady: Hope," *Al-Ahram*, Apr. 4–10, 2002.

15 "Musician Clarifies Jewish Remark," *BBC News*, Nov. 13, 2003.

16 Uri Avnery, "Immortal Heroes of Jenin," *Guardian*, Apr. 15, 2002.

17 Nicholas Watt, "MP Accuses Sharon of 'Barbarism,'" *Guardian*, Apr. 16, 2002.

18 "Israeli Citizens Appeal: International Intervention in the Israeli-Palestinian Conflict," Palestine: Information with Provenance (PIWP database), Apr. 27, 2001. http://cosmos.ucc.ie/cs1064/jabowen/IPSC/ php/art.php?aid=592.

19 Andy Beckett and Ewen MacAskill, "British Academic Boycott Of Israel Gathers Pace," *Guardian*, Dec. 12, 2002.

20 Ibid.

21 "About-Face: Cambridge Confirms Hawking Is Boycotting Israel," *Algemeiner*, May 8, 2013. http://www.algemeiner.com/2013/05/08/ about-face-cambridge-confirms-hawking-is-boycotting-israel/.

22 Dennis Overbye, "Hawking Takes Beijing; Now, Will Science Follow?" *New York Times*, June 20, 2006.

23 "Stephen Hawking Due in Iran," *Press TV*, May 14, 2007. http://edition. presstv.ir/detail/9774.html.

24 Jenny Gross, "University of Johannesburg Cuts Ties With Ben-Gurion University," *Huffington Post*, Mar. 24, 2011.

25 Harbin Institute of Technology, "About Us." http://en.hit.edu.cn/about .asp.

26 Daniel P. Moynihan, "The Politics of Human Rights," *Commentary* 64, no. 2 (August 1977): 24.

27 International Court Of Justice, Reports Of Judgments, Advisory Opinions and Orders, *Legal Consequences Of The Construction Of A Wall*

In The Occupied Palestinian Territory, Advisory Opinion of 9 July 2004, paragraph 139.

28 Jeffrey Goldberg, "In the Party of God," *New Yorker,* Oct. 14, 2002.

29 "Address of the Secretary-General of Hizbullah 'Sayyed Hassan Nasrallah' on the Day of Ashouraa 10 Muharram 1419 = 6–5-1998." This is from Nasrallah's website, www.nasrollah.org, which seems no longer available, but it can be found at http://web.archive.org/web/20021001075054/http://www.nasrollah.org/english/indexeng .htm.

30 Badih Chayban, "Nasrallah Alleges 'Christian Zionist' Plot," *Daily Star,* Oct. 23, 2002.

31 "Annan Condemns Israel Atack in Lebanon," *Ynet News,* July 12, 2006. http://www.ynetnews.com/articles/0.7340.L-3274607.00.html.

32 "EU accuses Israel of 'disproportionate use of force in Lebanon," *USA Today,* July 13, 2006.

33 "Chirac Questions Israel's Intentions," *Al-Jazeera,* July 14, 2006. http://www.aljazeera.com/archive/2006/07/200849131648790685.html.

34 Quoted in Manfred Gerstenfeld, "Europe's Mindset Toward Israel as Accentuated by the Lebanon War," *Jerusalem Viewpoint,* no. 507, Jerusalem Center for Public Affairs, Oct. 1, 2006, http://www.jcpa.org/jl/vp547.htm.

35 "Middle East: On the Brink of Chaos," *Guardian* (London) July 17, 2006.

36 "Paradise Lost: Robert Fisk's Elegy for Beirut," *Independent,* July 19, 2006.

37 Tom Gross, "The Media Aims its Missiles," *Jerusalem Post,* Aug. 3, 2006.

38 Ibid.

39 "Danish Lawmaker Wants Livni Detained," *Jerusalem Post* (Associate Press), Aug. 28, 2006. I am grateful to Robin Shepherd's *A State Beyond the Pale* (London: Weidenfelt & Nicolson, 2009), where I first saw this story.

40 "Key Republican breaks with Bush on Mideast," *CNN.com,* July 31, 2006. http://www.cnn.com/2006/POLITICS/07/31/hagel.mideast/.

41 See my "America's Worst Ex-President," *Commentary* 122, no. 7 (February 2007).

42 Jimmy Carter, "Stop the Band-Aid Treatment," *Washington Post,* Aug. 1, 2006.

43 Steven Erlanger, "Palestinian Leader Orders Force to Find Seized Israeli," *New York Times,* June 27, 2006.

44 Human Rights Watch, *Fatal Strikes: Israel's Indiscriminate Attacks Against Civilians in Lebanon* 18, no. 3 (E) (August 2006): 3.

45 Government of Lebanon, Presidency of the Council of Ministers—Higher Relief Council, "Lebanon Under Siege," http://web.archive.org/web/20060927025252/www.lebanonundersiege.gov.lb/english/F/Main/index.asp; United Nations, General Assembly, Human Rights Council, Third session, *Implementation Of General Assembly Resolution 60/251 of 15 March 2006 Entitled "Human Rights Council": Report of the Commission*

of Inquiry on Lebanon pursuant to Human Rights Council resolution S-2/1, 23 Nov. 2006, 3.

46 Benjamin M. Lambeth, *Air Operations in Israel's War Against Hezbollah: Learning from Lebanon and Getting it Right in Gaza* (Santa Monica: Rand Corporation, 2011), 79, 81.

47 Human Rights Watch, *Fatal Strikes,* 3.

48 Al-Manar, May 27, 2006. Quoted in Reuven Erlich, *Hezbollah's Use Of Lebanese Civilians As Human Shields: The Extensive Military Infrastructure Positioned And Hidden In Populated Areas,* Intelligence and Terrorism Information Center at the Center for Special Studies, Israel, Nov. 2006.

49 Human Rights Watch, *Fatal Strikes,* 5.

50 Ibid., 26–7.

51 Lee Keath, "Israeli Troops Fight Guerrillas in South Lebanon, Warplanes Flatten Buildings, *Associate Press,* July 20, 2006.

52 Clancy Chassay, "The Yesterday the Israeli Jets Came to Srifa," *Guardian* (London), July 20, 2006.

53 Hassan M. Fattah, "Hostilities in The Mideast: Destruction; As Cease-Fire Holds, Lebanese Dig for the War's Victims in the Rubble of Many Towns," *New York Times,* Aug. 16, 2006.

54 Avi Bell, "Human Rights Watch Has Some Explaining to do," *Opinio Juris,* September 1, 2006. http://opiniojuris.org/2006/09/01/human-rights-watch-has-some-explaining-to-do/.

55 United Nations, General Assembly, Human Rights Council, Ninth Special Session, "The grave violations of human rights in the Occupied Palestinian Territory, particularly due to the recent Israeli military attacks against the occupied Gaza Strip," A/HRC/S-9/L.1, Jan. 12, 2009, 5.

56 Hanan Chehata, "Exclusive MEMO interview with Colonel Desmond Travers – Co-author of the UN's Goldstone Report," *Middle East Monitor (MEMO)* (no date). http://www.middleeastmonitor.org.uk/downloads/interviews/interview-with-colonel-desmond-travers.pdf.

57 Hamas Says 300 Fighters Killed in Gaza War, *Agence France Presse,* Nov. 1, 2010.

58 Richard Goldstone, "Reconsidering the Goldstone Report on Israel and War Crimes," *Washington Post,* Apr. 1, 2011.

59 "Nobel-Winning Elders Deplore Gaza Flotilla Attack," *The Hindu,* (Johannesburg), May 31, 2010.

60 European Parliament, "Israeli Military Operation Against the Humanitarian Flotilla and the Gaza Blockade," Texts adopted, June 17, 2010. http://www.europarl.europa.eu/sides/getDoc.do?type=TA&reference=P7-TA-2010–0235&language=EN&ring=P7-RC-2010–0345.

61 "Gaza: From Blockade to Bloodshed," *Guardian* (London), May 31, 2010.

62 "Israel: Full, Impartial Investigation of Flotilla Killings Essential," Human Rights Watch, June 1, 2010. http://www.hrw.org/news/2010/05/31/israel-full-impartial-investigation-flotilla-killings-essential.

63 United Nations, General Assembly, Human Rights Council, *Report of the International Fact-Finding Mission to Investigate Violations of Inter-*

national Law, Including International Humanitarian and Human Rights Law, Resulting From the Israeli Attacks on the Flotilla Of Ships Carrying Humanitarian Assistance, Sept. 27, 2010, 53 (para. 264).

64 See Rael Jean Isaac, "*TIME* Against Israel," *New Republic* 183, no. 16 (October 18, 1980): 18–20; and Joshua Muravchik, "Misreporting Lebanon," *Policy Review* 23 (Winter 1983): 11–66.

65 Karl Vick, "Why Israel Doesn't Care About Peace," *Time*, Sept. 13, 2010.

65 Ross, *The Missing Peace*, 549–90.

67 Ethan Bronner, "Israel Holds Peace Talks with Syria," *New York Times*, May 22, 2008; Shimon Shiffer, "Report: Netanyahu Agreed to Full Golan Heights Withdrawal," *Ynet News*, Oct. 12, 2012. http://www.ynetnews.com/articles/0,7340,L-4291337,00.html; Efraim Halevy, "Israel's Man in Damascus," *Foreign Affairs*, May 10, 2013. http://www.foreignaffairs.com/articles/139373/efraim-halevy/israels-man-in-damascus.

68 Ron Bousso, "Saudis Back New Peace Drive, Shun Israel Call for Ties," *Agence France Press—English*, Nov. 27 2007.

69 Glenn Kessler, "Rice, Israeli Official Share Perspectives; Both Women Cite Pariah Treatment," *Washington Post*, Nov. 29, 2006. I am grateful to Joshua Teitelbaum, whose paper, *The Arab Peace Initiative: A Primer and Future Prospects*, published by the Jerusalem Center for Public Affairs, brought this quote and the next to my attention.

70 Ross, *The Missing Peace*, 756–7.

71 "Chief Palestinian Negotiator Saeb Erekat: 'Abbas Rejected Israel's Proposal at Annapolis Like Arafat Rejected the Camp David 2000 Proposal," Middle East Media Research Institute, special dispatch 2313, Apr. 14, 2009.

72 Ethan Bronner, "Olmert Memoir Cites Near Deal for Mideast Peace," *New York Times*, Jan. 27, 2011.

73 Ibid.

74 Matti Friedman (Associated Press), "Former Israeli Premier Details Failed Peace Offer," Sept. 19, 2010.

75 George W. Bush, *Decision Points* (New York: Random House, 2010), 410.

76 Condoleezza Rice, *No Higher Honor: A Memoir of My Years in Washington* (New York: Random House, 2011), 724.

Conclusion

1 Roi Mandel and Yaron Druckman, "Protocols of Golda Meir at Agranat Commission Released," *Ynetnews.com*, Sept. 12, 2013. http://www.ynetnews.com/articles/0,7340,L-4429143,00.html.

2 Mitch Ginsburg, "Golda Meir: My Heart Was Drawn to a Preemptive Strike, But I Was Scared," *Times of Israel*, Sept.12, 2103. http://www.timesofisrael.com/golda-meir-my-heart-was-drawn-to-a-preemptive-strike-but-i-was-scared/.

3 Lydia Saad, "Americans' Sympathies for Israel Match All-Time High,"

   Gallup Politics, Mar, 15, 2013. http://www.gallup.com/poll/161387/
   americans-sympathies-israel-match-time-high.asp.
 4 "March 2013 Post-ABC Poll: Israel and the Palestinians," *Washington
   Post*, Mar. 26, 2013. http://www.washingtonpost.com/politics/polling/
   march-2013-postabc-poll-israel-palestinians/2013/03/26/ce601246-
   8f7d-11e2-9173-7f87cda73b49_page.html; "Public Remains Supportive
   of Israel, Wary of Iran," *Pew Research*, Mar. 19, 2013. http://www
   .people-press.org/2013/03/19/public-remains-supportive-of-israel-
   wary-of-iran/; HART/McINTURFF, "NBC News/Wall Street Journal
   Survey," Study #13061, Feb. 2013. http://online.wsj.com/public/
   resources/documents/wsjnbcpoll-02262013.pdf.
 5 "Video Clip #3689, Suha Arafat, Widow of Yasser Arafat: The 2000 Intifada was Premeditated, Planned by Arafat," Dubai TV, Dec. 16, 2012,
   Memri TV, Middle East Media Research Institute TV Monitor Project.
   http://www.memritv.org/clip/en/3689.htm.
 6 David Horovitz, "When They Become PM, They Realize How Utterly
   Dependent Israel is on the US," *Times of Israel*, Sept. 18, 2013.

Index

Benvenisti, Meron, 143–144, 144n, 151, 169

Bernstein, David, 185

Bernstein, Robert L., 181–82

Bevin, Ernest, 4

Biletzki, Anat, 147, 148–49, 169

Birnbaum, Ben, 188–89, 191

Birth of the Palestinian Refugee Problem, 1947–1949, The (Morris), 152–153

Bischof, Gunter, 90

Black September, 42–43, 59; as a Fatah organization, 48–49; hijacking of Sabena airline by, 43; "Operation Abu Daoud" of, 46; terrorist attacks of at the 1972 Munich Olympics, 44–46

B'nai B'rith, 68

boycotts, divestment and sanctions (BDS), use of to pressure Israel on the Palestinian issue, 81, 82

Brandt, Willy, 45, 59, 94

Brit Shalom, 168

British Petroleum (BP), 57

British Trades Union Congress (TUC), 193–94

Bronner, Ethan, 153, 226

Bseiso, Atef, 50

B'Tselem, 147–48, 151, 158, 170, 208; duality in the work of, 148–49; lobbying of Europe to refrain from relations with Israel, 149–50

Buber, Martin, 137–38

Burg, Avraham, 142–43, 151, 169; comparison of Israel to Nazi Germany by, 143; renunciation of Zionism, 143

Burg, Yosef, 142

Burma, 76

Bush, George H. W., 66, 69

Bush, George W., 226

Butler, Judith, 180, 195, 198, 231, 258n43

Caetano, Marcelo, 54

Cameron, Bruce, 182

Cameron, David, 197

Camp David Accords, 96, 224–25

capitalism, 86, 87, 125; "global capitalism," 197

Carmel, Moshe, 37

Carter, Jimmy, 131, 132, 133, 139, 207, 219; criticism of Israel's blockade of Gaza, 221; criticism of Israel's refusal to exchange prisoners with Hezbollah, 215–16

Castro, Fidel, 78

Ceausescu, Nicolae, 131

Ceylon, 73

Chagnon, Jacqui, 182

Chambers, Whittaker, 178

Chancellor, John, 135

Chavez, Hugo, 180

Che Guevara Brigade, 38

China. *See* People's Republic of China (PRC)

Chirac, Jacques, 215

Chomsky, Noam, 119, 159, 196, 198, 231

Christianity, 21, 116, 180

Christians, 2, 21, 27; Maronite Christians, 134

Church of the Nativity (Bethlehem), 174, 175

Clinton, Bill, 141, 201, 206

Clinton, Hillary, 189

Cobban, Helena, 49, 238n15, 238n18

Cockburn, Alexander, 101

Cohen, Eliot A., 165, 255n90

Cohen, Raphael, 176

Cohen, Roger, 196

Cold War, the, 17, 30, 62, 73, 85, 151, 182, 183

colonialism, 29, 30, 69, 117, 179; effects of, 99; European colonialism, 101–2; neo-colonialism, 69

Commentary, 149, 150

Committee for Accuracy in Middle East Reporting in America (CAMERA), 156, 160; policy of *Ha'aretz* toward, 167–68

Communism, 98, 196, 210; in the Third World, 182

Communists, 28, 124

Convention on the Prevention and Punishment of Genocide, 189

Convention Relating to the Status of Refugees, 84

Corrie, Rachel, 171–72, 174, 175, 221, 231; death of, 171, 177–78; justification of Palestinian violence by, 176, 177; leftist ideology of, 178–79

Couve de Murville, Maurice, 17–18

Covering Islam (Said), 119

Cuba, 28, 29, 36, 67, 150

Cuppers, Martin, 7

Cyprus, 46